FLASHBACKS

THE FLASHBACKS SERIES IS SPONSORED BY THE
EUROPEAN ETHNOLOGICAL RESEARCH CENTRE
CELTIC & SCOTTISH STUDIES
UNIVERSITY OF EDINBURGH
27-29 GEORGE STREET
EDINBURGH EH8 9LD

FLASHBACKS

FLASHBACKS

Showfolk

An Oral History of a Fairground Dynasty

Written by
Frank Bruce

in association with
THE EUROPEAN ETHNOLOGICAL RESEARCH CENTRE
AND NMS ENTERPRISES LIMITED – PUBLISHING
NATIONAL MUSEUMS SCOTLAND

GENERAL EDITOR
Alexander Fenton

Published in Great Britain in 2010 by
NMS Enterprises Limited – Publishing
NMS Enterprises Limited
National Museums Scotland
Chambers Street, Edinburgh EH1 1JF

ISBN 978-1-905267-45-3

**British Library Cataloguing in
Publication Data**
A catalogue record of this book
is available from the British Library.

Cover design by Mark Blackadder.

Cover photograph: [front] Members of
the Codona family with colleagues and
friends at Kelvin Hall carnival in
Glasgow, photographed for the *Daily
Record,* 10 January 1973 © Mirrorpix.

[back] Wedding group, Portobello, early
1920s, featuring many of those men-
tioned in the book and also a very young
Gordon Codona and his older brother
Alfred. Back row (left to right): Albert
Biddall, Violet Codona, Billy Codona,
Frank Codona, Billy Codona, Billy
Codona (Snr), Johnny Codona, Nathaniel
Codona, Jimmy Niven, Florrie May
Codona, Harry Paulo.

Front row (left to right): Hannah Codona,
Albert Codona, Catherine Biddall (*née*
Codona), Alfred Codona, Florrie
Codona (*née* Broughton), Cissie Codona
(*née* O'Donnell), Minnie Codona (*née*
Broughton), Mary Ann Rankin (*née*
McArdle – bride), Becca Paulo (*née*
Codona), Lucy Hannah Codona (*née*
Graham), Beatrice Niven (*née* Codona),
Nathaniel Codona, Catherine Doris
Codona.

Children at front (left and right): Gordon
and Douglas Codona.

Internal text design by NMSE –
Publishing, NMS Enterprises Limited.
Printed and bound in Great Britain
by Bell & Bain Ltd, Glasgow.

For a full listing of related NMS
titles please visit:
www.nms.ac.uk/books

CONTENTS

ACKNOWLEDGEMENTS

I AM indebted to members of the Codona family who agreed to be interviewed, in particular the late Gordon Codona whose memories make up over half the book, as well as Barry Codona, Justin Codona, the late Mrs Cathy Macintosh and Mrs Catherine Codona Thomas. I would also like to thank Alan Codona for answering my very first query about the family and putting me in touch with his uncle Gordon, and other members and relatives of the extended family who added pieces to the jigsaw: Mrs Janet Cardownie, John Cardownie, James Codona, Mrs Janie Codona, Johanan Codona, Johnny Codona, Mrs Joy Codona, Mrs Judy Codona, Mrs Josephine Fox, Anne-Marie Gwynn, James McArdle (Snr), James McArdle (Jnr), Janice McHardy and Agnes Wilson.

I would also like to thank Jacey Bedford, Belfast Public Libraries, Blackburn Library, Bolton Libraries and Archives, fairground historian Frances Brown for many valuable suggestions, Mary Buisson, Joy Cann of York City Archives for exhaustive research into the story of William Codona, Sheila Campbell of Kirkcaldy Central Library, John Doune, Edinburgh City Archives, Edinburgh Central Library, the *Edinburgh Herald and Post*, Geoff Felix, Archie Foley for sharing his genealogical researches and collecting information on the Portobello connections, Tony Gee for Scottish fairground references, Tommy Green, Eleanor Harris of Argyll and Bute Library Service, John Hayes of Edinburgh Museum of Childhood, Marij Van Helmond of Argyll and Bute Library Service, Joan Hori of the Hawaiian Collection, University of Hawaii at Manoa Library, Jane Humphreys of Falkirk Library Services, Isobel Kincaid of

Stirling Central Library, The Living Memory Association – Edinburgh, John McCormick, Martin MacGilp who generously gave me early references from research into the history of puppetry in Scotland, Ally McGurk, Jim McHardle, Iain D. MacIver of Lanark Library, John McKillop for checking his archive for cinema-related references, Stuart MacMillan, Tommy Manson, Mrs J. I. H. Marshall, National Library of Scotland, June Morrison of Paisley Central Library, the late Paul Newman, North Eastern Education and Library Board, César Ortega, Philip Paris, Jim Pratt, Mona Rhone, The Showmen's Guild – Scottish Section, Stirling Council Archive Service, Melvyn and Gaynor Strand, Catherine Taylor of Aberdeen City Library, Joanne Turner of Dumfries Museum, the late Dr John Turner, Vanessa Toulmin and staff of the National Fairground Archive at Sheffield University, Emily Walsh of Bourne Fine Art, Mrs Cathy Whittaker, and Richard Youngs of the Glasgow Room at the Mitchell Library.

My thanks, finally, to Linda Fuchs, Mark Mulhern and Lesley Taylor for their work in getting the text to publication.

Frank Bruce
EDINBURGH 2010

LIST OF ILLUSTRATIONS

EDITORIAL NOTE

THE 'Flashbacks' series presents, in printed form, the words of individuals concerning aspects of – or the entirety of – their lives in Scotland. The content is variously composed of interview transcriptions, memoir or autobiography. The aim of the series is to gather in and re-transmit to a wider audience, fragments of the lived life.

Individually and collectively, the volumes of the 'Flashbacks' provide an account of 'what a life was' in different places. These volumes do this by allowing people to give their own account, in their own words. In this way the reader gains an insight to different lives in different parts of Scotland.

This particular volume adds a new theme to the 'Flashbacks' series – that of showfolk and 'the shows', through accounts of the members of one of Scotland's best known showground families: the Codonas and some of their relations. Through interviews, archival research and careful observation, Frank Bruce has produced a lively account of an under-researched aspect of Scottish life and society. The extensive use of first-hand accounts allows those interviewed to speak in their own way, thereby allowing the reader to hear of the life of showfolk as directly as possible.

The essence of the 'Flashbacks' series is the everyday life of as broad a sample of people as possible. Everyday life is often held to be that which is lived in between interesting events, with those events constituting our stories or our histories. However, it is in the everyday that we meet most people; that we prepare and eat meals; that we raise our children; and that we engage in work and other activities. In short, it is in the everyday that we live most of our lives. The accounts given in this volume add to the 'Flashbacks' project which will continue with further volumes by different people – perhaps even you.

Mark A. Mulhern
EUROPEAN ETHNOLOGICAL RESEARCH CENTRE
EDINBURGH 2010

Numbers in square brackets after a Christian name refer to the Codon Family Tree at the end of this book. Text in italics during oral testimony indicates an author question and [...] marks a cut or transposition of interview material.

SHOWFOLK
An Oral History of a Fairground Dynasty

I

Introduction

ONE July day in 1836 the *Glasgow Constitutional*'s correspondent stepped out of his office and elbowed his way through the crowds to sample the attractions of the Glasgow Fair:

> Well, now, this is something like life! What is that strong long fellow bawling about through the speaking trumpet? The Hottentot Venus! ... There is a learned pig here too. The pig and the Venus are together in the same box. ... Crowds of people press forward and climb the wooden steps. Oh, attractive beauty! – Oh, fascinating wisdom!

He gives a long, whimsical account of what he finds, including a lengthy mention of one showman in particular, Frank Codone[1]:

> Looking about, we recognise, in an opposite booth, that old favourite with the 'Glasgow chaps', Frank Codone. Is Frank never going to die? How we should like to perpetuate his life! We remember him since we could mind anything, and he was then, and has been since, the pet of the fair. He has never risen in his profession, this Frank – for want of a 'spirited and enterprising' patron, perhaps. He has stood stationary as to position, although no man changes his position oftener, or to less purpose. Why, he will tumble, and balance, and do a hundred things that no one in Glasgow can do at all, perhaps; and there he is, poor fellow, wearing out his body in this way, merely to catch a few stray halfpence. Where does he burrow – into what deep recesses does he penetrate and hap himself

during all the weeks of the year, save this one? Is Frank a lover of town or country? ... Alas! What do we know of poor Frank, or what should he care about himself, but that he is a show-man?[2]

Fan-maker, acrobat, puppeteer, animal-trainer and all-round showman, Frank Codone was – even if he never rose in his pro-fession – the founder of a fairground dynasty that has lasted for over 200 years in Scotland, and probably a good deal longer on the continent. The interviews that make up most of this book are with his fifth, sixth and seventh generation of descendants, all of whom worked in the same business. This is an impressive family tradition even by showland's multi-generational standards, and to a large extent this book is an exploration of what went into forging such a remarkable saga of occupational and com-munal continuity.

For the second hundred years of this saga, the evidence is in the strikingly direct form of individual oral histories. These vivid autobiographies overlap to form a composite history of the Codona family and the ever-changing world of showpeople at large. Evidence for the first hundred years is less direct, but for a nomadic community, outside the mainstream, unusually rich. A lucky combination of the very complete and accessible Scottish official records, and the rarity of the name and its variants – for the nineteenth century more or less restricted to travelling show-people – meant that searches of digital archives yielded results that were nearly always relevant and comprehensive. An outline of lineages and travels could be traced from the official records of birth, marriage and death dates and places, coloured by the items of news, reports of fairs and biographical anecdotes picked up in indexes and newspaper archives. It is enough to give us a rare insight into the life and times of a typical nineteenth-century fairground family.

The story is mainly of small-scale enterprise, always on the move. Within 60 years the trail stretches from Italy to Honolulu. The few who reached the highest levels of the circus profession did so in the Americas. Adelaide Codona appeared in the 1870s with a four-horse act as a major performer with some of the greatest North American circuses of the time – huge outfits by European standards. Half a century later her grand-daughter Victoria was topping bills as a tight-rope walker and her grandson Alfredo was one of the greatest trapeze artists in the world. It is in Scotland, however, that the family established its firmest and most lasting foothold. According to a close relative of the family, the Codonas were 'looked on as the Royalty of the showpeople' by the middle of last century, a sentiment echoed in a 1954 two-part newspaper feature 'Codona; the royal family of the fairground' which describes their prominent position in the business with 32 members in the Showmen's Guild owning a large number of the big rides that dominated the fairs.[3]

Of course, the notion of a 'Codona family' implies a greater degree of coherence than was the case: over the generations as the family tree spread, quite distinct groups of fairground Codonas emerged. Those in this book belonged to one branch of the family, and their reference group encompassed one or two degrees of kinship.[4] It was this branch that saw themselves as occupying a prominent position in the business. Beyond this, while other branches of the family were known of – inevitably, since they worked and lived in the same circumscribed world – the exact relationship was long-forgotten, and there were none of the close business ties that characterised more immediate relationships – strikingly extensive and well-maintained connections by ordinary standards. In any case the Codona story parallels and is intertwined with that of other circus and fairground families. Long lasting work/kin connections with the Brown and Rizarelli circus families can be followed in the nineteenth century. This was a closed world: like married like and few families did not at some point have a son or daughter marry a Codona and occasionally Codona siblings married siblings from another family. As Cathy Macintosh (whose Codona mother married a circus Paulo and who herself married a showman) put it to me, 'We're all the one family, really. I think we're all related if you go back far enough'.

As well as being true genealogically, Cathy's comment

reflects the strong sense of identity and interconnectedness felt by showpeople. They were linked by kinship and occupational ties and by a travelling lifestyle that reinforced the importance of mutual support to replace the support that the settled community got from its own institutions. Keenly aware of where opportunities might lie, most families traced similar paths through the business, faced the same ups and downs, experienced most of the same challenges and shared a common culture and heritage.

This is reflected in the themes and issues that recur through these oral histories, echoing the nineteenth-century evidence and expressing the common experience of showpeople as a whole. Perhaps the most obvious of these themes, and the one that most strongly echoes the nineteenth-century evidence, is the importance attached to vigorous enterprise and initiative in an ever-changing business. This is a theme embodied in the recurring tales of innovation and one-upmanship found in printed and oral autobiography from the nineteenth century to the present. More subtly, it is reflected in a certain tone or attitude – matter-of-fact, practical, direct – typical of these narratives.

Then there is the shifting, ambivalent and sometimes difficult relationship between showpeople and the settled community, or in more abstract terms, between insider and outsider status – as seen from both sides. This is given Manichean expression in frequent tales of fairground confrontations. Though these were based on actual events, such confrontations were a recurring part of fairground life and in the telling they echo and draw on the established narrative tradition that dealt with this; emphasising the unprovoked unruliness of the mob, the self-defence of the showfolk who come together in the face of a common threat and often win the day by some clever ploy or decoy. A sense of having to act in righteous self-defence, more or less in the place of the settled authorities, runs through this tradition. It is put at its most dramatic in 'Lord' George Sanger's account of riots at Lansdown Fair near Bristol: 'The few police about were utterly helpless, and the showfolk had to defend themselves as best they could. ... It was no use looking to the law to revenge the injuries they had received.' After the riots, the showmen exacted their own rough justice on the ringleaders of a mob by dunking them in a pond.[5]

Such fairground confrontations lay at the extreme end of a gamut of interactions that brought the sense of insider/outsiderness into play. Again and again this is expressed in more mundane accounts of the 'outside' as manifested in school, local authorities or hostile punters. Central to this fluid relationship is the positive showman identity articulated both for 'inside' purposes, as a prized status and source of esteem, and for outsiders as a 'unified front' (despite the high degree of internal differentiation in the show community based on factors like occupational group, status and longevity in the business).[6]

This pervasive sense of belonging and being separate bound up in this identity is perhaps not as stark as for other more marginalised groups of travellers but is much stronger than amongst other communities involved in entertainment. Though music hall and variety performers might have some family background in their business, and felt a strong sense of solidarity with their peers, again reinforced by a travelling lifestyle, they kept a strong sense of identity and connection with their public that they often drew on to generate a sense of 'closeness'.[7] This may explain why, despite having performing skills that could have transferred outside the circus and fairground, over the nineteenth century only two of the Codona family seem to have ventured into the music hall or variety business.[8] For circus and fairground showpeople, the life was distinct and all-encompassing, involving work, private and family life; it was a total way of life that was hard to leave.

This takes us to the most significant theme that appears in interviews, the crucial but complicated role of the family and the wider community of showpeople in terms of kinship, carefully managed co-operation, patronage and mutual support alongside fierce competition and prominent sense of hierarchy. This underlies all the accounts that follow, although it is not always directly stated. A strikingly overt exposition of how family and community could come into play, however, was given to me by showman Jim McArdle Senior and is worth quoting in some detail. Jim's father Michael was the son of Michael McArdle, a hairdresser – and so an 'outsider' – and William [3] Codona's daughter Beatrice (who subsequently remarried Jimmy Niven, an engine driver for the Codonas seen as another 'outsider') and was brought up alongside his Codona cousins. However, according to Jim, he 'wasn't taken into the family. To the showpeople he was Michael Codony but to the family he was Michael McArdle'. Although he worked for his four uncles 'the Codona brothers', 'they never treated him as a nephew but as a worker. This was because his mother married an outsider twice'; it would be first names behind the scenes but not on the ground – 'they had a reputation to maintain'. Michael went on to marry into the Paulo circus family (his wife Augusta was a dancer), and, according to Jim, this also affected his status. Only a generation out of the circus business, the Codonas saw themselves as fairground, not circus people; they 'thought they were it – they were the cream of it. The Paulos were circus people'.

It was only when Michael was gravely ill with pneumonia that his uncle Frankie changed his attitude: 'When uncle Frankie visited him in hospital, it took that visit to make Frankie realise that this was his sister's son laying there dying – his only nephew from the sister's side of the family. After my father pulled through, Frankie took him under his wing; after that visit uncle Frankie was an uncle in every sense of the word. Frankie taught my father many things about being a showman, how to be a lessee and act like one. How to treat his fellow showmen as tenants, every aspect of a lessee's [business] was taught him ....'[9]

Jim McArdle himself grew up in Portobello with his aunt Rebecca (née Codona) and her husband Harry Paulo and so his observations are shaped not only by his father's experiences but by his own position, close to but outside this branch of the Codona family. As we will see, speakers' positions in the family geography – more or less near the 'centre', more or less settled and so on – play a significant role in how they slant the shared themes that run through this book.

This, of course, is something best left to discover in context, since the richness and vitality of individual narratives lies in how at any one time there are a multitude of overlapping themes and personal nuances being played out. Witness Gordon Codona's tightly packed encapsulation of several themes as he talks about the wife of his great-uncle Tommy:

> His wife Hannah ... she was a flattie, that means she wasn't born in the business, that's a flattie, and – it's not derogatory, I mean it's just a term – if you're not a showperson you're a flattie. And he married Hannah and she was interested in the name and the heritage because she was outwith the business. Our own family, I wouldn't say we were very particularly bothered about where we came from. We was more interested in carrying on with the business and getting on with it, you know.

Fig. 1 *The Showman*, broadside, Edinburgh, c1824-29.
Before inviting the 'bonny bairns, come here an' see / A wondrous sight for a baw-bee' the showman makes a plea: 'In this Town I'm not a stranger, / Yet my life is in great danger, / With these wretched black-guard boys, / Where'er I go, who me annoys. / Cannot the Police make them yield? / 'Tis such as me that they should shield; / I gave them no provocation, / Tho' they give me great vexation.' Showmen have long continued to feel left to fend for themselves when it comes to dealing with trouble. (*Copyright:* Reproduced by Permission of the Trustees of the National Library of Scotland)

2

*The Fair
Familiar Faces*

G OING back to the first Frank Codona, a lengthy description
of the 1837 Fair seems to answer the 1836 *Glasgow Constitutional*'s question about his mortality:

> Our Fair had but one point of attraction – the foot of the
> Saltmarket and thither we wend our way. As we go along,
> we cannot but feel sorry that the poor people at the stalls are
> apparently doing so little business. ... We have now got down
> to the shows. What a falling off is here! Wombwell with his
> fine menagerie has not dared to visit us. There is no circus, no
> dramatic troop worth speaking of. But let us bustle through
> the crowd, and take a look at the 'old familiar faces'. Well,
> positively there is Hughie Watson in the front of Mumford's
> show, joining in a country dance with the clown and two little
> girls. ... We would give something now for a sight of Frank
> Cadone. This will be no Fair at all without him. Alas! A friend
> at our elbow has just told us that poor Frank is dead. Poor
> Frank! – he could balance a cart-wheel upon his chin – and yet
> he is dead! Well, well – to think that Glasgow Fair could be held
> without Frank Cadone! It makes us consider ourselves of little
> account. Frank Cadone is dead, and Nelson's monument is still
> standing, and the jail has not toppled down into dust, and the
> Saltmarket is still the Saltmarket. ... We must positively enter a
> *show* to get rid of our thoughts. ...[10]

When and whereabouts did the Codonas first arrive in Britain
and where did they come from? Scottish-born Geordie showman
Billy Purvis, who met them in 1826, described them as Italian,

as did juggler Pat Feeney, who worked for the 'Cardonis' when appearing at Glasgow Fair in the 1820s. After recounting the various circuses and shows that appeared in the 1820s – Pollito's wild beast show, Anthony Powell's Circus, Ord's Circus, Bartley Minch's show, Kit Newsome's Circus – he comes to the 'Cardoni family':

> Then there was the Cardoni family had just come to Glasgow. They was Italians. The sons was then practising jugglery, and old Cardoni assisted me to get some apparatus and I practised with 'em, and he engaged me, and I became pretty clever. The sons, except Frank, is still living. Old Mr Cardoni died about 35 years ago [c1836]. He was 102 years old when he died; a tidy spell, warn't it? By-the-bye, his was the first Punch and Judy show ever exhibited in Glasgow. Once he was specially engaged to perform Punch and Judy before George the Third and the Royal family, and that was a honour he boasted of the longest day he had to live.[11]

Within recent family memory, however, rival claims have been made for Spain, Italy and Switzerland. According to Cathy Macintosh, her cousin Frankie Codona always used to say that the family was Spanish. She remembered one particular incident:

> Well, we were at a dance one time and my cousin Frankie ... he always thought we were Spanish, we were definitely Spanish. Nothing to do with the Italians. And, of course, this person says, 'Go away! For goodness sake, Hannibal came over the Alps with the elephants and at the back of him there was an old man with an ice-cream barrow and he was a Codona!'

The name itself offers little clarification. Frank Codona and his immediate descendants were almost certainly illiterate and the spelling 'Codona' was a literate third party's approximation of the family name that only became the most commonly used form in the 1870s. Early accounts of Frank's activities give various spellings – Cardoni, Cadone, Cadoni, Codone, Candone, and other variants are given of his descendants' names throughout the nineteenth century. This makes it hard to use the name as a geographical clue; the variants suggest Spain, Italy or Switzerland, and of course, Frank or his forebears might have passed through, married in or been born in all three countries. Multi-national backgrounds are common in the circus and this probably lay behind a 1909 publicity story about Mexican tightrope walker Victoria Codona having 'Castilian blood' and being not only the daughter but great-grand-daughter of the circus.[12] 'Castilian' was really an exotic way of saying 'continental'. Her father Eduardo was Mexican, her mother Hortense French, her father's father William was born in Lancashire, his father John was born in Scotland and her father's mother Adelaide was born in France but was frequently billed being Spanish or Andalusian.

There is tantalising evidence for a shared family tree from which the Codonas who settled in Scotland early in the nineteenth century may have branched off; that of the Cardona/i family who crop up in various records as performers in Spain, Italy and England.[13] English clown Harold Whiteley recalled a 'Cardona and his cage of lions' with Circo Price setting off from Madrid to tour Spain in 1882, a mention made interesting in this context since in the author's manuscript 'Cardona' is written above a crossed-out 'Codona'.[14] He may have been one of three animal trainers in Bostock's menagerie who took this performing name but this still suggests that there was an original by this name. More recent representatives of the Italian circus and puppet traditions are acrobat Enzo Cardona and his family and Pulcinella puppeteer Francesco Cardoni (c1893-1977).[15]

'Cardoni' is the name used above by Pat Feeney and 'Cardona' is used on an 1823 billing for Glasgow Fair (see Fig. 4) and given on at least three statutory certificates.[16] It also corresponds well with an alternative name still used by some descendants of the original Frank, and given on the 1859 death certificate of one 'Francis Cardownie, an old showman, mendicant'. 'Cardownie' appears as often as 'Codona' in the statutory

FIG. 2 Pulcinella glove-puppeteer Francesco Cardoni performed in the Borghese
Gardens in Rome for decades after World War I. Pulcinella is a close cousin of
Punch, and this Francesco could well have shared a common ancestor with the
Francis 'Cardoni' alleged by showman Pat Feeney to have been the first to bring
Punch and Judy to Glasgow. See Appendix 1 for more on this performer.
(*Source:* Frank Bruce)

records until the 1870s, when 'Codona' becomes more or less
fixed. If Cardownie was, as seems likely, partly an attempt to
give a more accurate rendering of actual pronunciation then it
would support the case for a Cardona/i connection (this certainly seems to explain the 1871 census having 'Cardownay' as
an entry). On the other hand, Cardownie could simply have been
an attempt to give a Scottish look to the name.[17]

As to when they arrived, Frank's son William was born in
Lancaster in 1804 and according to a 1838 report in the *Glasgow
Constitutional*, 'Frank Codone' – probably Frank the second –
'who has always been a favourite – as smart and light-hearted
as ever' had appeared at every Glasgow Fair for the last 25 years,

in other words, since 1813.[18] Pat Feeney's account confirms that he was a performer when he arrived, and suggests that he came to Scotland from Italy after a stay in England since any perform-ance, however indirect, in the presence of King George III, who never came to Scotland, would have had to have been there. This seems to match the claims made by two great-grandsons, from separate branches of the family, in one account having an ancestor performing for a King George and in the other account as having come from Italy.[19]

Migration from northern Italy in particular grew from the end of the eighteenth century, primarily as a result of the collap-sing rural economy. Many of these dispersed rural migrants turned to street performing of various types, most commonly a quite limited musical or animal act – a vagrant occupation that was the best of the available alternatives – and by the mid nine-teenth century such performers, particularly organ-grinders, had become ubiquitous.[20] The first Codona might have come as a result of the economic push driving these compatriots, but more likely he was one of the much longer tradition of skilled, profes-sional itinerant performers. In other words, he was a migrant more pulled than pushed. He arrived decades before the large late-nineteenth century waves of migration and seems likely to have been a skilled performer when he arrived, given his wide range of performing and circus skills. These were not quickly or easily acquired – puppetry in particular was a skilled and competitive business in Italy – but it was normal and probably essential for the professional showman to have a wide reper-toire; other well-known faces at the Scottish fairs such as David Prince Miller and Billy Purvis had puppetry, theatrical and circus skills.[21] As a 'professional' plying the European circuit of fairs he would have been aware of the growing opportunities for entertainers across the channel. Most obviously, in the last three decades of the eighteenth century London was at the centre of the modern circus business pioneered by Philip Astley that drew talent from across Europe. Performers connected with Astley were working in Scotland by the 1780s and he and his rivals opened purpose-built amphitheatres across the United Kingdom

FIG. 3 Early advertisement for circus in Edinburgh, *The Caledonian Mercury*, 28 March 1791. The Amphitheatre or Edinburgh Equestrian Circus was opened on the corner of Broughton Street in 1790. This style of purpose-built entertainment was in the vanguard of a proliferation of commercialised amusements. (*Source:* Frank Bruce)

(and in Paris in 1782), including in 1790 the 'Amphitheatre or Edinburgh Equestrian Circus'.[22] The same three decades also saw a craze for elaborate full-scale 'Fantoccini' shows that drew a number of Italian puppeteers and their companies.[23]

What is certain is that the Codonas were not the first continental entertainers to visit Scotland; these had been appearing at fairs and in public squares for hundreds of years. A survey of popular entertainers appearing in the seventeenth century concludes that the mountebanks who appeared with the medicine shows of the period were almost all from the continent.[24] Most visitors were transient, a notable exception being Signora

Violante (1682-1741), a 'rope dancer' who had appeared at fairs abroad and in England before settling down in Edinburgh in 1735 at the end of her career, where she performed in the 'new theatre' in Carruber's Close, and the old Assembly Hall, and opened a dancing school.[25] Further up the social scale were the many foreign classically trained musicians who set up shop, entertainment entrepreneurs just like the humbler fairground folk, notably the Corris: Domenico Corri's various enterprises included opening an Edinburgh pleasure garden in 1776, one of the polite antecedents of the modern amusement parks run by settled showmen, and his brother Natale ventured briefly and unsuccessfully into the circus business in partnership with comedian John Bannister, converting the family concert rooms into the 'Pantheon' in 1817. Other Italians who appeared in Scotland in the early nineteenth century included strong-man and 'wonder-worker' Belzoni who toured in 1810 and the menagerist Polito who appeared in Aberdeen and Dundee in 1816 and in Glasgow and Aberdeen in the 1820s. The families of Italian origin with the closest occupational resemblance, however, were the Paris and Salvona families who, were involved in circus, fairground and penny geggies but only seem to have settled in Scotland in the mid to late 1800s.

The earliest direct, 'official' reference from the old parish records to a Francis 'Codone' being in Scotland seems to be his marriage to Elizabeth Buchanan in July 1823 in Glasgow, at the time of the fair, coinciding with a billing for 'Mr Cardona', most probably Frank [1], in an 1823 advertisement for 'Brown's Pavilion' at the fair.

This billing is significant because it is the earliest record of a Codona-Brown connection that can be followed across North America and until the 1890s when this Brown's great-grandson (or possibly grandson) married circus artist Harriet Codona in Buenos Aires.[26] It also gives us a useful snapshot of his circus skills:

The two originals and Favourite Rival CLOWNS, *Mr James and Mr Cardona*, will particularly exert themselves through the

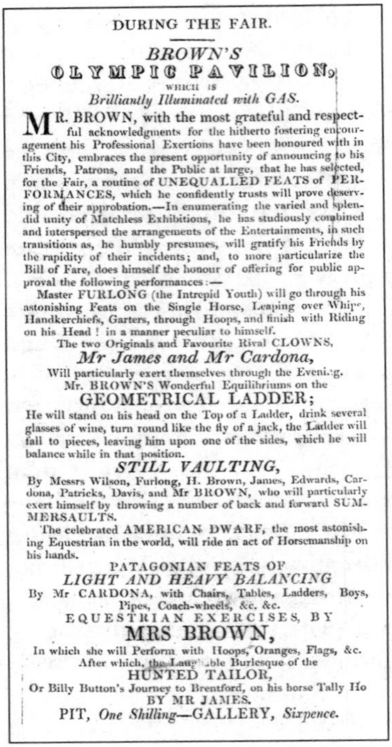

FIG. 4 Advertisement for Brown's Pavilion appearing during Glasgow Fair of 1823. 'Codoni' also appeared in Brown's 'Olympic' during the fair of 1826. His employer seems likely to have been the Mr Brown, 'Principal rider at Astley's Amphitheatre', billed at John Bannister and Natale Corri's Pantheon Theatre Circus Venture in Edinburgh in 1817 (see note 27). (*Source: Glasgow Free Press*, 16 July 1823. *Copyright:* Reproduced by Permission of the Trustees of the National Library of Scotland)

Evening ... STILL VAULTING, By Messrs Wilson, Furlong, H. Brown, James, Edwards, Cardona, Patricks, Davis, and Mr BROWN .... PATAGONIAN FEATS OF LIGHT AND HEAVY BALANCING By Mr CARDONA, with Chairs, Tables, Ladders, Boys, Pipes, Coach-wheels, &c. &c. ...[27]

Two years later, Francis 'Cadone' (possibly father or son) was in Pittenweem for the baptism of his daughter Ann on 11 May.[28] One of Pittenweem's three annual fairs fell on 26 March, but probably more of a draw were a number of major fairs around this time in Fife; Kirkcaldy Links and St Andrews Lammas Fairs remain amongst the most important funfairs.[29] Anstruther Lintseed Market, the subject of William Tennant's comic epic *Anster Fair* (1812), was held on 11 April or one of the six days immediately after and could well have been one of the sites they visited. The second canto of Tennant's poem is a vivid description of the 'vast tumultuous jovial rout' including a troupe of actors, bagpipers, fiddlers, ballad-singing women, 'many a leather-lung'd co-chanting pair of wood-legg'd sailors' as well as some acrobats, maybe not the Codonas but just the sort of act they started out with:

> ... tumblers, in wondrous pranks, / High-stag'd, display their limbs' agility, / And now, they, mountant from the scaffold's planks, / Kick with their whirling heels the clouds on high, / And now like cat, upon their dextrous shanks, / They light .... [30]

The first appearance of the 'Cadoni' family to be described in any detail is showman Billy Purvis' account of a run-in at Kilmarnock Races in 1826:

> The Fair opened at one o'clock, at which time we commenced taking *our fares*; and to fare better than usual, I send for one of the bottles of brandy, and treated myself and company to a glass, drinking, 'success to the new booth'. Opposite to us was an exhibition, the property of an Italian named Cadoni, who, with his family, displayed their feats of tumbling and postures extraordinary, and who sneered at the humble style of your friend Billy. 'Ha! You come up to my grand show, and see de real dancers, and not de dancing dollies of dat man of de mountain!' I let him go on for a while, and then, by George, I opened out in such as style as you little expected. 'Here you will see all that is grand, surprising, delightful; naen o' yer common, outlandish [foreign, alien, strange] men! If you come into my show, you'll come into a respectable situation; I am a Scotchman born, and this is my pride. I made my first appearance at Glasgow Fair, where I made as much money as bought this new show; and if my performances were not worthy of notice I had never dared to have shown my face at Kilmarnock. I did not come to Scotland for money, it was to visit the land where I first drew breath. I am no Italian, and never went about the country with dancing dogs, monkeys, and Punch and Toby. Here boy (calling Gordon to me), go to the Inn and bring me a bottle of the best French brandy, (whispering as he went away, "go to my lodgings for it".) The brandy was soon brought, I drew the cork, and filling a glass, went forward to the front of the stage, and said

aloud, "And here's to the town and trade of Kilmarnock, may they flourish!" The people gave three cheers, and then I arranged my company in a row, filling each a glass and telling them to repeat the toast ... the Scotch folks were delighted by my display of nationality, and the performers licked their lips.'

Imitating this manoeuvre, Cadoni's clown was despatched for two bottles, and he returned with two bottles of ale. He poured out a glass and repeated my words: but I soon put a stopper on his freak [caprice]. Holding up my bottle, 'this is brandy, real cognac, gentlemen; naen o' yor sma' yell [small ale or beer, i.e. weak beer],' I cried. 'Let any person taste that likes! Here,' handing a bottle and glass to a person in the crowd, 'drink it among you and satisfy yourselves.' This crowned the business; for a magical effect seemed to rouse the people, and crowds on crowds came to see my show, Cadoni actually shed tears of vexation, but it was his own doing. ... Many a time the Italian has said to me since the spree, 'Ah! You did shut me up Mr Purvis: dat brandy business did me brown [to do brown – to outwit] entirely.'[31]

This story clearly illustrates the energetic, competitive world of the showmen, a world that put a foreigner at a double disadvantage, as an outsider both to his audiences and his peers. It also gives a good idea of the Codona family business at this point: it involved an 'exhibition', probably a canvas and timber booth, the whole family was involved, and it included dancing, acrobatics, performing dogs and monkeys, a puppet show and there was a clown; in other words a miniature family circus of a type found at fairs across Europe well into the nineteenth century. Even with all these performing skills – as well as those listed on the 1823 bill – business, as Purvis' anecdote suggests, was never certain and had to be fought for. At Paisley Fair in 1828 Francis Cadoni 'the well-known mountebank' had to turn to a more basic ruse to generate income:

At the conclusion of Paisley Fair, Cadoni finding his ordinary tricks beginning to fail, resorted to the expedient of a lottery, as a means of raising the wind; the prizes of which were a boll of meal or 20s, and a fat pig or 40s. The bait took, and the shillings poured in. A barber gained the meal, and the prize ticket for the pig was drawn by a female.

Unfortunately, the female was Cadoni's landlady, who was in on the scam – as was the barber – and they all ended up before the magistrates.[32]

The *Paisley Advertiser* carries a long report of this incident a month after the fair giving more clues about Francis Cadoni, 'tumbler and itinerant fan-maker' (presumably a standby or supplementary skill), and his working environment. He must have arrived as one of the 'nomadic hordes who itinerate with all their household goods attached to the flanks of some sorry jade', observed – in an earlier report of the fair – pouring into the town to set up camp in the square opposite the county buildings. Despite this unpromising arrival, the writer goes on to remark on the transformation of the town centre: 'Here in a twinkling were flaunting the splendid blazonings of the wonders each rival establishment for the public favour contained. Griphons and Hippogriffs, and mermaid ... the decorated streets of glaring canvas are groaning with.' Cadoni, we are told, was 'deputy manager for one Brown, the head of a company of ground and lofty tumblers'. This must have been the same Brown he was working for in 1823 and 1826 at Glasgow Fair – suggesting a long-standing connection – though not one that prevented him from telling the court that the handling of the lottery had been done 'by desire of his master, Brown; and that he had pocketed nor profited anything save the disgrace of the present exposure'.[33]

Despite the occasional dud pitch, the Codonas had arrived in Scotland during a period of sustained growth in various branches of the entertainment business. The range and scale of spectacles appearing in cities and at fairs was expanding by the end of the eighteenth century with the arrival of large travelling menageries, purpose-built and travelling circuses and 'show-fronted' theatre booths. Glasgow Fair in particular saw a period of rapid expansion in the 1820s.[34]

The expanding entertainment industry was sustained by a general increase in spare cash in the pockets of the swelling urban populations. These were a draw for showpeople not only at statute fairs but wherever they could muster a crowd. David Prince Miller, a friend and associate of Billy Purvis recalls arriving in Dumfries after a 13 mile walk in the rain:

> We in a very short time commenced operations, purchased some coals, made a large fire, erected a temporary platform, composed of boards and trestles which we borrowed, and in less than an hour after we arrived in the town, I was mounted on the aforesaid platform eating fire, &c., my companion thumping away at the drum and blowing the pandeans. The hall we had obtained was exceedingly well fitted for our business, and our success repaid us for the unpleasant journey. ...[35]

Numerous semi-permanent ventures supplemented the seasonal fairs. Writing about Aberdeen in the 1820s, William Buchanan recalled that every available space was occupied by shows and exhibitions: 'Union Street, Castle Street, Frederick Street, King Street, George Street, John Street, all in their turn.'[36] Robert Chambers remembered the Leith Walk of his boyhood in the 1810s as 'a scene of wonders and enjoyments' from top to bottom. Apart from the transient panoramas and caravan-shows:

> There were several shows upon Leith Walk, which might be considered as regular fixtures. ... Who can forget the wax-works of 'Mrs Sands, widow of the late G. Sands,' which occupied a *laigh* [basement] shop opposite to the present Haddington Place, and at the door of which, besides various parrots, and the sundry birds of Paradise, sat the wax figure of a little man in the dress of a French courtier of the *ancien regime*, reading one eternal copy of the *Edinburgh Advertiser*![37]

Edinburgh printer James Smith (b.1824), describing the vigorous pranks of his youth, mentions going to 'Rory's Show' sometime in the late 1830s:

This booth, which was exceedingly popular among the working classes of Edinburgh, was situated in the Old Physic gardens, on the site now occupied by the North British railway station. Rory was a famous Merry-Andrew, who played his antics on the outside platform for the purpose of inducing visitors to the inside, aided by the inspiring sounds of a drum, clarionet, and pan-pipes; and the exertions of the inimitable Rory were generally well rewarded.[38]

Long-established fairs in Glasgow and the cities were gradually given over almost entirely to entertainment. Newspaper reports of Glasgow Fair in the 1790s devote few if any lines to it, usually only to mention livestock prices, making it hard to draw conclusions about the entertainments on offer. The following note from the *Glasgow Courier* suggests that in 1793 they were still limited:

On Tuesday the annual Fair of this city commenced. Yesterday, the day usually appropriated for the sale of horses, exhibited but a sorry show, and there were few or no purchases. On this occasion the following curious inscription was exhibited on a sign board in the Trongate: 'Penny reels danced in this clofs [*sic*] up two stairs.'[39]

Three decades later, the 1825 view of Glasgow Fair given in pioneering pictorial magazine *The Northern Looking Glass* is not of the great influx of livestock for sale earlier in the week, but the booths, stalls, and other amusements which took over at the end of the week.[40]

At country meetings, however, the trading element held comparative sway and at Falkirk Tryst in 1867, it is this that provides most of the colour rather than the rather modest, down-at-heel shows:

... I came upon a crowd of people looking at a mountebank in the act of swallowing a bayonet, which he did as far as the hollow hilt. Then he made a short speech, collected a few

FIG. 5 Glasgow Fair, mid-1820s. A vigorous woodcut showing the variety of amusements – dwarfing the crowds – available by the 1820s that foregrounds some of the perils of the fair: brawling, drunkenness, gambling and pickpockets. (*Source:* reproduced in C. A. Oakley: *The Second City, Glasgow*, revised 1967 edition)

coppers, and announced his intention of eating a quantity of 'burning fire' by way of dessert to his steel dinner. Besides this clever artist, there were others of the same kidney, with cards, dice, lucky-bags, wheels of fortune, and rowly-powly concerns, but they did not appear to be largely patronised. One old Irishman, with three pins, a wooden ball, and some gingerbread in a dirty pocket handkerchief seemed to be doing very well, but I soon discovered that the old boy was on the high road to ruin. He was setting his pins too close in fact, and one young fellow, in the garb of a clod-hopper, was knocking them down at every throw. ... The refreshment tents are full of farmers, cattle dealers, and stock breeders from all parts of Scotland and the North of England, making bargains, or discussing bargains already made. ... The bank booths are nearly filled with stout substantial men in greatcoats and thick mufflers, carrying riding whips and capacious pocket books, clamorous for cheques, drafts, or bundles of bank-notes. Outside the tents and booths

FIG. 6 'Oldhamstocks Fair', 1805, Alexander Carse, watercolour.
One of at least three views of this fair by the artist. The emphasis is on the
buying and selling of domestic goods – crockery, drapery, shoes – as well as
livestock. Amusements are provided by a small troupe of circus performers
drumming up business under an advertising board, as well as a fiddle and
singer, game of dice and the inevitable drunken brawl.
(*Source:* Private collection courtesy of Bourne Fine Art)

great fires are blazing under pots and goblets of potatoes and
broth, while hungry drovers gather round and regale themselves
with bowls of the savoury liquid and potatoes piping from the
pot. And still the routing, barking, bellowing, pushing, thrashing,
bustle and excitement continue without intermissions. ... Blind
and lame beggars, ballad-singers, apple-sellers, mock auctioneers,
sweetie-wives, piemen, and huxters of other kinds ply their
vocations, and add very considerably to the Babel of sounds.
It is altogether a scene of indescribable uproar, bustle, business,
and confusions, which must be seen in order to be realised.[41]

Fairs may have provided a rare and welcome splash of excitement in the otherwise hard-working lives of their patrons, but
for others they were a source of considerable concern. In part,
this was a response to the hard drinking that was a traditional

35

element of fair holidays (the cause of perennial trouble for the showmen up to the present). Popular poems about the fairs habitually have the day's fun ending with a drunken binge and a high proportion of the booths and tents at fairs provided 'refreshments' to this end. An 1827 report of Edinburgh's All Hallow Fair notes that, although the sale of cattle was slow,

> ... in every other department all was sunshine and vivacity. Showmen and sweetie-wives, gamblers, hawkers, itinerant musicians, and people in a dealing way of every description. There were in all fifty-four tents for retailing refreshments. Some were twenty, and others only twelve feet in front. Taking the average at fifteen feet, as they paid at the rate of 6d a foot, this would be a balance of upwards of £20 to the proprietor of the field for tents alone.[42]

Another source of concern was the inevitable appeal of flush fairground crowds to the criminal fraternity as indicated in the following, otherwise relatively sympathetic, description of the same 1867 Falkirk Tryst:

> ... During the three days of the market, the Tryst ground, as usual presented a busy and picturesque appearance; and was largely frequented by visitors – especially on Tuesday. Of travelling mountebanks there was, as on former occasions, a brisk turn-out; and we are informed that the light-fingered gentry, and others who delight in the society of persons with heavy purses and light beads, were also present in considerable force. In the centre of the moor the 'shows' did a good stroke of business during the three days, as also did the itinerant confectioners, wheel of fortune men, gingerbread dealers, &c. The card sharpers, however, were strictly watched, and were quite unsuccessful in their nefarious calling – a circumstance which is to be attributed to the energy of the police. ...[43]

More strenuous, however, were the objections mounted by those who regarded shows and exhibitions of any sort as inher-

FIG. 7 A rural tryst (possibly by Smailholm tower in the Borders),
*c*1820s, oil. Note the two performers on their simple stage with
canvas wings. (*Source:* Private Collection)

ently immoral. This was a well-rooted religiously based attitude
in Scotland. One parish minister, Theodore Gordon of Cabrach
Parish, Aberdeenshire was compelled to 'express his sorrow to
the Presbytery' on 10 November 1736 for having gone to see a
rope dance at the Brick-hills of Old Aberdeen.[44] This position took
on new life a century later as audiences for entertainment grew
in number and spending power. Typically forceful exposition is
found in the Rev. J. H. Wilson's *Our Moral Wastes, and How to
Reclaim Them*, London, 1859. The author vents his prejudice
against 'the low travelling caravans', 'cheap theatre', its actors
and audience, and includes an engraving showing Aberdeen's
Albion street with a booth theatre as a scene of dissolute revelry,
and an 'after' scene with the street refurbished and devoid of life
and the theatre replaced by a Mission Chapel.

The attitudes of those in authority to popular culture in
general appeared to have hardened by the middle of the century
with attempts being made to curb many of the events where
showmen found audiences. Leith Races, the occasion for a week-

37

FIG. 8 'The Statute Fair – Hiring', John Faed, 1871, oil.
According to the *Art Journal's* contemporary review, this picture should be
read as a 'protest against the reputed domination of whisky at all popular
assemblages'. This reading follows a long-standing strand of public moralising,
but is a narrow take on the artist's intentions. What is clear, however, is the
sheer visual impact of the booth-theatre dominating the background.
(*Source:* Wolverhampton Art Gallery)

FIG. 9 'Campbeltown on Fair day', A. Mackinnon, 1886.
An acrobat and dancer perform on a bare stage by the clock tower.
(*Source:* Argyle and Bute Council Museum Service)

long 'saturnalia', were for the second and final time moved to Musselburgh in 1856 when, as one local historian put it: '... through the refusal of the Magistrates and Dock Commissioners to sanction the erection of drinking booths and similar pernicious concomitants ... they were brought to an end, not a year too soon for the public good.'[45]

That the mid-Victorian city was a less amenable place for showpeople was, however, only partly due to the moral crusaders. It probably had more to do with the prolonged construction boom that filled in many of the empty spaces used by showpeople. Of Aberdeen, William Buchanan noted that 'as street after street was filled up with buildings' room for the shows 'grew scarce' and the site of Polito's 'grand menagerie of wild beasts' had become a church-yard. The Leith Walk of Robert Chamber's youth became 'a plain street, composed of little shops of the usual suburban appearance ...'.[46] Moreover, by the late 1850s new forms of permanent, highly organised and capitalised urban entertainment began to lure audiences, notably music hall, and increasing numbers were able to take their holidays outside the cities. According to the *Glasgow Herald*'s 1878 report of 'The Fair Holidays':

> In almost every street, and more especially those leading to the railway stations and the Broomielaw, were to be seen large numbers of people, tired of the city with its smoke and din, hurrying away to enjoy the fresher atmosphere of coast or country. ... It is within the mark to state that between 120,000 and 130,000 left the city by one mode of conveyance or another.[47]

The roster of possible venues was further affected with the ending of many rural fairs as changing agricultural practices made them unviable. Falkirk Tryst was already on the wane by the 1860s.[48] A general decline in the business seems to be confirmed by the nostalgic colouring of many accounts of the fairgrounds from the mid- to late century. Of the ancient Dumfries Rood Fair, local historian Joseph Irving observed:

Elderly fair-goers have a habit of contrasting the splendour of the fair nowadays with what it was in past times, when the seven incorporated trades turned out with their gaudy trappings on the Thursday, or town's holiday, and a glimpse might even have been obtained of King James' famous gift, 'the Siller Gun', as it was borne in triumph to their own hall. In 'the shows', especially, the falling off is described as a local calamity. And certainly with Jerry Wombwell on the White Sands, and old Ord on the Green, a poor substitute is presented by a gaudy show of shooting ranges and a rickety caravan or two, even though they do happen to contain Peruvian Pangythans. ...[49]

The widespread nostalgia for the shows of yesteryear is clearly seen in the following account of Glasgow Fair in 1887 as the writer compares the hand-powered rides of his youth with the steam-powered rides that had appeared from the late 1860s:

We live in a fast age, and even the amusements of our children must be fast. ... In the old times the hobby horse was like a gigantic bicycle wheel laid on its side. The bloated aristocrat who had sufficient bullion to pay his way sat on horseback on the outer rim of the wheel, while between each spoke ran two or three boys, who shoved for all they were worth, with their reward being the privilege of surreptitiously swinging on the spoke when the proprietor was not looking and the legitimate enjoyment of sitting on the spoke when the proprietor cried 'Three merry rounds and a jump up'. ... Now all this is changed. The hobby-horse of today is a mighty machine, which would scorn to be driven by boy-power ... the modern machine rushes round so fast that one has no time to cast scornful glances around – it is a mad, whirling dazzle, which stops suddenly when its wheezing snorting engine ceases, and the rider is jerked off. ...[50]

What was being described – with a retrospective bias – was simply another stage in the long series of transitions that have continued in the amusement business up to the present. The 'shows' moved from the city centres only to spring up on the

Fig. 10 Dumfries Rood Fair, series of postcards, *c*1890.
(*Source:* Dumfries Museum)

new wastegrounds created by urban spread in the form of the long-running seasonal 'shows' that were a feature of many working-class neighbourhoods. According to James Leatham, writing of the Aberdeen of his boyhood in the 1870s, 'shows were all over the city and environs' and within living memory, Edinburgh had these at Tollcross, Jane Street, Dalry Road and Iona Street, Leith as well as Portobello's Fun City and New Year carnivals at Waverley Market and Meadowbank.[51] From the showpeople's perspective, flexibility and initiative in finding new ways to draw the crowds and seeking out new pitches had long been a way of life and was something to be celebrated, as we will see, in the stories of problems solved, obstacles overcome, disasters averted that form a significant part of their occupational lore.

In the case of the Codona family, the story during the twentieth century is one of innovation and change. This can also be seen in the fragmentary evidence of the family's fortunes from the time of the obviously adaptable immigrant acrobat, puppeteer and animal trainer Frank Codona up to the 1890s when the story enters living memory with one of his great-grandsons, William [3] or 'Billy', proprietor of a chain of small cinemas, Scotland's first permanent funfair and several travelling rides. What we find is a remarkably strong continuity of venerable performing skills being gradually supplemented and finally discarded in favour of mechanised attractions.

After the death of Frank Codona, the statutory records provide a map of dates and places from the 1850s. As to where they were working, there is a predictable concentration across central Scotland, particularly around Stirling, conveniently within reach of the most lucrative centres of population. Not surprisingly for this highly mobile occupational group there are exceptions, although these are harder to trace outside of Scotland with its more comprehensively searchable records. 'Francis Codony' is noted in Birmingham for the 1841 census, which would have been in time for the Whitsun Fair and holiday business and he died there in 1849. John [1], probably his younger son also travelled widely (as did several of his children – see Appendix 1). He was possibly working in Lancashire in 1841[52], Yorkshire in 1848 or 1851, meeting his English wife Louisa Lightfoot, and was in Wales on at least two occasions. The *North Wales Chronicle* gives a short description of an appearance at Pwllhel market in 1847 that in its almost archaic simplicity could stand for hundreds of years of such small-town marketplace performances (and is a reminder of the important role played by children in show business):

During the past two weeks, the town, as the evenings drew in was in a state of excitement, it being visited by Mr. John Codona's travelling showman [*sic*], accompanied by his little girl and boy, and though they are considered of low degree, yet their performances manifested a high degree of cleverness. The little girl, only 4 years old, in her tight rope dancing showed skill and talent which seems destined for a higher patronage than she now receives. And Codona in his tumbling feats with the boy was truly clever.[53]

Other traces of his travels left in the official records are for 1853 when he was back in Wales for the birth of his son Elijah, in Tobermory where he is recorded in September 1859 probably having appeared at nearby Salen for the important late-August horse fair on Mull, and in Aberdeen in 1877 (for the marriage of his son John).

There is also a tantalising account of a Signor Cardoni appearing in London's East End in 1856, who was surely connected to the 'Scottish' Codonas, given their long tradition of performing with puppets and the fact that John was working in England in the 1850s and his brother William was probably in England for the birth of a daughter Mary Ann around 1856:

'This way, ladies and gentlemen – just going to begin – the ingenious Fantoccini of Signior Cardoni!' Such is the appeal that greets us from the side-door of a small house in the eastern quarter of the town. The house is that of a slopseller, whose wares crowd the shop. Over the fan-light of the private entrance, which stands open, a small transparency bears the inscription 'Cardoni's Fantocinni! – Pit 4d., Gallery 2d'.

The house had been turned into a little theatre with three rows of red stuffed seats for the pit and gallery of bare benches rising to the ceiling and the hour and a half variety programme included trick marionettes, dances by a sailor, highlander, and 'Paddy', finishing with juggling and songs, with music on piano and violin. Most evocative as described by the author was the first act:

After a short overture, the curtain rises, and reveals an area in
the centre about seven feet square, carpeted with green baize,
and backed by a dark space into which the eye cannot penetrate.
... There is no note of preparation, not a sound being audible
from behind the curtain – but suddenly steps out from the side
the figure of an Italian peasant-girl in the Tyrolese costume of
laced bodice, short skirts and circular hat. You know it is not a
living figure, for it is but three feet high; but you are puzzled:
the girl looks round and smiles, glances at you with a pair of
black eyes, dashes the ringlets aside with her hand, bridles up
with a little feminine toss of the head, clears her throat with
just one 'h'm', and begins to warble very prettily a Tyrolese air
to Italian words. ... When it is finished, she bows gracefully to
the audience in return for their applause and retires.[54]

Then there is equestrian William Codona and his wife Adelaide, who reached the higher echelons of the circus profession.[55]
William's movements over the 1860s are unclear, but in 1867 he
appeared in MacFarland's Circus in Dundee and from 1868-71
they both toured the continent. Back in England they travelled
particularly with Charles Adams' Circus around the North of
England. In July 1873 they performed in Adams' substantial and
elaborate timber theatre in York, billed as 'Mr. W. Cadona, England's Peerless Somersault Rider', along with Madame Cadona
'the accomplished Equestrian, from the Principal Continental
Cirques: and late of Metz and Strasburg'. Three months later
William died at the age of 27. Adelaide continued to travel with
Adams, across Europe and in the United States. In 1879 she toured
with 'The Great London Circus', part of a 'monster combination' of three shows that visited dozens of towns across the States.
Billed as 'the celebrated Andalusian sensation' making her first
appearance in America at the sizeable salary of $200 a week she
was puffed as follows:

This beautiful young Spanish Equestrienne is without peer in her
profession, and as a Bare-back Hurdle Rider, is without an equal
in the Old World or the New. Senorita Cordona will also intro-

duce for the first time in America her original Melo-Equestrian Creation entitled Poland, Spain and Italy, a novel, refined and classic *act du manege*. This versatile young Artist will also perform her unrivaled Equestrian Four Horse Specialty [sic], entitled The Amazon's Flight, and using for this purpose Four Native South American Steeds.[56]

According to the *St Louis Despatch* she seems to have merited the salary:

In the evening the monster canvas tent was literally packed with people and there was scarcely any room to accommodate the thousands who came pouring in. Before the arenic scenes began fully 10,000 persons were present ... Senorita Codona proved that she is the most intrepid and finished rider. On her bareback steed she leaped through thirty-one hoops without a mistake. Her feat of riding four bareback steeds was also received with enthusiasm.[57]

FIG. 11 Adelaide Cordona, Empress of the Flaming Zone poster for her tour of the United States. (*Source:* John and Mable Ringling Museum of Art Circus Museum, Florida)

45

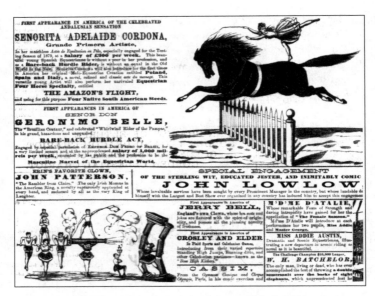

FIG. 12 Detail from a poster for Senorita Adelaide Cordona
appearing with the Great London Circus in 1879.
(*Source:* Circus Poster Collection. Manuscripts Division. Department of Rare
Books and Special Collections. Princeton University Library. *Copyright:*
Reproduced by kind permission of Princeton University Library)

William and Adelaide's story again reminds us that Scotland
was only one stop on the pattern of wider wanderings that was
typical of performing dynasties. British and continental performers had toured the United States from the start of commercial circus there. John B. Ricketts who established the first
modern circus in the States in 1793 had come from Scotland the
previous year and Circus Codonas had arrived by the 1850s if
not earlier.

By March 1855 a Henry Codona had crossed north America
to California. This was 14 years before the journey could be done
by rail, and he had followed in the footsteps of thousands of
Gold Rush migrants by making an overland crossing of Panama
(a week long trek through jungle by canoe and mule) and then

taking a steamer to San Francisco.[58] In California he joined Lee and Marshall's National Circus appearing as 'Mons. Codona' in April as one of three clowns in the Gold Rush town of Placerville, possibly as part of a French troupe 'late of Franconi's Hippodrome in Paris'. By October, Lee and Marshall's were in San Francisco, from where they set sail for the Sandwich Islands, appearing in Honolulu that winter, and then returning to San Francisco in the New Year.[59] 'A large and well-appointed company ... together with a full band of music', they were recollected as having done 'a large business opposite the Commercial Hotel' in Honolulu, in the face of nearby competition from another circus on the lot behind a saloon.[60] Typically versatile, Henry is billed performing 'la perche' (on the end of a pole held by a partner, an act recently introduced to Western circus), as a trick clown and trapeze artist.[61]

Henry Codona continued to appear with Lee and Marshall's, particularly in Sacramento, now billed as 'trick clown and double sommerset thrower'. Lee and Marshall are described in the 1856 city directory as having $40,000 invested in the 'paraphernalia of the Hippodrome' and as erecting 'an extensive and substantial brick amphitheatre' capable of holding 2000, and their artists are listed as including Cordona (Vaulter).[62] In Sacramento, he married Elizabeth Maria Freeth, almost certainly the rider 'Miss Freeth' who was with rival outfit 'Risley's Vatican' in California in 1856.[63] What makes this especially likely is that Risley's Vatican at this time included 'the Caroni family' who had been in San Francisco in October 1855, at the same time as Lee and Marshall's. Signor and Signora Caroni had staged a publicity stunt in direct opposition to Lee and Marshall's of walking a tight-rope from the ground in front of the International Hotel to the top of the building. As the *Daily alta California* observed, 'This will surpass the feat of Madame Austin, of Lee & Marshalls Circus as she only walked to the fourth storey window'.[64] Could the Signor Caroni, described as performing 'wonderful gymnastic feats on the Spanish Column' have been another Cardoni/Codona and have been a link between Henry and Miss Freeth?[65]

All these performers were lured by the opportunities offered by Gold Rush California. Just as Henry Codona's predecessors must have been drawn by the growing urban audiences of industrial revolution Britain, so the demand for entertainment created by the mushrooming populations of cities like San Francisco and Sacramento must have been tantalising. By the time Henry crossed the Atlantic circus links between the continents were well-established but a more specific clue as to why Mr Codona might have travelled from Scotland is offered by the mention that some of Lee and Marshall's performers were late of Franconi's Hippodrome. We can trace Franconi's Hippodrome's route back east. In 1853 and 1854 it was based in New York and before that Franconi's troupe had toured Britain. Members of the family worked in Scotland in 1850 when 'Franconi's Cirque National de Paris' was based in Glasgow and then Edinburgh under the management of Henri Franconi and in the winter of 1852/3 when he and his wife were working for Pablo Fanque's Royal Amphitheatre.[66]

The relationship between Henry Codona and equestrian Harry, the next of the family in the American sources, is unclear but both seem to have appeared in 'Sheldenburger's European Menagerie and Grecian Circus'. The trade journal *New York Clipper*'s listing of various circuses' line-ups for the 1871 season has H. Codona as 'Equestrian director' and as a rider, along with his wife, but also has H. Codona as one of the gymnasts.[67]

Harry Codona and his wives, Amelia an equilibrist and gymnast and Lizzie Marcellus an equestrian, appeared with circuses from Cuba to California between 1863 and 1881.[68] A puff for an 1869 appearance with Ames' New Orleans Circus tells us that he was 'England's champion somersault rider'.[69] He worked several seasons with the famous American clown and circus proprietor Dan Rice, meeting his second wife Lizzie in Rice's Paris Pavilion Circus in 1873 where he performed 'classical riding' as well as pad riding and 'a ludicrous stilt act'.[70] Harry and Lizzie married that July but divorced in 1876 when they were working with Cook's Circus on a riverboat going up the Mississippi. This was not long after an incident possibly fuelled by jealousy during which Harry Codona pulled a razor on his wife and Dan Rice intervened.[71] Things had obviously blown over by 1878, when Harry Codona was working with Rice again appearing in Kansas billed as 'as one of the most memorable of circus performers' in another riverboat circus travelling the Missouri river.[72]

Making a later trans-Atlantic crossing was the step-dance specialist John W. Cardownie. According to one obituary he was 'the son of a travelling showman and was left in Aberdeen practically as "nobody's child", had an eventful career and "dragged himself out of the gutter"'.[73] After a decade of mainly Scottish semi-professional appearances, he had turned professional in 1887, billed as 'champion all-round dancer of the World' and forged a successful music hall career across the United Kingdom with his wife and three daughters in the 'Cardownie Troupe'. In 1896 he travelled to the United States where the Troupe was booked on the top Vaudeville circuits for four years before a tragic boating accident near New Haven took his life in April 1900.

John's daughters continued performing after this as the 'Cardownie Sisters'. The 1900 New York census lists a Janice Cardownie, born about 1882, a La Cardownie, born about 1880, and a Phoebe born about 1881, all born in Scotland, and who must have been the 'Cardownie Sisters' who appeared in June 1900 at New York's Casino Theatre roof garden just a couple of months after John's death.[74] From then until 1915 they appeared regularly in vaudeville, billed variously as 'the Cardownie Sisters, National Costume dancers (more or less what the Cardownie Troupe did), 'Cardownie Sisters, America's foremost quick-change artists' at the Acme Theatre, Sacramento in 1905, in 1907 as 'The Cardownie Sisters, international dancers' at the Savoy Theatre, Hamilton, Ontario and as the 'Cardoni Sisters' at the Dewey Theatre in New York.[75] Phoebe and Jessie (possibly the 'Janice' above) also made appearances in Broadway musicals between 1905-1911.[76]

The most famous American Codona, however, was trapeze artist Alfredo Codona (1883-1937) of the 'Flying Codonas', together with brother Lalo, sister Victoria, and father Mexican-born trapeze artist Eduardo Codona. The obituary of Adelaide and William Codona's son Louis describes him as brother and uncle of the Flying Codonas, making Eduardo Adelaide's son.[77] However, according to a direct descendant, Eduardo's mother was Victorine Regnier, a young dancer who ran away to Mexico with other French showfolk having got pregnant in Glasgow during the winter of 1859 (there is no evidence that the father was ever actually in Mexico). Soon after she arrived in Mexico and gave birth, she was befriended by Jose Bocanegra Aguilera, a floor acrobat from South America (this relationship lasted until at least 1873 when 'El Ñino Condona' is billed in Buenos Aires alongside Aguilera and Garcia as 'Los Tres Mejicanos').[78] Victorine and Jose met up with the Buislays, a French circus family and arranged for Eduardo to be their apprentice. How the two stories fit together is unclear but Adelaide was most probably French, and would have been a very young mother to Eduardo – and William a young father, so perhaps the Victorine of this account and Adelaide are the same person. Adelaide may have been a stage name (one disproportionately adopted by circus equestriennes of the time) and we do not know her maiden name. The rest of Eduardo's story is more straightforward; after a tragic accident ended the Buislay's interest in the show business Eduardo the apprentice, having married one of the Buislays daughters, inherited all of the circus gear and the rights to the show which he developed into the Gran Circo Codona.[79] His children started performing at an early age, Alfredo making a debut balanced in his father's hand aged less than a year. 'The Flying Codonas' reached the highest level of the profession, having been booked by Ringling Brothers Circus in 1917 where Alfredo met his future wife, aerialist Lillian Leitzel. They married in 1928 but Lillian died after a fall during a performance in Berlin in 1931. Alfredo then married Vera Bruce (who had replaced Victoria Codona in the family act) in 1932, but injury ended his career in 1933. His marriage to Vera Bruce disintegrated and while in the process of a divorce he shot his wife (who died of her injuries) before killing himself, a tragedy that almost overshadowed his reputation as a circus performer, renowned for his execution of the triple somersault, 'el ángel del trapecio' according to a recent history of Mexican circus.[80]

As to what the Scottish Codonas were doing, they remained in the circus-performing tradition. Some left the business, moving sideways, often into horse-related occupations where skills could be transferred, or arguably down a notch on the occupational scale, but most seem to have stayed. Over the middle part of the nineteenth century they – or at least the men – are described in the official records not only as 'itinerant showmen' but 'acrobat', 'circus player', 'travelling exhibitioner', 'exhibitor of mechanical figures', 'travelling performer', 'equestrian' and 'gymnast' (the last two common terms for circus performers) and 'professional dancer' with, from the 1880s, 'actor' and 'comedian' being used, probably in reference to involvement with 'penny geggie' theatres – although popular performers had always combined acting and more athletic types of performance.[81] Far fewer occupational labels are given for women but most were from show backgrounds and those marrying into the family inevitably worked in the business – the case up to the present. Those whose occupation is specified include Louisa Lightfoot (second wife of John [1]) given in censuses as a travelling actress in 1861 and equestrian in 1881. In the 1851 census Margaret McKellar (second wife of William [1]) is given as strolling actress, and on their marriage certificates Laura Caddick (married William [4] in 1908) and Selina Pinder (married John [2] in 1909) are actress and circus artist respectively.

A much more detailed account emerges from the six different occupational descriptions of Frank's [1] son William given in his children's marriage and birth certificates; 'acrobat', 'itinerant showman', 'comedian', 'gymnast' and 'itinerant violinist', 'travelling performer with mechanical figures' and finally at the end of his career as a horsebreaker. He is a typically versatile showman of the time, the product of the overlapping circus and popular theatrical arena of the nineteenth-century fairground. This mixed performing tradition remained strong up to the end of the century but is hard to trace in much detail outside the brief occupational labels of the official records. Circus bills and programmes only survive for the large, permanent, purpose-built circuses or Hippodromes found in most major cities and name only the most important visiting performers. Apart from the sequence of billings that can be followed for notable exceptions like William and Adelaide Codona and some of those who worked in the Americas, named appearances are very rare and one-off. They include 'Mdlle Codone, who is allowed to be by all the most extraordinary and graceful performer on the Tight Rope in Europe' at Astley's Amphitheatre in December 1849, 'Mons. Cadoni the Antipodean wonder' with James Cooke's Circus in Newcastle in 1854 and 'Codone' with Risarelli Brothers Circus in Paris in 1879 (one of a number of connections between the Codonas and Risarellis over the 1860s and 70s).[82] Others may have appeared in such venues amongst the unnamed clowns, acrobats and equestrians but the evidence (or lack of it) suggests that – as we have seen for the 1820s and 30s – they plied the more modest but still lucrative show-fronted fairground booths. In 1843 'Codona's Lilliputian Circus' is listed in a description of Glasgow Fair. Less grand than attractions like Springthorpes 'magnificent collection of wax-figures', the 'Imperial Roman Exhibition of Moving figures in Alabaster, as large as life' or Cook's Circus 'a respectable building' which had stood for several years at the foot of the Saltmarket, but more substantial than single-attraction caravans, the Codona enterprise – a small-scale circus or possibly a marionette show – is described as one of:

> By far the most numerous class of booths ... those devoted to the drama, singing and dancing, &c, a style of cheap amusement for which the charge is only one penny. We have here Miller's Eastern Pavilion, Codona's Lilliputian Circus, Chambers' Royal Pantheon, Mumford, the Prince of showmen, Purvis's unrivalled dramatic and ballet performers, and a host of others. The booths contain several hundred persons, and as there are from eight to ten performances in the day, an immense amount of money, in penny subscriptions, comes into the general treasury. The audience, of course, consists almost entirely of the lower orders, of both sexes, two-thirds of whom are masticating 'speldrins'

[split and dried smoked fish], or drinking cheap ginger-beer, and the other third smoking tobacco.[83]

Over 30 years later Frank's grandson William is described in his son's 1879 marriage certificate as a 'circus proprietor' and he was the likely proprietor of 'Codona's Lilliputian Circus' advertised as 'on tour' in the *Ross-shire Journal* for 28 June 1878, suggesting a long, either intermittent or permanent, history for this enterprise. He (or possibly his father) was also the likely subject of a poetical reminiscence by Chryston schoolteacher George McIsaac that provides a detailed account of a typical show:

> Cardownie wis a showman born,
> Likewise a showman bred;
> The rovin' life he dearly lo'ed,
> An' sae this life he led.

> Expert he wis at slicht o' haun',
> Yea, did outrival far
> The feats an' freak, aye, ev'n the breeks
> O' puir auld Malabar.   [Old Malabar – Irish showman juggler
>   Pat Feeney, see above]

> Inside a yellow wooden box   [Showmen's living wagons were
>   traditionally painted yellow]
> Upon four wheels that ran,
> Cardownie ate, Cardownie drank –
> A puir but honest man.

> Its brods were geyzened, frail an' auld,   [*geyzened* = leaky, warped]
> Clean innocent o' pent;
> While through its seams in gushin' streams
> The fitfu' breezes went.

> In it he lived – wife, weans, an' doug,
> Nor rent nor tax had he;
> Secure within his wooden wa's
> They huddled happily.

But we maun haste – the show's begun
An' lood the maisic's clashin';
A wheezy hurdy-gurdy grunts,
An auld burst drum they're bashin'

He's placed some callans in a raw,
And wi' them terms he's made –
Wha first shall bolt a treacle scone
Will get a saxpence paid ....

A comic scone-eating race is described, followed by a show:

The gruesy shed wis quickly filled,
Folk bent on fun an' mirth;
'Twas easy seen baith lugs an' een
Ware for their penny's worth.

Bress balls an' forks an' knives he pitched
A' airts wi micht an' main;
Like homin' pigeons aye they cam'
Back tae his haun' again.

Sic balancin', sic jugglin' tricks,
Sae great an' wondrous feats;
Inside his mou' he ken'led tow,
On canes he birled plates.

An' O! the sangs, the funny jokes
Adoon oor cheeks brocht tears,
Sides like tae split – thus did he get
Oor coppers an' oor cheers ....[84]

This William's four sons William, Frank, John and Tommy
continued in the performing traditions: Frank was a highly
regarded Punch and Judy exponent and William was involved
at some point with marionettes, continuing a family tradition
and following popular theatrical fashion that saw an upsurge of

marionette theatre activity in the late nineteenth century.[85] By the 1890s they were still heavily involved in the 'penny geggie' business, but now of a more purely dramatic type, a line pursued by several other show families at this time across Scotland. These dramatic entertainments were provided for a 'penny' entry and produced in ad hoc permanent or portable canvas and timber booths. They were popular throughout the century and were key attractions at the fairs. At the time of the *Glasgow Constitutional*'s 1836 visit to one such circus-style booth the drama offered ranged from cut-down Shakespeare to melodrama, often garnished with song, dance and other non-dramatic fare:

> The booth is large, in the centre of which is a circle, strewed with sawdust. The gallery is crowded. We presume we have the good fortunate to be in the pit. What a noise! – buz, buz, buz! – cries, shouts, yells, – flourishes of drums and trumpets! ... Enter a *lady and gentlemen* (of course) the lady is hoisted up to a tightrope and treats us to a dance ... this is far better than the tame stalking and elocution in the theatres – it is all down-right passion, pure earnestness! Edmund Keane, when he had such audiences, never played better. What need? These people must get alarmingly furious, knit their brows, stab and poison with effect and energy, and foam at the mouth, if they don't wish to be hissed.

By the 1840s, at Glasgow Fair at least, theatrical shows were taking over, and by 1849 the *Glasgow Herald*'s reporter concluded that 'the penny theatricals have almost entirely taken the place of the ground and lofty tumbling and fire-eating that used to make citizens amazed in the days when Katterfelto and Cadonni were in their glory'.[86] Columnists generally saw this as a bad thing, especially because penny theatres attracted large (the Royal Hibernian theatre seated 3000 in 1848) mainly adolescent or younger audiences. For the proprietors, they were very good business. Showman James Calvert was prosecuted in 1846 for presenting stage plays without a licence in a large canvas-covered wooden booth in Low Green Street capable of holding 1600. After a trial lasting six months he paid penalties amounting to £150. According to the *Herald*, there were four such venues near the foot of the Saltmarket performing regular stage plays three or four times a night and five or six times on Saturday nights 'to audiences consisting of several thousands of boys and girls, averaging from 5 to 15 years of age'.[87] Less than a year later, despite the costs of a trial and fines, Calvert was back in business.[88]

The geggies were often either treated with condescension or mocked, as in music hall writer Alexander Melville's 'The nicht I did my actor in the penny gaff':

> I'm no Sir Henry Irving noo,
> Nor am I Beerbohm Tree;
> But a bigger star than ony is
> The actor that you see.
> I got a rare engagement,
> Jist aboot a month ago,
> Tae murder William Shakespeare
> Down in Weaver's penny show.[89]

Nevertheless, according to one patron, 'The geggies were sustained by actors often of a high standard but down on their luck, generally through a weakness for the bottle.' He recalls one at Vinegar Hill, a Glasgow pitch favoured by geggie owners, starring 'Beaumont Hughes, who I believe at one time in his career had played prominent parts in London theatres. Hughes had the reputation of having once, in the geggies, played right through a scene with a dagger through his hand, pinning it to the table. Apparently, either through malice or by accident, someone had substituted a real weapon for the property dagger that usually did duty.'[90]

Whatever the standard, the geggies were often the only source of dramatic entertainment for their working-class audiences outside the big cities. Hughie Smith's company was gratefully remembered as an important source of amusement in Arbroath in the 1860s and 70s:

FIG. 13 'Fun of the Fair', *Quiz*, 15 July 1881. Two drawings to go with a lengthy description of the year's attractions and fairground characters to be found at Vinegar Hill. The emphasis is still on performances of various types: melodrama in the geggies, circus turns and marionettes.
(*Source:* Archie Foley)

By day his old 'soap box on wheels' trundled through the streets bearing in great, thick, black letters the announcement of the night's performance, a stoppage being made at each conspicuous corner to give voice to the purposes so artistically foreshadowed on the primitive waggon. ... At night, under the light of blazing lamps, the actors lined up on the front pavilion arrayed in all their glory. Young 'Hughie' relieved his parent at the drum, the while his sister – the oppressed heroine of a hundred plays – resplendent in spangles which glittered under the flares like a princess's jewels, danced divinely and sang what sounded in our ears like the sirens' seductive song.[91]

Scottish comedian and film star Will Fyffe started his career in the geggie run by his father, a carpenter by trade, and was proud to recall his humble start:

We used to build up our own theatres – in snow very often and many a time during a storm. They were wooden, built in sections with canvas tops. They were all on lorries and wagons. The stage was a wagon with two back flaps which we let down and then built round it. It used to take us about three days to build it, but we would stay in the town for months at a time playing a different drama each night, followed by a laughable farce. ... It would do our present-day actors a power of good if they could hear and see the actors of those days. Their voices were distinct and robust, not the inaudible murmurs we hear now. The actors in those days had to work harder and in the face of great competition – when the fair was in full swing. The roundabouts and side-shows often used to steal our thunder. ... The fairground's steam organs used to blare out in the middle of our most dramatic speeches. We had to shout to be heard. Often our lines were interrupted something like this: 'Tell me, my darling, what do you see?' – 'Coconuts! Mulky coconuts!' Then, small boys would throw stones on to the roof of the geggie and they would go clattering down just when somebody was playing a big death-bed scene![92]

The Codona involvement in the geggie business was extensive. In addition to a Portobello venture recalled below by Cathy
Macintosh from the memories of her Aunt Catherine, the family
also had three portable geggies around Glasgow; one in Dumbarton, one in Pollockshaws, and the most famous in Springburn.[93]
According to Gordon Codona's mother Florrie May interviewed
in 1954, each play would be performed for three nights and then
the cast and scenery moved on to the next. The repertoire seems
to have been the heavy melodrama that was the staple of the late
nineteenth century geggies, the Codonas' most popular being
'Uncle Tom's Cabin', 'Reddy's Bonny Daughter' and 'The Collier's
Dying Child' and, as was the case with most geggies, the whole
family appeared in the plays:

> The grandfather was famous as Marcus in 'The Sign of the
> Cross.' We would do that play one night, and 'Maria Martin'
> the next, and then go on to 'Rob Roy'. The Codonas could do
> any play.[94]

Further detail about an unnamed geggie in Springburn –
probably the Codona venture – appears in a lecture given by the
headmaster of Springburn School, Charles Forsyth in 1940,
remembering the 1890s. He recalls that the audience sat on
planks and the show lasted for three hours with an hourly change
of show and a charge of 2d being made at 7 pm, 8 pm and 9 pm:

> The house was usually packed and we were enthralled by the
> plays. The only one I can recall was 'Burke and Hare', the ever-
> green favourite. The acting was good and the delivery was good.
> At that time I would be in the toils of learning a verse or two
> of poetry and I marvelled how the actors could remember the
> words of their parts. I expect the explanation would be the
> natural one. Good actors for one reason or another had lost
> caste in their profession and were glad to earn a pittance in
> their usual way of doing so. The plays always had a high moral
> tone. Virtue always triumphed over wrong and how we cheered
> when the hero got the better of the villain.[95]

These types of amusement began to lose ground around the turn of the century, however, and William Codona [3], who had started his career in Scott's Circus, had already begun the transition away from being a performer to being a proprietor by 1891, by which time he owned a 'steam-yacht'.

In the census of that year his brother Frank was described as a 'gymnast' and Tommy and John were still giving their profession as 'circus artist' on John's 1909 marriage certificate to Selina Pinder, of the Pinder circus family, but over the next decades most Scottish Codonas became the proprietors of rides or 'side stuff' and, in the case of William [3] or Billy Codona as he was known, the Fun City and a small chain of cinemas. By the 1930s, the principal exponents of the long performing tradition in Scotland appear to have been descendants of Henry Codona who had worked as a musician and acrobat with the Pinder-Ord Circus.[96] One of Henry's sons (William Codona [4]) gives his profession as 'gymnast' on his 1899 marriage certificate and is most likely the William that appears, still a gymnast, on the 1908 marriage certificate of Henry's other son Henry. This William's granddaughter remembers him as an acrobat and trapeze artist. Born in 1924, she can recall the circus horses and being in the caravan with 'auld Willie' and being told to tell nobody where the money was kept. William and his family had their caravans in the Vinegar Hill site to the north of Glasgow's Gallowgate that was a permanent funfair and winter ground from the 1870s until well into the twentieth century. The circus at this point was 'part of the family', but was eventually lost.[97] Another source takes the circus performing tradition to the 1940s when the second of Henry's grand-daughters worked with the 'Pinder Sisters' for a short time when the family was based at Seafield near Leith.[98]

The outstanding performer was another of Henry's sons (by a second marriage) John, born in 1895, who continued performing as a musician and puppeteer until the 1960s and was keenly aware of his performing heritage. In one interview he proudly stated that when his great-grandfather came over from Italy to present a marionette show to one of the King Georges, the musical 'commentary' was provided by the pan-pipes, and since then there had always been a Codona playing the pan-pipes.[99] In a manuscript handbill he describes himself as follows:

> John Codona Punch & Judy Performer established since the 17th Century. Performed then by my Great Grandfather. Patronised by Royalty. Then by my Grandfather then my father then by me. Open for engagements for children's parties, house parties or any musical entertainment including marionette figures & dog Tobbie performance.[100]

John had started busking as a boy and after being gassed and wounded during World War I, went back to busking on his bass drum and pan-pipes, dressed in a distinctive glengarry. A familiar figure around Edinburgh and Fife, he presented a Punch and Judy show for 50 years until his death in 1964. In an interview from 1963, a year before he died, he stakes his claim:

> I've busked for a living since I was a laddie of 11. I supported my wife and five bairns on my takings right through the depression and I've hardly ever taken a penny of Government assistance. … There isn't a street in old Edinburgh I haven't played in, and I've been asked into some of the swankiest homes in the country. But people, particularly the working class, have changed. … Take my picture now, I tell them, for John Codona, the greatest one-man band who ever lived, will soon be gone for ever.[101]

His passing marked an end of the family performing tradition in Scotland, but also a particular type of street performing as a whole that was more typical of the previous century and that he had done well to prolong.[102] The pan-pipes and bass drum, as he was well aware, were the instruments of the Victorian showman, a fixture, as we have seen, of exhibitors' parading platforms used to draw crowds, most famously described over a century earlier by Henry Mayhew in his Punch performer's show, and also used independently by his 'Performer on Drum and Pipes'.[103] John Codona seems to have been much like the Victorian predecessors described by Mayhew, working hard for his living

Fig. 15 John Codona: series of photographs showing him in action on Dumbiedykes Road, Edinburgh, 1954. As the caption given by the original photographer states: 'John Codona, the one man band acting Pied Piper to the local children lead by Peter Bottomley (with stick).' (*Photograph:* Jean Bell. *Copyright:* Courtesy of the Living Memory Association)

Fig. 14 (*right*) 'One-man band; a quaint Edinburgh character', Tony Wasilewski. (*Source:* Mrs J. I. H. Marshall)

and exploiting every possible opportunity to perform; as well as his street rounds, he is remembered entertaining at football matches, gala days, shows, fêtes, taking advantage of Edinburgh Festival crowds, playing in the New Year at the Tron church, performing with his Punch and Judy show in Princes Street gardens, at hospitals and children's parties.

One Edinburgh resident recalls that when he found out that she was dating a soldier in the King's Own Scottish Borderers he would start playing 'The Blue Bonnets' just as he rounded the corner into her street, assured that he would be rewarded for his efforts. Being an ardent communist, according to my source, he would then play on with 'The Red Flag'. As this anecdote suggests, he was a regular visitor to certain streets around the city.

Ally McGurk remembers regular visits to Warrender Park Road in the southside:

> ... whether it was weekly or less often I can't be sure. He would stop outside each stair in Warrender Park Road where we lived, and start playing. Of course his bagpipes were loud enough to rouse everyone, and we all made our way to the front windows to watch. My mother would take some small change and wrap it in a piece of silver paper (to keep it together) and throw the little package out of the window to land near his feet. I think this was the usual way of giving him contributions – I seem to remember our neighbours doing the same thing.[104]

Mary Buisson remembers him visiting middle-class Ann Street on a weekly basis in the mid-1950s when she was seven or less:

> On Wednesday nights, after eight o'clock we expected the arrival of Codona, the One Man Band. ... even when he wasn't actually playing music, Codona's movements were musical and we would hear him long before he was actually at our gate. We would press our noses onto the cold window panes in the sitting room, clean after our bath, dressed for bed, unable to go until we had heard our fill of the Scottish ballads. The windows would steam up and we would have to wipe them clear with the arm

FIG. 16 Hand-written handbill for John Codona's Punch and Judy, undated. (*Source:* Museum of Childhood, Edinburgh)

of our dressing gowns. Codona would look all blurred out in the dark street, his feet performing a strange kind of jig on the damp cobbles. His arms pumping in and out in rhythm to his music, his head nodding from side to side as he reached for the distant notes for his tune, the feather in his cap bobbing cheerfully. When the tune was ended if he was asked into the house, he would walk up the path, the drum beating his every other footstep, the bells on his ankles jingling, his other instruments strangely silent. As he reached the front door he would bend down and loosen the drum pulley and put his drum and his bagpipes down where we used to lay down our school satchels. He would follow daddy into the sitting room with only his bells tinkling. In the sitting room he would unhitch his mouth-organ and lay it down on the table beside him, he would smile a broad grin. ...

After a few drams and tales of the First World War, he would set off on his round; 'his drum beating his every other footstep, he would pause outside our gate to blow into his bagpipes to re-fill the air sack'.[105]

Mary Buisson's next-door neighbour on Ann Street employed him for a children's party (presumably a Punch and Judy show, since, as the letter shows, he could not see the audience) in 1956, and her thank-you letter to him survives:

Your son could see, and you yourself could hear, how much delight you gave the children; and you have left these 29 five and six-year-olds with an experience which they will remember all their lives. We congratulate you on your skill and artistry.[106]

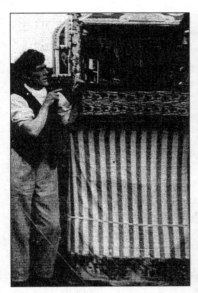

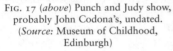

FIG. 17 (*above*) Punch and Judy show, probably John Codona's, undated. (*Source:* Museum of Childhood, Edinburgh)

FIG. 18 (*above, right*) Codona's Royal Punch, performing for South Morningside Primary School, *c*1942-44. This comes from a very short clip in a film made by Edinburgh Corporation 'holidays at home' Committee to promote local holidaymaking and avoid wasting wartime resources. In the scene immediately before this, John Codona stands beside his striped booth with a woman, presumably his wife and assistant. (*Source:* 'Holidays at home', Scottish Screen, 1944)

FIG. 19 (*right*) John Codona busking on Ann Street, Edinburgh. (*Source:* Jacey Bedford)

3
Geggies, Gallopers
and the Ghost Show

O RAL history takes us back, initially at second-hand, to the
1890s – the decade of John Codona's birth, when showmen
were increasingly abandoning the performing tradition that
John was to maintain for another 70 years. The story is taken
up with the third generation of Frank's descendants – William,
Tommy and Frank – three brothers who, (as well as a fourth un-
recollected brother, John), followed careers encompassing what
was a fairly typical range of experience from horse-drawn travelling circus and booth shows, to steam-powered rides, traction
engines and fairground bioscopes. Frank, like his brother
William, spent part of his career in the geggies, being principal
Scotch comedian in his own booth and latterly working with his
brother William.[107] Tommy started with wax-works proprietor
Mark Purchase, aged ten, was later with showman George Biddall as a parader and was a clown known as Handy Andy with
Pinder's Circus and ended his career travelling with a ghost show,
a type of attraction that still retained a good many theatrical
and performing elements into the age of cinema and electricity.
An anonymous poem, 'Codona's Ghost Show', probably from
around 1920 and referring to a flower show held on Dundee's
Magdalen Green pays tribute:

> As usual down to Magdalen Green I went to see the shows,
> Of course it's at the Flower Show time that everybody goes
> And at the very back I saw, what I thought a new Intrusion
> But when I got there 'twas Codona's Ghost Illusion.
> Good Luck, Tommy, the game is good, your name still to the
>   fore

Like your open air shows years ago was a credit I am sure
So may your patrons rally round you and make it quite a host
And bring again to memory the old time Pepper's Ghost
I am certain it will come again
Keep trying and you'll find the Dumb Show of the pictures you
    will leave it far behind
There is nothing like the old show to make the people laugh
Like Rumbo Jumbo and the Ghost with their witty, funny
    chaff[108]
It may take time, but wait a while
You'll find it all serene
The peoples' getting tired of the Dumb Show on the Screen
So good luck Tommy Codona, may your name prove quite a
    host
By keeping up the memory of the old time Pepper's Ghost.[109]

Gordon Codona was Tommy's great-nephew and remembered a personal boyhood involvement in the ghost show:

[*Gordon Codona's words*]

The ghost show travelled. It was an illusion, it consisted of a black area at the back on a board and there was a mirror set above this black board at that angle so that when you sat or stood in the show you were looking at the mirror, you see, you looked up and you saw the mirror. You didn't see what was down here on this floor. The board was sloped a bit to correspond to the angle of the mirror, you see, and the idea was that you saw the head without the body and the body without the head and all they did was got a black cover over the body and showed the head and all you saw in the mirror was the head. But it was a good mirror, you couldn't realise what you were … this was the illusion. And one of the – the head without the body – one of the things was the flying angel. Usually the flying angel was one of the showmen's kids used to get the job of, bring them in, put them on the board, used to do this. They were the angels going about the ghost show. Little things like that. Simple, simple things.

FIG. 20 Tommy Codona's ghost show, c1920s. Tommy Codona is at the bottom of the steps pointing to what looks like a bill of fare, whilst various paraders – contortionist, dancing girls, bass-drummer and what looks like a cowboy performer on the right – all try to draw the public, with music no doubt provided by the organ. (*Source:* Codona Family Collection)

I think perhaps on one occasion I got the privilege of laying on the board amongst the other children and posing. We didn't do very much; we just lay on the board and moved our arms about. We were supposed to be angels as far as the ghost show was concerned, you know. Usually the showmens' kids all got the chance to go into the show and become angels. It was a great experience for us just lying on this board here and pretending that we were flying through the air which was the vision that you got through the mirror, laying on the boards you see. But that's about the – it wasn't a regular thing – I think I only done it once. Couldn't have been a very good angel!

... They showed you different scenes ... there couldn't be a lot of movement, because you were on a board, you know, and if you moved the wrong way you'd probably break the illusion a bit. Because it was black to black to hide the form. It showed

you heads on their own and bodies without the head and visions
of somebody flying through the air, which was somebody over
the top of somebody underneath sort of thing, you know. It was
more of a – the only movement was a movement of arms or of
legs not a movement of a body as far as I remember.

That was just the type of show that you saw. A canvas show.
Wooden frame, with a tilt, we called them tilts, tilts over the
top, canvas over the front and there was a parading platform
at the front where they could draw the crowds and shout, bang
the drum and things like that. That was the ghost show.

There wasn't a lot of illusion, ghost shows, illusions. There
were a few. I think there was only one in Scotland playing that
I know of. Late twenties. That was about as late as it would go.
I can remember and I was born in '21 and I can remember the
show and I was only young boy, so I think it was about the late
twenties.

William Codona was the most successful businessman of the
four brothers, but he was also a versatile performer. J. Wilson
McLaren met him towards the end of his life and records:

> He played Conn in 'The Shaughraun', Miles in 'The Colleen
> Bawn', Jakes in 'The Silver King,' Bailie Nicol Jarvie in 'Rob
> Roy,' and Marcus, along with the late Wilson Barrett, in 'The
> Sign of the Cross.' Besides, he could tell a good funny story, do
> a song and dance act, a juggling act, and play a cornet and trom-
> bone, and was an accomplished marionette manipulator.[110]

William started his career with Scott's Circus, where he met his
first wife, Mary Ann Kennedy.[111] He progressed from a simple
horse-drawn travelling show, to running a small chain of penny
geggie theatres, moving into the large powered rides by the
early 1890s, and gradually taking over a run of fairs from one
of the Evans family, (a showman who according to Gordon
Codona, had no sons to take them over). By 1897 his ghost show
was listed in 'The Showmen World' column of *The Era* magazine
as being amongst 'The big shows at Glasgow and now doing the

FIG. 21 William Codona with wife Mary Ann Kennedy and daughter Rebecca, cabinet portrait, *c*1903/4. (*Source:* Cathy Macintosh)

Scottish round'.[112] Like several other Scottish showmen William made an early entry into the 'bio-scope' business. *Showmen World* had noted his 'Kino-moto Theatre of illustration' alongside the ghost show at Irvine Races in 1899 and he eventually developed a chain of small cinemas across the Lothian area.[113] However, the venture for which he was perhaps best remembered, was establishing Scotland's first permanent funfair at Portobello in 1908.

Although described in his obituary as 'of a quiet disposition, to those who knew him intimately he was lively and witty', in family memories he emerges as an innovative, decisive and determined showman.[114] These last two qualities emerge very clearly in the reports of what was described as 'one of the most extraordinary occurrences that has ever fallen to be chronicled' at Carstairs sports day on 26 August 1905:

> When during the course of a collision between a number of young men belonging to the district and the proprietors and attendants of the roundabouts, shooting saloons, etc., which were for the time stanced on the village green, the latter seized hold of the rifles at the saloons and fired at the crowd for some considerable time, the result of which was the wounding of a boy named Brock … in the left shoulder.[115]

The event that eventually lead to this dramatic conclusion was

FIG. 22 William Codona and family outside living wagon, *c*1905.
From left to right are sons Frank and Johnny, then William and wife Mary Ann,
Nathaniel, Catherine and Rebecca Codona at the front. The pony (a typical
showman's Appaloosa) and trap belonged to William and Mary Ann. Note also
the 'Kicker' in the background. (*Source:* Cathy Macintosh)

a disputed payment for the shooting range that escalated with
blows exchanged, a further scuffle with a policeman injured,
rushes by the showfolk to defend their own, then stones thrown
by a crowd of locals and the alleged indiscriminate shooting of
the crowd by showfolk from under their caravans. Not surprisingly, each side saw things their own way. The local papers,
mindful of their readership, are clearly biased, saying little about
the locals but 'the showpeople seem to have lost their heads', a
squabble in Carstairs years earlier that had caused them to fear
for their safety 'had been a trumpery affair, and had arisen from
the same cause, alleged cheating on the part of the showfolk',
William Codona, the principal proprietor, and one of the main
players, is described as being 'sarcastic' after his trial. Nevertheless, he and his co-defendants were found not guilty by a large
majority of 'culpably or recklessly' discharging guns or other
weapons.

His evidence to the court gives a clear sense of the man himself – determined and direct – and how he saw this particular

case and the long-standing issues it embodied. Like all travelling groups, showpeople could be subject to prejudice, which in the heightened often drink-fuelled atmosphere of a fair or carnival could turn hostile. Showpeople saw it as an important part of their business to smooth things over with punters but often felt unprotected by the authorities and were not slow to look after themselves and were perhaps predisposed by history to fear the worst:

[*William Codona*]

I am the proprietor of a number of shows, and have been for a number of years. My shows include merry-go-rounds, shooting galleries and the like. I was at Carstairs village ten years ago. We met with some disturbance at that time. We were attacked by some of the Carstairs people. If it had not been that some strangers interfered on our behalf we would have fared very badly. We visited the village again on 26th August. I saw Scott [the police constable] at the Carnwath races, and asked him if I could get the show ground. He said he did not want of any of us ... rubbish there. I got permission from the factor. We opened about four o'clock in the afternoon. From about seven o'clock at night the people seemed as if they had something in their mind, and they kept refusing to pay when the attendants asked them to pay. About eight o'clock I was talking to Scott, when he said that we had better take care of ourselves, as there was trouble brewing. He said also 'There's to be a row here tonight' and I appealed to him for protection. He said 'I will see you all right'. About ten o'clock I was speaking to Scott when a girl came to me and said a party would not pay for his shots. I thought it was a good chance when I had the policeman with me, and went over to the man and asked him to pay. This man said he did not owe me anything, and then Scott turned on his heel and walked away. I caught this man by the coat and asked him again to pay his shots, when he struck at me twice and I had to strike to defend myself. I knocked him down. A party then threw a coconut at me, and struck me. My son was struck at the same time on the head with a broken shaft ... his head

had to be stitched. We came to the conclusion that the policeman was taking the side of the people. We saw there was trouble
brewing and Broughton pled with Scott to stay amongst us or
some of us would be murdered. Scott said he would go out and
calm the people down but it did not take any effect. They commenced to throw stones, with the result that our caravans were
all more or less broken, the electric globes were smashed, and
two mirrors in the shooting saloon. I became in terror of my
personal safety and the safety of my wife and people belonging
to me. Several of our folks were running about with guns, and
I ordered them to be taken from them. I took guns from the men
myself. I never fired a shot, nor did I encourage any one to fire a
shot. I simply endeavoured to keep my own men from going on
to the road. There was a man Newsome at a shooting gallery
next to us and he fired two shots, but in the air, for the purpose
of frightening the people. I was in a state of alarm that night,
and the others were too. I thought the villagers were going to
leave us nothing to go away with. My property is worth £3000
to £4000. It was all on the ground that night. It's my interest
to keep on good terms with all villagers, as I have to live by
them.'[116]

Though his grandson Gordon did not know 'Billy' directly, the
memories passed down from his father give a strong sense of the
respect in which the man and his abilities were held.

[Gordon Codona]

His name was William Codona – Billy Codona – basically the
background was that he travelled about fairgrounds with his
family – four sons and three daughters – and in those days they
used to travel round in horse and cart to small shows. And he
operated amongst other things a show that they call the penny
geggie at that time; a penny because that was the charge that it
cost you to get in ... the old penny. They used to perform little
one act plays – Maria Martin, Sweeny Todd the barber. My
father used to be able to rattle off a few of these little one-act
plays that they used to do. My father performed in these along

with his other brothers and sisters. It was a family thing, and very often my father would start reciting out of the blue bits and pieces from these different acts that he used to do, you know. And he done all this prior to the First World War – in those days they dismantled everything. ... [The geggie] was canvas top, wooden proscenium that was put on. They were all canvas wooden structures with a false front and the music, if there was any music at the time was supplied by an organ, you know the old fairground organ.

Before the First World War he was over in Ireland and they were a bit of a rough lot and the Irish was Irish in them days, Scots were Scots, and never the twain shall meet and my father got wind of that there was going to be real bit of trouble with some of these Irishmen. My grandfather got wind that they were going to burn the show down. So he announced – he was there for two or three days – so he announced that tomorrow night he was giving something away that was ... free – free gifts, this, that and all the rest of it, you know. And that night went off quite alright and during the night, he pulled it all down, wrapped up and disappeared. He said that was the only way

FIG. 23 Codona's 120-key Limonaire barrel organ, Glasgow, 1906.
(*Source:* Frank Bruce)

they could get away without getting the place burned down, you know. And it was a threat, it was a genuine threat, you know. But these was the things that they had to do. My grandfather was in typical showman style, he told them what they was going to get for nothing tomorrow night, but tomorrow night never came, they was packed up and away that night![117]

They travelled about with that, then when the cinematograph era came on the go, this was when all the big cities had the cinema shows but the provinces had never, ever seen these, so that was something that my grandfather jumped on very quickly and converted his geggie shows, particularly in the wintertime to cinemas, silent movies.

He had small roundabouts, he had the kiddies' roundabouts. At that time there wasn't any big roundabouts because they didn't have the power to drive them or to take them about the country because it was all horse driven stuff. It had to be small, light equipment used. And this is when the cinematograph shows started. They converted again, moving on to different lighting systems and so on. And that was because of the advent of the traction engine – steam – just about the turn of the century. And my father, he told us he used to operate the cinema. And he said that one of his jobs with my grandfather was – silent pictures – they got a piano, and he said to my father, 'You'll play the piano'. Didn't know how to play the piano. 'What do I do?' He said well, when there's a slow scene on the screen there, just tinkle it lightly, and when there's a train coming' – fast action – he said 'go fast' you see. So that was my father's job, so he actually learned to play the piano, watching the pictures and doing this. And as a matter of fact, my father had a piano, an upright piano in his caravan years after. He played by ear and it runs in the family a wee bit. None of us are musicians as such, but we played by ear and that was his start of the cinema job.

When the cinema got going he played the piano for the music and one of the places he operated in was at Queensferry during winter. ... The cinemas was a wintertime thing. I think places – because they needed the current – you know, they needed somewhere that they could get the power at that time. This wasn't always available on the fairgrounds, you know. And that was most of the wintertime. And it was a good thing for the fairground folk because number one, they were closed up anyway so they converted the show to cinema.

And it was the showmen that really brought the cinema to the provinces. People got the interest through the showmen because they couldn't go to London or Edinburgh or Glasgow. They brought the cinema to them and that's agreed; it's established that it was the travelling showmen that really got the cinema going. So my grandfather was pretty quick on the job there. He was a clever man. I just remember him as a boy. ... I remember my mother and father taking me to see him in Edinburgh, Portobello, he wasn't well at the time and that's my only recollection of him unfortunately.

He married twice. The second wife was Williams, Becca Williams. I didn't ever know his first wife. He married in the business. That was the usual thing in them days, even until recently, you married within the business. Basically because that was the only people you met, long-term; you travelled about so much that you were only a week in a place or a fortnight in a place and you didn't meet the local inhabitants. The people you did meet were your own fraternity that were moving about all the time. You met them at different fairs – you didn't travel with them all the time. You'd meet someone here and a month would go by, couple of months, and some of the others at a different fair, with the changing. But everybody knew everybody else, that way.

My grandfather travelled mainly in Scotland. He spent quite a lot of time round about the Edinburgh area. That was part of his operation: by this time now he was getting into the larger roundabouts, this is the turn of the century because traction engines were coming on the go, plus the fact that his family was growing up and were more help to him and in 1908 he opened an amusement park in Portobello in Edinburgh, on the promenade. ...

By that time he started up the amusement park there and he

also at that time, he opened up a number of cinemas, permanent cinemas at Haddington, Prestonpans, Tranent, Portobello – I think there were another couple. That was permanent cinemas, that he, from his own experience he realised that this was the way to go, you know. That was at the same time as Greens, Greens' Fairs was on the go, you see. He was level with Greens. Greens was dabbling a wee bit in the fairground business and my grandfather was dabbling a bit in the cinemas.

At that particular time he would have the galloping horses, he had the switchback which was the big ride and golden dragons, motors which were large motors; in them days cars were a bit of a novelty and these went up and down over hills, and dragons was the same thing.[118]

They were all driven by steam at that time. There was a steam engine in the centre to drive them round. And swing boats, roll roundabouts, swinging roundabouts, and small things. But when the War started, he had the Figure 8 at Portobello. He just got that before the War and that came from Germany, it was a wooden structure. I'm not going from memory here; I'm only going by what I've been told. And, well, I remember the Figure

Fig. 24 William Codona's Dragon Scenic. (*Source:* S. Thackray: *British Fairgrounds; A photographic history* [Norwich, 1993])

8. But when the War started and he had these rides and he had four sons, he was branching out from the fairground business into the cinema business with his cinemas that he had that he developed during the war years too and two of his sons went to the forces. My father went to the Royal Engineers.

There was four of them. The eldest was William, Billy, and there was my father John, there was Frank and the youngest was Nathaniel. That was the four sons and there was daughters – Catherine, Beatrice and Rebecca.

And things went through a bit of a stop during the war years, obviously, with the War on but Fun City carried on as much as it could. But I remember sometime during the War before my father entered the forces he was operating the cinema, the cinematograph show at Queensferry. This was the time we spent quite a bit of time at Queensferry. It must have been because they weren't travelling about a bit then. And he did tell me that while he was at Queensferry he got involved in playing billiards, in one of the local clubs and he entered a competition there, billiards competition, and it always peeved him, he was in the final and he had to leave Queensferry, the fact he never ever got to play them. He said, 'I think I could have beat this bloke too'. He said, 'We had to leave, they were starting to move again'. He had to leave and never got to finish the final of his competition.

When the War finished, my Grandfather decided they were going to stop at Portobello, with these other activities that he had and he formed his four sons into a separate company, Codona Brothers, and they started out with the various rides, by this time now with dragons and chairoplanes, galloping horses, carousel, jumping [? ...] and mountain glide was another thing that they had: you walked up and you come down a dip, just a straight come down, you know, but it was a good height, you know, went over the bump and came down to the bottom, you know. Fairly simple, some of your rides at that time. The complicated ones with the huge motors ... the scenic railways as they called them, the dragons, they were pretty complicated. Expensive too.

We were actually on traction engines prior to the War. This is just before the War started. I said to you that they were getting the equipment round about that time; galloping horses and that. And as a matter of fact my father, when the War started, he went into the forces he finished up driving a traction engine during the War. ... He knew that, and the army was using traction engines to shift heavy equipment. ... There was a premium on all that type of ability.

I think he [William senior] had a good relationship with the banks. I'm gonnae say that because I saw a clipping and I don't know who's got it now, but it was the time of his funeral, there was a bit in one of the Edinburgh papers, and it gave you a list of mourners that went to the funeral and there was about four or five bank people there, I mean bank manager, bank manager, regional manager, general manager; this was listed in amongst these people. So he must have had a good relationship with the banks and probably he had a good reputation. He was a man of considerable means by that time. ... Portobello was a major act. It was the only one in Scotland at the time and it the only place that Edinburgh people went to. ... So he was well established and well known and he had a big funeral when he passed away. So I would imagine that finance and things like that would be the banks at that time, you know. When he formed the Codona Brothers, he had quite a bit of equipment then. They had the Figure 8, and they had the carousel and the galloping horses in the Fun City, and a Helter-Skelter and two or three juvenile rides. Continually changing as time went on. Quite simple rides at that time. ...

Cake-Walk was another one they had. That was two shutes went like that motion [contrary to each other] and you walked along them, or you tried to walk along them. You come in at one end, you walked along that one, you come off, walked across a platform, got on and you walked back this way. And you were just rotated like that. ... You didn't walk easy, you know, you had to hold on to a couple of bars. If you were clever you could use the motion to skip along, you see. I know that at one stage one of the stories used to be that when the people got

FIG. 25: Codona's Fowler traction engine, no. 1430, *Fearless*,
Glasgow, 1906. (*Photograph:* George Dawson. *Copyright:* National
Fairground Archive, University of Sheffield)

to that end, when they were coming out, one of the employees
would get back to that end and shove to make sure that everybody went out, when they were busy, otherwise they would stay
there for ever. It needed somebody at that end to keep them
moving off, off the shute, you see, when they were busy. That
was the old Cake-Walk. That was the sort of thing ... in them
days. We're talking about between the war years, 1920s.

The four brothers travelled about then. They all had their
own – my grandfather had this equipment divided out between
the four brothers who were married by this time. He was in
charge then. When he formed the Codona Brothers, the Codona
brothers were partners. And they were all the same type of
person as what my grandfather was. They were all ambitious,
they all had their own ideas, they were all good showmen, but
they couldn't agree! You see, so this went on for a few years
and eventually the partnership broke up. They all wanted to do
their own thing, obviously, you know and they split – that
would be about maybe middle 1920s – split up. Codona
brothers I don't think it lasted that very long, maybe ten years
or so, can't be sure. But eventually they all went their own way,

but they all done well, you know, they all branched out. My grandfather was the only one that stayed in the cinema business with his halls round Edinburgh.

The late Cathy Macintosh's mother, Rebecca, was the second youngest of William Codona's children. Rebecca married Harry Paulo of the circus family, a wire-walker, but did not take to the circus life and returned to Portobello where she brought up her daughter. Though a youngster at the time, Cathy had clear memories of her grandfather and some of the stories told about the family business around the early 1900s. She also had an impressive grasp of the extended Codona genealogy.

[*Cathy Macintosh*]

Well, we had the geggies, the Tower along the prom. My grandfather, he used to have the geggies in there in the winter and he couldn't read nor write, neither could my aunt. I think Frankie was the brainiest, he wasn't the brainiest but he was the one that could read and write. And there was a family called Whittaker, and Mrs Whittaker used to read the parts to my grandfather and Aunt Catherine and they had to pick it up from there. They had marvellous memories and that was the show and they were very good.

They had Burke and Hare, Maria Martin, Rob Roy, all those type of plays, you know. I remember we went to the Kings one time and Will Fyffe was in the audience and it was Burke and Hare that was playing, and one of my older cousins, we always called him Uncle – one of the audience stood up and said that Will Fyffe was one of the first ones to play some part [Daft Jamie], and Uncle, he went mad, he said, 'No, it was my grandfather, he did it'. So there you are, that was going back a bit.

Auntie Catherine, she was always the leading lady. My granddad, he was the leading man. Auntie Beatrice, she was second lead, she was pretty, she was a funny woman, she was. And the boys, I don't know much about the boys because it was more my aunts I was beside, you know. But I do know Auntie Catherine, she was in it, my gran, my granddad, and Auntie

Beatrice and then there must have been Uncle Johnny, I think he was in it, and Uncle Billy. There wasn't much between them, you know, between Uncle Billy and Uncle Johnny I don't think, there wasn't many years between them, you know. And uncle Frankie, he didn't, I don't think he did, he did the business. He didn't do anything on the stage business. ... It seemed to be very good as far as I could make out. ... Family, just family. Or they'd have, as I say, there was that man used to play Rob Roy and maybe Mrs Whittaker or one of them would play a minor part.

It was in the Tower, this one, the one here was in the Tower, the Tower Amusements, and that, I don't know what like it was, probably would be a wooden hut when my grandfather had it. But that's where they played, in the Tower. ... All winter probably.[119]

And then they would travel at different times?

Well, they did and they put on the geggies maybe there and then they'd go to another place and show at another, the same thing maybe at a different place, you know. ... They did quite a lot of different things my grandfather and grandmother, they really, they tried everything.

... I don't know what show it was in but it was a dying child and this person ... and that's who she was supposed to be and she was no good so she got the heave, my mother did. And then another thing was Maria in the barn and somebody was hitting one of her sisters, it must have been Auntie Catherine, and my mum was sitting there, she had to sit in the audience because there was nobody to mind her, 'Don't you hit my sister', and my grandfather threw her out again. So that was that. But she said they always had to, her and Uncle 'Thaniel, had to sit in at the show, because there was nobody to mind her. So they had to watch every show, so they knew where they were and that was it, you know. So that was her life. ... She wasn't really up to it, mum, she remembers some names and then that was it, but Auntie Catherine, she said she was a great actress, she was good. So was Auntie Beatrice, but Auntie Catherine was very good, so was my grandfather, he was very good. ...

My mother ... used to say that the boys would go on the geggies and one night it came – there was a big man that used to play Rob-Roy and Uncle Billy and Uncle Johnny – used to have this plank and he'd break it, and they decided that they would saw it – the plank was sawed, they used to saw it through so it would break easy, so when it came to putting the plank on his back they put it on the wrong way and he couldn't break it at all. So that was one story my mother used to tell. She didn't know a lot, you know, I'm going back a lot of years with her, she couldn't remember much because she wasn't – I think the geggies were over and done with by the time mummy got to about fifteen. And then they went on to the picture house. We had a few halls here, there and where have you. There was one at Abbeywell[120], there was one at Queensferry, ... I think Uncle Johnny, Gordon's father, looked after Queensferry. There was one at Prestonpans; that was a proper picture hall. There was one at Tranent, that was a proper ... I think there was one at Haddington, it must have been just a ... Corn Exchange or something, but there was one at Haddington ... [Queensferry] was over the winter but Prestonpans and Tranent, they were all the year round. They were proper picture halls.[121]

... My mother, she was no much good as an actress ... but she used to help with the picture halls and things like that, and the Fun City. But she was only, what, fourteen when my grand-ma died and my grandfather married when she would be about fifteen or sixteen so she was thrown into the Fun City or the business. Then she married and she married my father, he was a Paulo – circus – and she tried that for a year and she was no good at that, so they come back to Fun City.

... My grandmother died when she was 52 and not long after that my grandfather married again. And mother had two sisters and she had four brothers but she had two sisters and she was between the two of them. They had a picture hall in Prestonpans, they had one in Tranent. My grandfather had one in Tranent and one in Prestonpans and Auntie Catherine, Auntie Beatrice and my mother used to look after the one at Prestonpans. When my grandfather married again my mother –

she was between the two sisters – she stayed with one, one time and one another and there was always a bit of friction of who was taking the money, who was looking after the money, so they all landed out, seemingly. And I don't know what, my mother just left, she said, 'That's it, I'm nothing to do with it, I'm not going back'. But she had to go back because my grandfather made her. But during the War [World War I] my grandfather had the Fun City and his boys, it was a family concern, but the boys had to go to war, they went all these different places. Well, while they were away my grandfather took Fun City back off them. And Auntie Catherine, Auntie Beatrice and my mother and Auntie Beatrice's daughter Marianne, she was ages with my mum, they looked after the Fun City with my grandfather during the War. And when the War was over, my grandfather just kept the Fun City and that was it, he was the head of the family and he did as he wanted to with it, so he just kept it. And he kept it for a good while and then he decided to sell it, so he sold it to Aunt Catherine, she bought it. But the family didn't get anything from it, and what it was sold for my grandfather just kept, that was his. He'd given it to the family and then he decided to take it back. He was a topper! ...

And can you remember your grandfather?

Yes, just ... He was stout, a fat man. He was lord of the manor and I remember he lived in Tranent with his picture hall in Tranent they had and they had a house above it. And that's where he died there. And he always had a parrot and this parrot he taught, it could mimic him you know, and he used to talk and make the parrot mimic him and then he'd his grandchildren, he'd get you there and you had to perform, you had to 'twinkle, twinkle little star', or sing ... and if you couldn't sing, it didn't matter, you just had to do your piece when you went to see him. I would be what, about five or six when he died I would think, but I always remember that.

And did he have a distinctive way of dressing?

No – black clothes, just a suit, always a dark suit that I can remember.

They all met at this cottage. It must have been the cottage my grandmother died in and the cottage was at the foot of Figgate Street. ...where the Tower Amusements are. Well next to that there must have been a cottage and my grandfather had that cottage. ... I think he lived there when they had the geggies in the Tower. ... And every Sunday the whole family, they had to all come together in this cottage and tell them what that hall took and what this hall took and how they did with that. My grandfather kept reins on everything, you know, until I think the War and then he married again and then of course they all went their different ways. But my mother always said she can remember on a Sunday, they always used to land and there was all these brothers and the ones that were married, the married ones come and their kids and my grandfather used to go in the room with this lot and do the business. So that was that. Uncle Frankie, he was the scholar seemingly. And this was a great meeting on the Sundays; a real old fashioned way – that's how he was, he was the head of the family and he stayed the head of the family until he couldn't any longer, till that he got married to Auntie Becca and then I think the boys just got a bit fed up with it. ... My mother kept telling me about it. She says, 'Oh, I hated the Sundays', she said, 'all this lot came in for their dinner and their tea ...'.

... My grandfather seemed to have homes everywhere. My mother went to school in Leith. So they must have had something in Leith to live in somewhere. And then she came to Portobello; I think she must have maybe just left school, I don't mind of her talking about school here. And they went to Glasgow; he had something in Glasgow. And then he opened a Christmas fair in Glasgow somewhere. I remember mummy saying but where I don't know and he came back to Edinburgh. ... But mummy said, 'Oh what a miserable winter it was in Glasgow'. And he decided to open a Christmas fair or Christmas show or something and he had this big Christmas tree. Oh, she must have been tiny; she just remembered it and no more.

*I have heard … that your grandfather could do puppets …
marionettes.*

He did. … I don't know where they went. I don't know who got
the marionettes. … I remember hearing about them and when
he died I don't know what happened to them. I remember some
of the family wondering what had happened to these and I still
don't know what happened to them. … I think he had them at
Tranent. So whether they were parked away somewhere in
Tranent and forgot about, I don't know. But he did, he had the
marionettes because I remember them saying, years after, 'I
wonder what happened to the marionettes my grandfather had?'
Interesting to know what happened to them.[122] He used to have
a penny whistle, you know, these flutes.

Pan pipes?

Uhuh, and he played those… I remember my grandfather's was
black. I don't know what happened to those pan-pipes and he
could fairly play a tune on them and I remember Auntie Lucy,
and the one man band used to be in Princes Street and she stopped and she listened and she gave him money, I don't know how
much she gave him, and she said, 'You know, you're a Codona,
I'm a Codona too, I married a Codona'. He said, 'Well, I don't
want to know', and he just walked away and left. She thought
he was going to tell her something or explain something but
no, he just off and left her. He didn't want to be connected.

… My grandmother … she was a Kennedy and she was
from Gateshead. … My grandmother Codona … her mother
died young and she was brought up by the Scotts. She was
Mary Ann Kennedy. …

That's show families as well?

Yes, circus family Scotts and she and my grandfather ran away
and got married when they were very, very young and seemingly
when they first got married, they had a flat trailer thing and a
tilt over the top, and that's where they lived, that's what they
lived in and then they got a bit better – they had a horse, of
course, and then they got a bit better off and they got a wagon

FIG. 26 Studio portrait of Catherine Codona
taken around the time of World War I.
(*Source:* Cathy Macintosh)

as we call them. They went to Ireland and they – granddad and grandma used to recite or something, you know, they did shows before they had a family and this is how they got a living. You know, they went to Ireland and went all over and they did all these things, and then they got a wee bit better off and they got a wagon and they had their family.

I don't think her father was circus but I think her mother must have been because when she died, my grandmother was brought up with the Scotts and she, Scotts are the circus, they were circus people in England and that's about all I know about them really. Mother was only fourteen when she died.

... and your grandpa's second wife?

[His second wife] Becca, Rebecca Williams. ... That was her

married name. She was really an O'Connor, Rebecca O'Connor. She was cousin to my grandmother but my mother wasn't called for her, my mother was called after Auntie Becca Scott, she wasn't called after Auntie Becca Williams. But, seemingly, not long after my grandmother died, Auntie Becca Williams was never away from my grandfather, so they got married. So that was that. ... She was cousin to my grandmother, so whether that was to do with the circus, it possibly would be. She married a Williams. This was her second marriage.

I see ... complicated.

Oh, we're a rare fun family. ... They all, well, this was it; Alfred, he was called after his grandfather, Broughton, his mum was a Broughton and Auntie Minnie and Auntie Florrie were sisters, Gordon would tell you that, two brothers married two sisters. Uncle Johnny and Uncle Billy married two sisters; there was Auntie Florrie and then Auntie Minnie. They were Broughtons, that was their maiden name. Auntie ... Uncle Johnny's family was Alfred, Catherine, Florrie May, Gordon, Joyce, was that them? ... Alfred, our Billy – Billy was the oldest. That was six of a family and then to Minnie's family, Uncle Billy's family, there was Albert, Violet ... Norman, Rosemary, Minnie, Douglas. Both had six children. So there you are, twelve.

So was Gordon's mother ...?

A Broughton.

Was that a show family?

Yes, oh, yes. Yes, yes. Fairground. We're all the one family, really. I think we're all related really if you go back far enough.

4

The Fun City

PORTOBELLO was an obvious choice for William Codona to open the Fun City, the first permanent funfair of its type in Scotland. It was one of the earliest seaside locations to develop as a middle-class resort in the 1790s with villas being built, bathing machines for hire and showmen coming to entertain in the form of Ord's Circus which began several decades worth of annual appearances. By the end of the nineteenth century it had evolved into a major seaside destination for working-class holidaymakers, complete with pleasure-pier (built in 1871) followed by the extensive Marine Garden complex in 1909.

FIG. 27 Programme (1910) for the Marine Gardens complex shortly after its opening. (*Source:* Frank Bruce)

William Codona had already put a set of gallopers opposite the 1000-seat 'Tower Pavilion' (erected by the magician Harry Marvello in 1907), which was lucrative enough to be known as 'the goose that laid the golden egg', the golden egg presumably being the Fun City which followed in 1908. In its heyday, it was patronised by the many summer holidaymakers who would visit year after year, but also by more local visitors.[123] Among the attractions recalled by an Edinburgh office worker was the fortune-teller:

The offices all went together in the evenings ... at Portobello fairground there was Mrs Smith, and she was absolutely wonderful. She told me, I was 23 at the time, no I was younger, she told me that I would marry when I was 23, and I would marry a man with brown eyes, and he would walk with a roll, because he was from the sea ... and he was in the Merchant Navy to begin with. Every word was true.[124]

The Fun City also became the main base for William's immediate descendants. According to Jim McArdle (Snr) who grew up there in the 1930s, 'Portobello was the home – Billy, Frankie and Johnny all started out from the Fun City'. It was also a base for other show families including the Paulos, and Jim – related to both families – remembers all the show children going round the caravans for 'Sunday money'; from the Paulos he got one penny, but from the Codonas it was two pennies; 'they had money'.[125] According to current owner Melvyn Strand who grew up there in the 1950s and 60s, there were 18 families living on the site in the fairly small – 32 feet – caravans of the time, but it ceased to be used as a winter ground in 2001 when only two families stayed.[126]

For almost a century the Fun City weathered Portobello's changing fortunes (the Pier was demolished in 1917 and the Marine Gardens suffered a protracted decline and became a bus garage in 1960). Owner Melvyn Strand bought the site from from Cathy and Solly Macintosh in 1987 by which time it had been closed for two years. For him it was the fulfilment of a life long ambition as his family had always been tenants on the site (also, Melvyn's wife is a descendant of William Codona). According to Melvyn it was a typical small fairground with rides, sideshows and Dodgems and was in need of modernisation. It was renamed Fun Park, new rides were introduced and an amusement arcade with video games and shooting galleries opened in 1991. Later, more amusements were moved under-cover and a 20,000 square feet indoor section that contained a tenpin bowling alley along with Dodgems, a carousel and a children's train was opened in 1998. This was a £1.1 million invest-

FIG. 28 The beach and the Fun City, postcards. These holiday-season shots show the Figure 8, and in the distance the bustling beach of the inter-war summer season. (*Source:* Gordon Codona)

ment, but for Melvyn the insoluble problem remained – the site was too small to meet the needs of a modern fairground. Apart from the arcade, the buildings have now been demolished and plans to build flats on most of the site submitted. A new and improved amusement arcade is included in the plans to keep a link with the family fairground history in Portobello (a link also

FIG. 29 Catherine Codona Thomas
playing amongst the supporting
timbers of the Figure 8, *c*1942.
(*Source:* Catherine Codona Thomas)

shown in the fact that several families who once stayed on the site have put their names down for particular flats on the proposed plans).

In 1966 Michael McCreadie, who together with wife Hannah (*née* Codona) ran the Fun City until the early 1970s, was interviewed by Bill Tennant for his television show 'Time out with Tennant' in 1966, and gives a snapshot of the business at a time when there was already talk of the redevelopment of Portobello.[127]

[*Bill Tennant: Were you born into the business?*]

[*Michael McCreadie*]

No, it's about 33 years ago I came into the business. I was an engineer at the time.

What made you go in?

Well … just, I liked the thing and gradually worked my way into it and then I married into it.

How difficult is it to make a showground pay in 1966?

Oh, very difficult. There's such a lot of different factors come into the thing. It's very expensive to run a showground.

What's the expense, what's your main expense?

Well, repairs and the actual costs of the machines themselves when you purchase them.

What does a Dodgem cost you?

Well, in the region of ten thousand pounds ... for each machine and each car; each car will cost you about £380. ...

And how long will each car last you?

Well, that again is debatable; how they're used or abused by the public ... Four or five years.

Now, do you yourself own all the major equipment – the big machines?

Yes I do.

Now, all the side-stalls – what about them?

Well, they're all tenants that – I let them out, I let them out to tenants.

Now, I saw a kiddies' machine up the far end of your city which is now sixpence. What would that have been before the War?

A penny. So that's a substantial increase there.

And are youngsters – are the youngsters who go on them today the same sort of youngsters who went on them years ago?

Oh aye. They'll go on them, but they're not satisfied with them. It's more speed and thrills they're out for today. They'll go onto them but they're not satisfied. They'll want to enter the likes of these big machines – these big machines at the back of me.

Alright ... Ben Hur. Before the War what would the youngest kiddies be who went on that?

Oh, in the region of about ten years old.

And nowadays?

Och, you're talking about tots that were sitting on them there today. And we have to have a staff member holding these

93

kiddies now. You never had that before ... we find that the kiddies and that – the youngsters of today are more daring than what they were, you know, you go back pre-war or wartime.

Now, is the fairground still the same sort of place where the youngster brings mum and dad in with them?

Very much so, yes. If it wasn't for the kiddies there's quite a lot of them we wouldn't get into the ... it's the kiddies that sort of entice the adults into the fairground.

The public used to quite often complain about things in fairgrounds like the guns, you know, the guns they used for firing and they always used to sort of say 'ah, they just bend the sights, I mean they're not accurate guns'. How true is this charge?

Well, you see, it's not true at all because we send these guns up to a gunsmith and that's a local gunsmith, like, and he sorts up all these guns, we get them back again and then the human element comes into the thing. It's like Jock saying to Willie, 'I was a good shot during the War', and then they go to the shooting stall and then he finds out he's not such a good shot and sooner than take the blame himself he naturally puts it onto the guns.

Showpeople were sometimes not very well looked upon by the police or local authorities when they travelled because it was often felt they encouraged trouble around the shows, you know, they acted as a magnet for troublemakers. How do you feel about this?

Well, I think it's a little bit unfair that. I mean ... we don't find that at all, that they encourage the rougher element. As a matter of fact, since the War we've discovered that we've got ... class barriers is down. We've got all classes into a fairground now, people that before would never come into a fairground come into a fairground now. That .... the class barriers is definitely down in the fairground.

Talking of things being down – is there any chance with this re-development of Portobello which is being suggested, that this place will come down.

> Oh yes, there is a suggestion that they make a new front, you see, that they widen the promenade and we hope to be incorporated with the thing, which I think that most seaside places will eventually have to come to that way of thinking – incorporate a funfair in their seaside front. As I said, with a seaside the likes of Portobello, that I think is eventually is coming back, you know, Portobello is … I can see a great future in Portobello.

From 1973 until 1986, the Fun City was owned by William Codona's grand-daughter Cathy Macintosh – who spent most of her working life there – and her husband Solly. Cathy's mother Rebecca also spent most of her working life in the Fun City, starting work before World War I. Also briefly interviewed in 1966, Rebecca gives a typically pragmatic response to questions about a life spent in the Fun City:

How different do you find things in fairs nowadays?

> [*Rebecca Macintosh*]
> Well, I think they're better really.

Why?

> Well, I think people have more money to spend, you know.

In your day was it the fashion for the younger members of the family to work?

> Yes, yes.

What age did they normally start work?

> About ten I would say.

What sort of things would you do?

Well, in stalls, something easy, you know, Helter-Skelters and all these sort of things.

Now, what happened if the show was on while school was still in?

Oh, we had to still go to school. We had to still go to school.

You weren't given time off school?

No, no – just holidays.

Did you ever want to do anything other than this job?

No, no … [laughs]

Nothing! Never want to be a nurse? … Every girl wants to be a nurse.

No, no … [laughs]

And what about now, looking back on those years – do you ever feel you've missed anything having spent so much of your life here?

Well, no, I don't think so. No, I think we enjoy our life and it's pleasant in some ways and …

But do you not feel it restricting because you've got to be here all the time?

Oh yes, you feel that – yes, you do feel that.

If you've to do it all over again, would you still be in this business?

Well I'd maybe try and get something easier, you know, an arcade or something like that. … [laughing][128]

Daughter Cathy takes up the story from Portobello's heyday in the 1920s and 30s:

[*Cathy Macintosh*]

... I was in there for years and years. It was great and when Portobello was at its height it was a great place. ... As you came in the gate there was the Helter-Skelter, there was the fortune teller on the other side, there was the Helter-Skelter on this side, there was the boats, swing boats, you know, the children's boats, then there was the stalls, there was a coconut shy, there was a darts stall, there was a Crash the Kitchen, you know, a throw balls and hit the plates and that. ... Happy Home, that's what they called it and then there was a shooter, two-two shooter, I used to mind the shooter, and then there was an ice-cream shop, Shenkin's ice-cream shop, that was next and then there was a side gate and down the bottom there was the Figure 8, and then you come up the side, there was the Dodgem, and in the centre there was a wee machine, and there used to be an organ in the centre, and it was great. And I'm going back before the Waltzer, so there was a set of Chairs and then there was the Cake-Walk. So that was going that way – and that was Fun City. And the organ played, there wasn't any [Panotropes] or anything like that, it used to be just organ and a friend of mine ... used to go in the back of the organ, and put the paper in the organ. That went on for a long while. Really until the last War. And then, of course, the Waltzers come in. Chairs went out and the Waltzer came in. And then a few years after that Auntie Catherine sold the Fun City, and sold it to Uncle Johnny, and that was our Gordon's father, he bought the Fun City. So that's where it comes round to Gordon.

I was there from what – I was a youngster. I did all my schooling at Portobello and I think I was four when I came back. Mother and father got married and she left for two years I think and then she came back to Fun City and even all my married life I was in the Fun City, except for a couple of years when I got married and then I came back again.

So it sounds as though the women in the show families played, you know ......

Oh, they all played their part. They do, all showpeople do. I

FIG. 30 Fun City in the 1930s.
(*Source:* Portobello Local History Society)

mean no matter what family you're in, all the women have their part to play. They clean up and then they go through and mind the stuff. They don't get off!

And did you ever travel ... do the fairs?

Just for the first year I got married and at that time you just had to take what you were given. There wasn't any big fairs you could go to because you were just married and so we tried it for a year, year and a half, and then we decided to come back to Portobello.

We had a caravan. ... It was always, I don't know, it was home and that was it. It was a great thing. It was a good life, in fact I was talking the other day about showpeople, how they see the country. You know, they travel from here and they go up to Inverness and they go to Campbeltown and they go all round Scotland and they see all this round the country. You don't need a holiday, do you?

... There was a kitchen and then there was a bedroom, kitchen, living room. It was just there, you know, there was nothing – I'm going back, what, my God I'm going back a few years, I think about 40 years because from that, after we sold the caravan we bought a prefab and built that in the Fun City, and that was the usual, two bedrooms, toilet, what have you, bathroom, kitchen, living room and it was quite comfortable.

Now, your husband ......

He was a Macintosh. He was a showman. ... He travelled before he went in the army, yes, he went round the country with his mother and father and had quite a good life too. ... After the War he travelled with his mother and father. ... He came out the War and I think it was the next year that we got married and we tried the travelling and – you've got [to] have the positions in the grounds. His mother and father had the positions. You know, you go to – say you go to Ayr and there's a space there and there's nothing walking up to it. It's no good; you don't get the people in that and if you're not in that good position, you may as well forget it, because you get nothing. You've got to work for all you get. And when you're first married, you start there and you've got to work yourself way up to round there and it sometimes doesn't work. So that's what happened to us. Go to wee places and making a living but just, not doing anything great.

And what was the routine, you'd be at a fair for how long?

Fortnight. Two weeks. Finish on a Saturday, pull down Sunday. Monday, Tuesday travel. Wednesday, Thursday build up. Open Friday, Saturday and all through the next week and pull down. A fortnight each place ... but it was a good, a good life. If you had the good places, the good positions, a great – you couldn't beat it. No way. I only travelled for a year, a couple of years. But he travelled until he got married, until he went in the army.

Well, we came back and we went in the Fun City and then we opened a bingo hall, a bingo shop, and then we decided to buy the Fun City, so we bought it. But we only had the one girl and it's a family business, you need the family and he strained his back at one time, and, I don't know, things weren't going so good for a while, so we decided to sell it because ... we were getting older and our Becca wasn't – she was going to marry eventually but she wouldn't marry into the business, so there was no point keeping it. Had we had a bigger family, more or less we would have kept it but we only had the one girl, so that was that. So we got out of it and we couldn't have got anything nearer. We bought, just bought the house here, just along the way from Fun City. We bought this and then, as I said, there's two [showpeople] went to Glasgow, the other girl bought the one facing me, and the other one was just there, but we were quite a gathering round about us.

So you sold Fun City in 1986 did you say?

But not sorry because I think we were a bit past it by then, you know. However, we quite enjoyed it while we had it. It didn't make any difference, really, whether we had it or we didn't have it. It was just, that was life. You try all sorts don't you?

[Fun City] It used to be, years ago, I'm sure they used to say it was a crematorium and there was a harbour, it's Harbour Road, and you could still see the stones of the harbour outside years ago and that used to be the harbour … somebody said it was a morgue, oh to heck, but anyway whether it was or not I don't know. … My husband thinks my grandfather's ghost was there. He definitely did and there used to be Buchans at the back, the pottery. And I think they must have had the let of the place at one time because there used to be a back gate and there was a horse and cart used to go down the beach and they'd lift all the sand and they'd come up Bridge Street and go through the back of the Fun City into the pottery.[129] They didn't go round that way, they went through the Fun City. So they must have had the let of the Fun City years ago from Buchans, you know. Well, that was allowed so I'm sure that's what happened.

And when you had Fun City what was in it?

Oh, there was the Waltzer, the Dodgem, weighing machines, we had the skelter at one time. What happened – the Figure 8 had to be pulled down and the wood was as good as new, it was a damn shame. The master of works must have had a … it was when Auntie Catherine died and Hannah McCreadie and Michael McCreadie took it over, that was Auntie Catherine's adopted daughter – and I don't know what happened but the master of works decided that the Figure 8 wasn't safe.

So, my husband and the others, they had to pull it down. And the wood, the wood was marvellous and what the devil happened to this man I'll never know; why he decided it had to come down because there was hardly a rotten bit in it. It was all pine, and he said it was ridiculous pulling it down, and it was. … This must have been the 1950s I would think. Anyway, it was a landmark, the Figure 8, it was on all the postcards and everything and this daft man had it pulled down and it was a shame because that was the attraction. There was the Big Wheel when we were there but there was nothing to replace the Figure 8. When that went, the lot went more or less, you know. That and the Marine Gardens and the rest all went to pot after the War.

FIG. 31 Hannah Codona at the front entrance to the Fun City, c1926/7. (*Source:* Catherine Codona Thomas)

Because the number of visitors would be dropping as well.

Oh, it did, aye. During the summer, in the height of the summer, our caravan stayed – that's the prom and our caravan was there right on the prom and there was a board you know to divide you and you could hear the melodeons and the people singing and it went on all night, and along the far end at Seafield end there was tents pitched, they used to come with their tents and stay there for the Glasgow Fair fortnight. You always knew it was Glasgow Fair – the women used to come with their hairnets, pink and the blue hairnets. They used to come in, on a Friday night, and we were open till nearly twelve o'clock because we were so busy, and they'd get on this Figure 8 and go up on the skelter and it was really, it was all fun. It was a great place and then the War came and that finished it. Of course, everybody goes abroad now, I don't blame them, because it's as cheap to go abroad as it is here.

And did they have any of the show-type things like the illusions or the ghost show?

Well there was, Uncle Tommy had the ghost show. That was my grandfather's brother, Uncle Tommy Codona, he travelled with that. I didn't see it, but I used to ... Uncle Tommy and the ghost show and Auntie Hannah, his wife, she always used to say 'the Codonas, they had a fortune in tripe mines' and mummy used to say 'that's Auntie Hannah on about the tripe mines'. ... It was just, it was used to say they were worth money, and they'd left money somewhere or other and mummy used to say 'oh that's the tripe mines she's on about'. ...

And did you ever have trouble with people coming in or, you know, anything like that?

No. ... Well, you get a few odd things, you know, but you get used – you handle it mostly. If you didn't handle it you were in trouble so you've got to try and handle it. I remember one year in the Fun City there was a lot of these, eh, these with the coloured hair and that type, and they decided to all come to Portobello. Oh, it was packed. And the police told us, they said, 'Look, there's going to be trouble so close the gates and keep the gates closed'. So we kept the gates closed at first and then all of a sudden they were banging against the gates and they want in. So my husband said, 'Oh, we better let them in. Just goin' to cause trouble keeping them out'. So we let them in and, right enough, the minute they got in it was okay because a lot of them listened and we had to say 'now you've got to take the time, because somebody's going to get hurt. If you start rushing everything, it's not on'. So you just had to tell them that they had to take time to get on the Waltzer, wait till it stopped to get off and wait till it stopped to get on and everything went okay. But you get the few. I was in the arcade and a chap was bumping the machines, and of course I had a big lad at the back. And I remember I said, 'Look, if you're gonnae do that, you may as well just go out', I said, 'because it's not going to work. The minute you do that, all the money goes to me, so you've had it'. So of course he seen the right of it, 'Alright missus, that's alright'. But if I hadn't of opened, it would have caused more trouble. Another – I think it was the same time – the police decided to come down with their dogs ... and it was just they were rowdy, but the police got a few of them and put them in the wagons, they must have been giving the police trouble, you know. ... But that was it. Fantastic.

But what about between the Wars...?

No hassle. No that I can remember. They were all out for fun. If you did get a needle, it was – they went outside and had their own bit – it wasn't with the people in the ground, it was among themselves and they used to go outside on the beach and have their fight and that was it. We didn't have any, fortunately we didn't have any of that, you know. ... You tried to smooth it over because you didn't want to have a commotion; it wasn't worth it. You know, if a man wanted a coconut and thought he'd got a coconut, you said, 'Well you didn't get a coconut', 'Well, I'll tell my pal and I'll do this over', 'Here have the coconut and away you go', you know, that was the best way to work. And there was always somebody there. If you were in trouble, you looked up and there was always somebody there beside you, you know, if it wasn't one of the men that you employed, there was always one or two of them there that if I was in trouble, they were at my back. There was that big tall one, that I told you about, you know, there was always somebody about. And I've been here all my life and I more or less knew who was what and what was not. You knew he was a ... keep your eye on him because he was a bit of a trouble-maker. But no, it wasn't bad.

Was Fun City open all year round or was it just over the ...?

Over the summer period, March till end of September. ... When it closed it closed. That was it. It closed in the winter and we just tried to keep ourselves on what we took in the summer. And if it was a bad summer we were in trouble, we just had to do the best we could.

... You had to go and look for a job during the winter or if there was any carnivals open in the wintertime – we used to go up to Waverley Market, open up there. And of course go to the Kelvin Hall, see and if you could get a stance there when you were there. Failing that you had to just go and look for work. What you took in the summertime didn't keep you over winter. Not until the War came; once the War came we were regularly busy. We had the fleet used to go into Granton or Leith and of course we got them, used to come down, because Portobello was a great place then. And, it was; it was quite good. ... Auntie Catherine had it. I know because I used to mind the shooter and if any of these – we got a lot of Norwegians seemingly and there was a few of them used to come down to the shooter and if they stood too long my aunt used to send one of the men over, 'Go and tell that girl to get rid of those men. They've been there long enough!' And I used to say 'But they're spending money'. 'Tell them to go away for a while. Let the guns cool' – we had cartridges, live ammunition, 'Let the guns cool down and they can come back after!' That was my aunt.

She had the Noah's Ark, she had the Figure 8, she had the Cake-Walk, she had a set of Chairs, she had a Dodgem, a wee machine – a children's ride, a set of boats and a Helter-Skelter. ... That we had to pull during the War because they put an Ack Ack gun outside the Fun City and the skelter used to stand at the corner and they had to pull it down and put it to the back so that the Ack Ack could get firing when the enemy came over ... that was the only amusement park. Joppa, Seafield, nothing. They used to come from all over, Glasgow, Falkirk – we knew Falkirk holiday, you knew people come year after year and used to stay in a certain boarding house and they'd come along and see you, you know. From year after year you met and you knew them. Glasgow Fair – there used to be a station here and there'd be trips and they used to come right down Bath Street, train loads, it was great.

It was such a great place. It's upsetting, because you walked along that prom and it was worth walking along. You walked along the High Street, now you look and you think, 'God, what's happened to the place'. Of course, it's all Edinburgh, this is under it and this comes down – Musselburgh's thriving and Portobello's had it. ...

They could do the prom, you know, there's a great potential in the prom, from Bath Street along and nobody's doing a damn thing about it, even if they made nice flats, you know, there's space for flats that would be quite nice and I'm sure they'd sell well because they look right onto the sea, but it's just bare land. It's a shame. Used to be ponies – Hunter's ponies – our Norman used to run with the ponies when he was a kid, they had a yard up Pipe Street and they had ponies and then there was Marshall's yard, they had the boats – you used to go out in the rowing boats, you know, everything was there. It is a damn shame.

Gordon Codona tells the story of how his father John bought the Fun City from his sister Catherine in the late 1940s. It was run by his son William for six or seven years before being sold back to Catherine not long before she died.

[*Gordon Codona*]

Auntie Catherine and Uncle Albert Biddall, who was her husband, they operated it and ran it.[130] And we used to pop in and see her now and again. At that particular time there was another showman called Joe Leonard, during the war years, who had come up from nowhere, and had some roundabouts. At that time it was the easiest thing in the world to move about with roundabouts and earn money because there was money to be taken. The local authorities were looking for stay-at-home-carnivals and they were throwing sites at you. So this guy come

FIG. 32 Alfred Biddall in front of the
Helter-Skelter, c1940. Note the row
of peep shows to the right; the first
one is designated 'men only'.
(*Source:* Catherine Codona Thomas)

up; he first of all opened up at the Central Bridge with an indoor carnival, just at the corner of the Central Bridge in Glasgow. He got himself a good bit of money there and then he branched out and started buying roundabouts and operating them. He was standing on everybody's toes. … You wasn't allowed to go on a site under the Showmen's Guild, you know, you were entitled – he wasn't in the Showmen's Guild.[131] That didn't apply to him, you see. He couldn't be dealt with. So he was standing on everybody's toes. And in particular, for some reason or other, he was standing on our toes quite a bit. That Dunfermline Fair that we had – he tried to go to Dunfermline and we finished up using legal methods, interdicts, to stop him from opening there, which we did manage to do. That upset him. When we went to Dundee, he was at Dundee. When we went to Aberdeen, he was at Aberdeen at the site. It was getting this, you know – a pain in the neck.

Anyway, this fellow Leonard – my brother Billy knew him quite well, you know, used to see him socially. He wasn't very happy about what he was doing, you know! And he told my brother Billy 'I'm buying the Fun City'. Billy come back, told my father 'Joe Leonard's buying the Fun City'. Him at the phone, 'What's this I hear Catherine about Joe Leonard's buying the Fun City?' 'Well, yes. Me and Albert were thinking about – we'll sell it now, you see.' 'And what's wrong with the family?' my father said. 'You're selling to bloody Joe Leonard, you know. What's wrong with the family.' 'Well I didn't think you'd have enough money.' My father said 'How do you know we haven't got enough, you haven't asked us about how much it is yet, or told us about how much you want for it?' 'Oh.' She was getting on a wee bit, old Catherine, but she wasn't all that dumb. Anyway, my father said 'How much is it?' 'So and so, and so and so.' 'We'll buy it.' 'Oh.' Now Joe Leonard thinks he's buying it now, you see, we're still at the stage where – he'd opened his mouth too soon with my brother Billy, you see.

Now, Joe Leonard doesn't like us less, now. So what does he do? There's a bit of land outside of Fun City, it's been there – open land – been there for donkey's years for a house; the house owned the land. What does Joe Leonard do? Joe Leonard buys this house and the land outside. And we've bought the Fun City now, you see, and my brother Billy's there, he's going to run it now. Joe Leonard gets a roundabout, a Moon Rocket and some other equipment. It's just outside the door of the Fun City, you know. The Fun City's there and this is this. And he builds up out here – he's opening up. This is Joe Leonard – typical. Can't do nothing about it. Except Billy, he says, 'You're going to be a pain in the neck to us Joe. Why don't you just sell us this lot here and forget about it.' So Joe Leonard put a big price on it, gave himself a bit of profit, and Billy said 'Well we'll buy it and get rid of him', you know. So all of a sudden we've bought the Moon Rocket now and these silvery tops on this land; I'm at Portobello now in the summertime! Looking after some of this stuff. I had three or four weeks there with the Rocket, me and Katie, and then the machine was at Arbroath. ... The War was over then. I was married then, I got married in 1948. It was about 1950 or something like that. ... I was on there for a couple or three weeks, I was looking after this Rocket. But my brother Billy looked after Fun City. Did a good job of it. He done a lot to it; it was a bit run down, it was very run down when we bought it and Billy really smartened it up. It looked well, it looked as well as ever it was.

... It was just the rides. And the first thing we did, we had a

– we put a Dodgem in it, a decent Dodgem. We'd bought a big Dodgem during the war years, just when the War finished rather, a new, iron Dodgem, 80 feet. But we only used 60 feet of it to travel with. We used 80 feet when we went in the Kelvin Hall, so there was a bit – 20 feet of it wasn't used and some cars. So we got another 20 feet and two ends from the same firm that made it and they were the type of people that everything that they made – it was an engineering firm that went into making Dodgem's tracks – and they were made out of metal. They were heavy but because they were made out of metal they had to be precise; you couldn't just plane a bit off like you would a piece of wood, you see. So they had to be spot on; it was all jigged. We knew this with the Dodgem; there was only two sizes on it, it was amazing, you know. It had no numbers; everything fitted everywhere else, you see. So we wanted another Dodgem, so we got two ends off Lang Wheel's people, and added to the bit that we wasn't using, and we had a Dodgem.

They were an engineering firm that were making all sorts of things during the War, army things. And then after the War, just when the War finished, you couldn't get timber, wood was a non-commodity, but because they worked in steel, obviously, they made a Dodgem out of, manufactured everything out of – mind you, it was well made, beautiful made, except it was heavy. Fabricated steel, you know, it wasn't solid. The pillars, they were ribbed and all sorts – looked well. But heavy, you know, and heavy, heavy work. If they'd made it in aluminum – in fact we bought another Dodgem which was made in aluminium, Supercar, some years later, when aluminium become – they weren't using it for aeroplanes anymore so it come on the market. The aluminium Dodgem was light, half the weight, but everything was numbered. It wasn't jigged. That was made for that and that bit fitted there and wouldn't fit nowhere else. I mean there was no comparison in the construction, you know. I mean we done it twice, we sent away for them and said 'Give us another 20 feet', 'Give us another 40 feet'. That meant everything; up-rights and rafters and girders and … you just put it on and it fitted. Just went in, it was marvellous; the engineering was great.

We just built it up from there. And he got another Noah's Ark, he done a lot of things. Renewed the equipment. The only thing he didn't do anything with was the Figure 8, just kept mending it, you know. And Billy had it looking well, really smart. But he got dissatisfied because they wouldn't let him open on Sunday. And Sunday was the best day of the week. Everything else is open in Portobello, the ice-cream shops, you name it, gift stalls and all the rest along the promenade, and the Fun City's shut and there were people knocking at the door wanting in. And after Billy tried and tried and tried and he couldn't convince the town to give him permission to open that time. That's the sort of thing that sent me to England, you know. I knew that and I wanted to settle down; so, I'm not going to settle down in Scotland. I'm going to go where they operate on a Sunday, where they're a bit more relaxed, which I did do.

Catherine Codona Thomas' grandfather Frank was one of Billy Codona's brothers. As she tells us below, Frank's daughter Hannah was informally adopted by Catherine Codona, who took over the Fun City after Billy's death. When Catherine died, Hannah inherited the business, which she and her husband Michael McCreadie ran and where her daughter Catherine worked from the early 1950s until 1973.

[Catherine Codona Thomas]

My mum, her father was actually Frank Codona and they had six girls and a boy of whom my mum was the youngest. And when she was a baby, about two, my grandmother died. And my aunt Catherine, who was the other brother's – my mum's full cousin: you know, there was Frank and there was. ... Well, William was my aunt Catherine's father. So my mum and my Aunt Catherine were actually full cousins, although she was much, much older than my mum. And my aunt Catherine wasn't married. She didn't get married until she was in her late forties. At this point she wasn't married and she asked my grandad if she could adopt my mum. And my grandad said 'no, he couldn't agree to that but if she wanted to take her and bring her up that would be good because, well, they had all these children and no mother'. So my Aunt Catherine took my mum when she was two. That's how I'm associated with the other side of the family that – I should really be ... with the Frank [side], but my mum from then was brought up by my Auntie Catherine and went to the Fun City and Portobello and that was that, where her family continued to travel.

So, do you know anything about your grandfather Frank ... were there any stories that you heard about him?

I heard that there was quite a connection with Green's in Glasgow. I think they had the cinemas and things in Glasgow and used to do some work. He was seemingly very clever with his hands, you know, joinery and all that, although he never served an apprenticeship, but he was seemingly very clever that way. The other thing was geggie shows, puppet shows, and amusements. ... He seemingly got married again ... to a women with quite a lot of children as well! Which seemingly the family weren't very happy about because they'd enough children of their own, you know, and the older sisters were trying to look after the younger ones and all that and there was only one boy, Uncle Frankie. ... I knew them all. ... There's, actually one ended up marrying my dad's brother, so it was like two brothers, two sisters got married.

So all of Frank's children, they stayed in the business did they ... your grandfather Frank?

The oldest sister Mary Ellen, nobody really seems to know an awful lot about her. She went down south somewhere and my Uncle Frankie, my Auntie Bella, my Auntie Beatrice, my Auntie Violet, my Auntie Rosie was the one that married my dad's brother and went into the Fun City then. My Auntie Harriet, she didn't go into the business.

But most of them ......

Did – stayed in the business.

And then you must have known Aunt Catherine then.

Well she was like a grandmother to me. She was the one that was like a grandmother. She brought my mum up, you know, so she was the only grandparent I knew because my father's parents were dead as well before I was born. So she was really like a grandmother to me. I was ten when she died. A lot of people thought that she was very severe, if you like ... but she wasn't really, she wasn't really. Because, I spent a lot of time with her because by the time I was born they didn't live in the Fun City all the time. Sometimes she used to go down in the summertime and spend a few months living in the wagon, but they had a house in Inchview Terrace, a bungalow, in Inchview Terrace, number 72. And when my mum and dad got married she bought not next door but the one again, number 68 for my mum and dad. So there was only one house in between us and I used to go in over there all the time and I used to spend a lot of time with Aunt Catherine, sleep over at weekends. She had a housekeeper ... who sort of looked after her and as I say I spent a lot of time with her. ... She was the nearest I knew to a grand-mother.

Aunt Catherine married Albert Biddall ...?

That's right. ... He spoilt me. He adored me seemingly and I can remember being spoilt by him. But he died when I was wee; I was only five or six. They weren't married very long, because she didn't marry until I think she was in her late forties and his brother, Uncle Victor, he was through in Annan. They had cinemas; one in Annan, one in New Cumnock and one in Langholm. The Biddalls – they were real old gentlemen.

And you started in Fun City then when you were how old?

Ten. ... I used to help to look after the little kiddies' machine that was – it did go with a motor but it went at walking speed and then from that progressed onto the bigger children's ride and from there I went on to, for years I looked after the Ben Hur, some people call it the Jungle Ride. They changed it into a Waltzer, but I looked after it for a long, for a lot of years. ... I just sat in the pay box and the boys would collect the money and bring it up to me, but I drove the thing. And then I ended up, the last machine I looked after was the Octopus – it's got eight arms – cars, and it tips. They all had a – you had, they called it a knife, that was what you put in to get the current running through. They used to say put the knife in, like a blade thing that went into this holder thing, and then you increased the – they had buttons and you moved the handle over the half-circle kind of thing from one button to maybe six or whatever, and that's how you drove the Ben Hur, it was similar. But with the octopus, to get it to tilt, you had a break and a tilt arm and you had to lift the tilt one, and then when you were stopping it you had to break it down gradually, put the tilt back off, then take the electricity gradually off and pull the knife out. You could stop it at any time – it wouldn't stop instantly – well you had to at times if children were feeling sick or things like that, get it stopped. But you couldn't stop any of them instantly. You would have tilted the whole thing if you'd have tried to put the break on right away like, kind of thing.

Originally there was the two children's machines, a Dodgem,

FIG. 33 Catherine Codona Thomas in the pay box of the Ben Hur, c1956.
(*Source:* Catherine Codona Thomas)

the Ben Hur, there was a Skid – Cheesecutter. Originally there was a Figure 8, when I was a child and that took up all the back part of Fun City there. When I got married I got a caravan for a few years in the back of the Fun City, over a bit from where the Figure 8 was, but the Figure 8 was gone by then.

And what about the Helter-Skelter?

That was when I was a child. But there was swing boats as well – there was the Helter-Skelter and there was swing boats there, and all the stalls and a snack bar, a candy floss shop and a Cake-Walk.

The whole family worked but we had to employ quite a lot of hands. I should remember because I had to pay their wages – round about thirty. A lot of boys that would be at college and that, you know, or staying on at school and they worked in the summer holidays because their summer holidays was our busy time. And they worked at weekends or some of them would come down at night after their training to be engineers or joiners or whatever and they'd come at the night times and that type of thing. There was a few who worked there full-time but just a few.

And what sort of side stuff did they have in the Fun City?

All the different types of stalls. It went right round the sides – there was the stalls and the arcade. ... They paid my mum a rent. ... It was also family. The aunt that I told you married my dad's brother, she was there. Spensers – they're another show business family, they were there. Cathy Macintosh, her and her mum and her husband and that, they were in as well, so it was mainly sort of family. Well it was all family, when I think about it.

Glasgow Fair it was absolutely chock-a-block – chock-a-block. Like where I used to sit, the Ben Hur was just inside the main front gate and you had a great view right along the beach and the promenade and I mean it was thick with people, you know, the beach and the prom until late at night because, I mean we closed at something like half past ten and it was busy still then. Buses – there was a car park at the Fun City, there was a car park and there was a bathing pool … but it was a big, big car park and all the double-decker buses and that used to come through from Paisley, Glasgow, all the west mainly. The Edinburgh trades – because people didn't go abroad like they do now, so I mean they'd bring their children, or from round about like Haddington, and all the places round about Edinburgh, they'd bring them to Portobello for the day, for the beach and fairground and that was sort of their holiday time. Because loads of people that I've known as I've got older have said 'Oh, we used to go there', you know, on a day trip and some people used to come and spend nearly a week. So it was the thing but obviously then things started to change.

We were very lucky really, for the amount of people, there must have been thousands of people that went through the place in the summer, you maybe had a couple of incidents, you know, when you had to call the police. But nothing really. Not like what you hear about today. I would hate to be in today, I would not like that. Any trouble we really had was with bus trips coming in but it was very, very seldom.

We opened in April, over Easter or whichever came first – you know, if it was the spring holiday in Edinburgh and we closed at the end of September. You'd be busy in the busy times … but the busy times were the different holidays until we got to June, July and August. Mainly July because that was the Edinburgh fortnight and the Glasgow fortnight. The first fortnight in August was busy as well. So it's a short season really.

When we first opened in April we weren't nearly as busy as we were in June, July and August. So what you would do in April and May, it wasn't – we opened later in April and May than what we did, you know, when Portobello was really busy we used to open at eleven o'clock in the morning in the busy time and didn't close till half past ten at night. So it was nearly a twelve-hour day, where in April and May you didn't open till two o'clock in the afternoon and closing time really was depending on how many people were around, what the weather [was] like and that, it could be maybe anything from nine o'clock till half past ten. But it varied then, where at the main time you opened every day at eleven o'clock no matter if it was raining or if there seemed to be many people about or not, because there always did end up by being, so you opened up regular then.

You did [the] same things; in the morning it was everything was got ready, you know, if things needed all washed down like the horses on the Ben Hur, the cars on Dodgem, you know, they were all washed over and what not. And if there was any mechanical things needing, well I don't know really what they would need, greasing or whatever maintenance they needed, that was done as well. And everything had to be got ready first before we eventually opened to the public. And then at night, when you closed at half past ten, we didn't – we used to come – sometimes we'd come home, sometimes we stayed down there. By the time we got actually home, or got round to – if you were staying in the caravan, there – you had to get the money and everything banked for the bank the next day, got your supper and what not – you didn't go to your bed till about one o'clock. So it was quite a long day and that, you know.

What did you do over the winter when Fun City was closed?

Well, in my Auntie Catherine and my mum's time they had a cinema in Prestonpans, so in the winter my mum used to go down and work in that and of course that brought income in. It was there all the time, they had a manager that looked after it but in the winter time my Uncle Albert and my mum used to go down there. Me personally, I didn't do anything. Well, I had – when I worked, before I got married, in my mum and dad's business, I also worked at home, you know, looked after the home and things like that. So we'd just catch up on different cleaning things and that in the home throughout the winter and do different bits and pieces that way, but that was all. I didn't go out to work, I just worked in the business, you know, and doing all the books and stuff like that.

So what you made over the season kept you for the rest of the year?

Yes. I believe before I was born there was more things. I think there was a fair they had somewhere round about Meadowbank way and I'm not sure.[132] I know that we had the Waverley market from what I can remember when I was a teenager. I used to go up there and give family, relations a hand, you know, but we didn't actually have anything that went from the Fun City there. Not in my time but maybe possibly there was before that there was, I don't know. I would say about, it was definitely there till 1963, '64, there was definitely a winter carnival there. It had to be after that. I can remember my husband and I, we earned actually extra money for getting married through working up there. Also when we were first married for the first couple or three years it was still going on. So it had to be after 1964, 1965.

When you first got married you stayed in the Fun City; were there many other people staying there?

Yes, uhuh. I had my Auntie Becca, that was my Auntie Catherine's sister, that's Cathy's mum, Rebecca Codona, well, Paulo at the finish up, but her own name was Rebecca Codona – she stayed there with her daughter Cathy and her son-in-law and her grand-daughter. And the other permanent ones that were there were a sister of my mum's and brother of my dad who married each other, like it was two sisters, two brothers that were married. They lived there. That was the only permanent ones. In the winter the travelling showpeople used to come in. You know, when we pulled all the stuff down in the front, you know, like all the machines and everything, packed them all away, then the people who travelled, they used to start coming in about the end of October and they'd come in throughout the winter. Some of them might go out a bit occasionally if they had a certain date to go to but they were more or less in from about November through to the beginning of March.

So it was quite a community there then?

And income for my mum and dad as well, because obviously they paid rent to park there kind of thing. So they used to come

in, not the back bit where we were, they were more in the front
bit. They had their own – I'm not sure what happens nowadays
– but I know that they had their own dances and different
things that – they had quite a few dances. Any weddings that
was coming off happened in the winter mostly and they used
to have quite a lot of small dances and then they had a big
ball. They had a circus ball years ago. That was when the
Waverley Market was on and they had a circus there, and they
used to call it a Circus Ball – I don't really know why Circus
Ball – and that was the main big dance then. But then, after
that, they had a big dance in Edinburgh and one in Glasgow.
That was the main event of the winter that they all went to.

The likes of the Whites, I think they stayed actually up at
the side where the Carnival was. But there was a lot of people
who wintered in the Fun City who, yes, they had different – be
it stalls or, yeah, Sharp was the name of it, Sharp – the mother
was a White, from Whites the showpeople who married Sharp,
and they had a machine up there, I remember that. They had
that and they used to winter in the Fun City. There was a few
who had stalls and that, you know, they were wintering in the
Fun City. Yeah, it was used for that and it was handy for them
for the Waverley Market.

*And was there a sense of a hierarchy would you say in the
show community?*

Yeah. Years ago – yeah, I think that's right. It's just like, you
know, in settled life, well, it shouldn't really be but there is
different class, or there was different class distinctions, like,
you know. Well it was the same in showland as well. The ones
with big machines and that were higher up the scale, if you like,
kind of thing, than somebody that maybe just had a little stall,
you know, that type of thing. And although they intermarried a
lot in those days, they were inclined to not cross; you know, the
stall-holders married stall-holder, machine people married
machine people. But it did happen, just like in any – it did happen when it was crossed at different times, you know, where
they did. But that type of thing definitely.

How long did you continue working in the Fun City until?

Right up until they sold it – 1972.

And how had things changed by then?

They were starting to change a lot I would say in the ten years, really, previous to that. Although we got Sunday opening which was great, and my dad fought for that for a long while and the Edinburgh fathers away up there would not grant it at all. And when I think what they do now – they close Princes Street and all the rest of it. They would not let him open on a Sunday. They'd let the snack-bar and that open, we had to cordon off at the first machine, the Skid and that shut off all the rest of the ground so that the public couldn't get in there. But eventually about 1963 or round about there they actually gave him permission to trade on a Sunday and that made a big difference, to open on a Sunday. But, yeah, latterly you could – the weather, the weather for some reason went through a really bad patch summer after summer and of course if you don't get the weather then you don't get ... and also the abroad bit had a lot to do with it as well.

So when did your mum have it until?

1973 and then she died in 1977. She never really got over coming out of the Fun City. That brought her health down a lot and she never really recovered from that and she died in 1977. Because it was all she had known all her days as well. So for 62 years that's all she had known. She did exactly the same thing as what I then ended up doing. She went from children's machines to the big machine, the Ben Hur with the horses, was the one she looked after, just exactly how I then did it, you know, when it came my turn. It stopped there because by the time our children – my husband and my children – were up, we were out of it. But it certainly did last through my mum's time and then my own. Most of the people in Portobello, it's my mum, Hannah Codona was very well known in Portobello, very well, everybody knew my mum. Not so much my Auntie Catherine, because she wasn't a person that went around an awful lot. She was a very reserved sort of person, you know, and then she was that bit older than my mum. But my mum from she came here at three and went to school and everything here and then was in the Fun City all her life, as I say, right up till just about three years before she died. So it was mainly her that Portobello people connected with.

I was heartbroken when I had to leave as well. Because it was all I had ever known and I was worried about what I was going to do as well. You know, because my husband had come into the business too.

You're a jack of all trades really. I mean I had to do God knows what but, you know, you're not qualified in anything and that's what worried me. But, however, I suppose I was just young enough to adapt. But it has a right soft spot for me. So much so that I've never been back. I've never set foot in the place. I couldn't. Umpteen people have said to me 'You should go because it's so completely different now it wouldn't upset you anymore. It's not like at all what it was', you know. But I just couldn't.

When it was sold for that four years, Uncle Billy managed it. He was another brother and he was quite a character, he really was. As I say, I was only a little girl and his family were quite a bit older than me and we used to be very close. And they used to have a house that was just outside the Fun City, there was ground there, there was one house and that's where they lived. They had three daughters and a son. He was really a bit like an old film star, he really was quite a character; quite a jokey, jovial person he was, you know … they travelled. Because, as I say, he was only here for about four years.

As I say, we were stuck here. We didn't travel or – really we didn't belong to any – like, see my dad, he came from Portobello, settled people but I didn't really belong in amongst that group completely and I didn't meet the rest of my family that were travelling because although I was in the business all the time, I wasn't like a lot of showpeople. I didn't seem to be able to communicate right when I met some of my cousins and things – they spoke a different language from me. Because, well, schooling for instance; my schooling was like a settled person's schooling, where their's wasn't. Even the way they speak; they speak with a bit of accent from all different places. So they speak different, where I just spoke like anybody that came from Edinburgh. But then you see it worked the other way, because at school a lot of people at school wouldn't mix with me because I came from showpeople. A lot of people no. But certain people definitely. I don't think so now because most of them are settled now, you know, even though they're still operating things to do with the amusement business. They live in houses, their children go to school, just like everybody else, so I don't think it is now.

So what would it be at school – would it just be that certain kids wouldn't play with you?

Gypsies, that kind of thing, you know, and I lived in a house, that was the thing! I did live in a house, in Inchview Terrace. In the summertime I used to stay in wagons down there, you know, just while we were open down there. But my dad, my dad was a Portobello man. But, you see, so I was never fully accepted in that side of it, nor in the other side of it because a lot of my cousins would say to me, 'but you're, you're …', well their expression for it was, 'you're more like a flattie'. I'd say, 'Well I'm neither one thing nor the other'. But I wouldn't let, the thing is, I wouldn't let the settled people run the showpeople down, and I wouldn't let the showpeople run the settled people down. Only certain ones, there again. It's like the settled people. It's ignorance really. But I don't think it happens nearly so much nowadays because there's not so much of a marked difference.

FIG. 34 The Fun Park on the Fun City site in 2004, showing the covered-in amusement arcade and café. (*Source:* Frank Bruce)

FIG. 35 Current owner Melvyn Strand among the debris during the last days of the ten-pin bowling site at Fun City. All that remains is the arcade. (*Source:* Archie Foley)

5

Four Brothers
and Thirteen Cousins

WILLIAM Codona's sons, John, Frank, Nathaniel and
William, all went into the business, as did their sons – 13
first cousins. Anne-Marie Gwynn is related to Nathaniel through
marriage and spent time travelling with the family when growing up at the time of the World War II. Both her account and
Gordon Codona's which follows, include vivid descriptions of
living wagons, the earliest being Gordon's grandfather's. To give
some more historical context to their descriptions, this 1894
report of St James Fair, Kelso reveals living arrangements at the
time of Gordon's grandfather. Note how well the diet described
here must have compared with an average meal of the time:

> Their caravans are ranged in a line for a great distance along
> one side of the park, and though these vehicles are necessary
> for travelling and as a store-room for goods and chattels, when
> stationed on such an occasion as this, the entire lives of the
> owners are lived out of doors. ... The culinary operations are
> publicly conducted at the door of each caravan; the cooking
> being done over a stick fire, which fills the atmosphere all about
> with a blinding smoke. ... Some of the fires were surrounded
> by pots and kettles, suggesting quite a variety for dinner; and
> being very curious, I take note of the menu, while the meal is
> partaken of in front of one of the caravans. Soup, beef, new
> potatoes and cabbage, sliced plum pudding fried over the smoky
> fire in dripping. The family is a large one, and being accustomed
> to dine in public, it does not seem to incommode them, though
> they are surrounded by onlookers. ... Before another caravan
> washing as well as cooking is being done, and even the boiling

of the clothes is not omitted. Several women are baking scones, kneading them on a tray, and firing them in a frying pan over the fire. ...[133]

[Anne-Marie Gwynn]

I really can't tell you when or why or from where the family originally came. I suppose, as a child, I just assumed they were always there – not much help there then! I wasn't brought up on the fairground, and am related to the Codonas through marriage. However, we all remained pretty close for many years and spent a lot of time with them. I was allowed to travel with them when I was very young, and was probably more of hindrance than a help – but I thought I was brilliant!

To start at the beginning – there were five sisters in the O'Donnell family – they lived in Portobello, and their father was a barber. I don't think Cissie could have been called a 'nanny', but I believed she 'watched the kids' and did a bit of housework for William Codona's family. What we did hear was that William had several side-shows (coconut shies – roll-ball, etc.) then came the Hobby Horses. I would think that once he had the Hobby Horses, his family would have worked them – but the story goes that Nathaniel (and possibly a brother) was working as a Pierrot at the end of Portobello pier. This next part I know is true. Cissie and Nathaniel fell in love, and eloped. Far from being dismayed, the Codona family were delighted and had a huge wedding party in the couple's absence. When they returned as man and wife, the family bought them a caravan, which, they said, was all they wanted. But apparently bit by bit, they furnished it with exquisite china, glass and linen – which, although it may have been in a later caravan, is one of the things I remember.

The caravan ... small and shiny, with a scroll all around the outside. The entrance ... fold down steps, up to a 'stable door' (but much smaller of course). This allowed Mary-Ann [Smith] to chat to passers by during a pause in cooking. The cooker stood on a cupboard (I think) facing the door, and was run on something like Calor gas. The meals were cooked here, though

there wasn't room to swing a cat as it was no more than a lobby.
I also remember young Nathaniel washing his hands and face
there, so the cooker must have been interchangeable with a tin
basin, and the kettle must have been boiled before the switch –
unless it was all done by magic.

On the left was a bedroom, Cissie and Nathaniel's, and it
seemed to be full of bed, but immediately inside the door was
the chest of drawers where the money was tipped, all in change,
all uncounted. But in one of the drawers above this were Cissie's
jewels – rings mainly – which I was once allowed to try on. My
mother later told me that some of the rings (Cissie's favourites,
by the way) were real diamonds, etc., but just as many came
from Woolworths. Cissie apparently didn't mind how much or
little they cost, but she did love a bit of glitter. The other room,
on the right as you went in, was wonderful. If you stand in the
lobby and face it ... on the left, a built-in mahogany cupboard,
drawers underneath. Alongside this was the fireplace. The grate
was very small and surrounded by a guard of slim, round,
elegant steel or maybe chrome uprights with spear-like tops.
The grate itself was quite high on the wall, and was surrounded by narrow oblong mirrors. The mirrors were set into
mahogany frames, a long mirror from the base, and a shorter
one at the top, with another under the mantelshelf. All of the
mirrors were bevelled, with a 'star' flashing in the centre of
each piece. Pure fairyland, I thought. On the other side of the
fireplace, more drawers and cupboards from ceiling to floor. On
the short wall, facing the lobby, was a small bay window, with
a lace curtain, and a bowl of fruit on the window-sill. Under
this was a seat, stretching the width of the wall. (A bed later, I
believe.) Starting from the bay window and coming back to the
door on the right-hand side, were built-in seats with cupboards
beneath them, and a table (with very good linen and china at
mealtimes), all of which turned magically into beds at night.
Can't remember much about the ceiling, except that it too was
shiny and I have a vague memory of lamps with very pretty
glass shades.

I don't believe there was ever a fire lit in that fireplace, by the way. It wouldn't have held more than a lump of coal, and I don't recall seeing a chimney, so maybe it was just for show. Don't care, I'm glad it was there.

All five sons were brought up there, and all of them worked on the rides, which eventually included hobby horses, motor bikes, Waltzer and swing boats. I would have said Chairoplanes too, but I think they belonged to either the Smiths or the Whites.

Gala Days in West Calder and the surrounding villages: coal miners had the day off work, and children were off school (may have been during the summer holidays – but the weather was warm as I remember). This would have been about 1940. Children were given a brown paper bag containing a sticky bun or two, and a bottle of school milk. There was a beer tent for the men, side-shows, and if I'm not wrong, the only round-about was Codona's Hobby Horses. Mad excitement about this, and the Codona family were making money – until about 3pm, when Cissie Codona told her boys they were to shut down because, 'It was time the men went home while they still had money in their pockets, because they need to feed their families for the rest of the week.' The boys shut the machine down.

Young 'Thaniel (Nathaniel's son) married Emily. They had three children. Cecilia, the oldest, then Emily, and I believe a son after that. Cecilia kept the books for her father – but when she grew up married a dentist, and removed herself from the business. As a small child she was always dressed in very expensive clothes – especially of the frilly party frock variety – in which she went 'out to play' on the muddy ground on the site, and you can imagine what she looked like when she came indoors. The second child – well, the women did the washing outside in a zinc bath, filled with water boiled in the wagon. The clothes were left to soak in soapsuds. On one of these washing days, Emily Codona had gone to do some other task, and when she came back and plunged her hands into the soapy water, she withdrew what she thought was a bundle of clothes, and found that among them was her small daughter. No more to say really, is there? I don't think she (or Nathaniel) ever recovered. It was after this that the son was born.

Winter ground was the Kelvin Hall Glasgow – don't know where the wagons were parked, but [I] do remember Cissie Codona being very ill, and still wanting to go to the Kelvin Hall one Christmas. Nathaniel carried her from her bed to his car and drove her there I believe for the last time. The atmosphere there was very exciting, and exhilarating. Good humoured. Hundreds of people went there as a Christmas treat. There were roundabouts, and a circus, and lots of money was made. I wanted to join the circus, because the ladies wore such lovely filmy dress. Actually I think they were probably a bit grimy but who cares?

Uncle Nathaniel had a car (old black Ford I believe), and I remember him as being small, fat, pleased look on his face, and wearing a pinstriped suit with waistcoat, black overcoat in winter, and trilby hat: cigar in his mouth ... ash down his waistcoat as he drove on pretty empty roads from Glasgow to Edinburgh.

Whoever was taking money on the machines chucked it all into an old leather shopping bag at the end of the night and hauled it over to the wagon, up the three folding steps to the lobby, and into the room on the left where there was a large bed, and a tallish, mahogany chest (built-in, of course) against one wall. The money was then tipped into one of the lower drawers till someone got round to counting it. (My mother kept the books for Nathaniel for many years, and as a matter of fact he loaned her £900 to buy our house in Edinburgh. 7 Eyre Place. She'd paid back all but the last payment when he died. It was run as a guest house while I was growing up, and my brother only sold it a few years ago.) That money. Well it was used for all the Codona family needs, and as they travelled around the country during the War, they could always buy butter, meat, eggs and such from farms as they passed, so I don't think they starved.

Mary-Ann Smith too was allowed to take what she needed, and sometimes she needed to take me to some posh shop in Sauchiehall Street and buy me an expensive dress. (She belonged to the Smith family, who were also travellers, and she was employed by the Codona's. She cooked and did the housework, and looked after the children. I loved her dearly. The Smiths were

the same ones who worked with John Codona's Fairs.) Young
as I was I remember the alarmed look on sales ladies' faces when
Mary-Ann marched in with her huge shopping bag and loud
voice and examined the merchandise. They could barely contain
themselves when she finally marched over to the glass-topped
counter, asked how much the dress was, then simply tipped the
bag up and emptied heaps of small silver and a mountain of
copper on top of it. The sales girl called her 'Madame', and had
to count it out. Mary-Ann swept the rest back into the bag,
snatched up the shopping and me, and swept out. It was great.

After Glasgow Green, the whole lot of us went to see the
last performance of Sophie Tucker, and when she sang 'There's
No Business Like Show Business', all the showfolk (fairground
folk) got up and cheered. They assumed that it was their shows
she was singing about, not the stage shows. Later we went for
fish and chips, and sat at a table to eat them. Big thrill for me,
especially when they bought me a knickerbocker glory, and I
felt very sick.

The trip to Fife. ... I believe the Codonas went every year
and travelled around, but although we may have visited them
there, I wouldn't know where. The only trip I really remember
was because of what happened. I think I was about eight years
old, maybe nine (and children of nine were much younger then
than they are now, that may be a contradiction in terms, but
I know what I mean) anyway – I was allowed to travel in the
wagon from either Edinburgh or West Calder to Kirkcaldy.
I recall kneeling on the 'window seat' and watching the trees
and fields. I also remember passing a crowd of raggedly looking
people on the roadside, and them waving and smiling and calling to us. Mary-Ann and I were leaning out of the half door,
but when I started to wave back, she hauled me away and
slammed the top half. 'Don't,' she said. 'They're tinkers!' Which
meant they begged, stole, and never washed. (This was a pride
thing. Showfolk were clean, tidy and honest. Not to be confused
with the likes of THEM.)

Well we got to Kirkcaldy, and the men set up, and women
cooked and gossiped, then the fair began. The people came, the

adult showfolk were busy with stalls and roundabouts, and the children left to their own devices, which meant playing in the mud, or doing their chores. My chore was chopping carrots for soup. One day, when my 'cousin' Cecilia Codona came in to the caravan – she was a bit younger than me – she was wearing one of her pretty party frocks, all frills and flounces, but very muddy, limp frills and flounces. I was wearing nothing special, having nothing special to wear. We had the wagon to ourselves, and were supposed to play together, so I was quite surprised when I was ordered to stand with her in front of a mirror, so that she could say, 'I suppose you think you're pretty – well you're not, and I hate you'. Upon which she seized the nearest carving knife, and told me she was going to kill me. (You don't forget things like this believe me.) I was so scared and so sure she would that I grabbed my coat, and headed for home. I had some coppers in my pocket given to me by Mary-Ann, enough to take a bus to the ferry, but no money for the ferry, so shaking, I attached myself to a couple, and sneaked on board. Got to Queensferry, and walked all the way home to Eyre Place. My mother looked surprised to see me, and asked 'What are you doing here?' So no-one had missed me and the police hadn't been called and I wasn't going to jail – I suppose they got it sorted in the end, but I never wanted to go and stay in the wagon again. By the way, Cecilia turned out to be a very nice person. She looked after her father, and did the books, and even-tually married a dentist, and was out of the business for good.

After his father died, 'old' Nathaniel and some friends were talking about what their late fathers had left them – wagons, lorries, entertainments, and Nathaniel said, 'Ah well, my father left me the whole of Scotland to earn my living in'.

Gordon Codona was one of John Codona's three sons and one of the 13 first cousins who went into the business. His account over the next few chapters covers his career and the world of the travelling showpeople from when he left school to join the family business in the mid-1930s to 1960, when he established a static funfair at Redcar on the Northumbrian coast. Gordon's skill as a raconteur has no doubt been sharpened by the showmen's performing heritage and tradition of story telling or 'say-so', and is shared with a number of Codonas remembered as being able to 'tell a good tale'.

[*Gordon Codona*]

At the time my father was bringing up his family, the living accommodation wasn't very big; none of the trailers and things were very big. I think my father when he got married, he had a twelve quid caravan, a new one that he'd got, you know, to bring his [family] up. That would be horse, horse-drawn at that time. It was horse-drawn because I remember eventually when I was younger he had a horse-shoe in the caravan that he kept and that belonged to one of the old horses … from one of his previous caravans, from one of his horses, an old faithful horse that he'd had, cannae remember its name, and he'd kept this

FIG. 36 Gordon Codona, Stirling, 2003.
(*Source:* Frank Bruce)

horseshoe all that time, you know. All the stories about the good old horse, you know.

After the War they began to get, what happened then, after World War I there were some motor vehicles become on the go then, you know, ex-wartime lorries and things and the showmen began to get those, the four-wheel-drive lorries that they used to pull the guns, you know, they used those and some of the other transport. That pushed along lorries for the showmen. The main stuff for our family was the traction engine because we had the larger roundabouts and the lorries weren't capable of taking that about. The engines were the thing that was needed for that particular work. Right the way up between the two World Wars it was the traction engines that was the main transport and the power. The thing about the traction was it developed the power ... electric power for the machines. The lorries couldnae do that at that time. So between the two Wars it was the traction engines that kept the fairgrounds going, right up until the late 1930s when diesel engines began to come on the go. But we operated and used our traction engines, and all the family, all the Codona brothers right up until the War started, although we began to get a sprinkling of diesel engines in just towards the late 1930s, just when the War started.

So the wagons when you were born, brought up were ...

They were a bit bigger, aye, I think they had gone about – my father went from his 12-foot caravan to one about 18 feet, 18- to 20-foot caravan, and he had that for quite some time and then, of course the family was getting a bit bigger and he had two caravans. ... Latterly, when he decided to split up and when I got married he got another wagon built in Cambuslang, the man is Dewar at Cambuslang. That was a bigger one, that was about 22-foot caravan, we had that when the War started, travelled about with that. ... He had heart trouble, and he stopped at Largs and went into a bungalow at Largs just when the War started. When I got married, 1948, I got my father's wagon, caravan, that's what I had when I got married.

It was a bedroom. It was 20 feet; it would be a ten-foot

bedroom and a twelve-foot living, kitchen area. Very compact. There was no room wasted at all. Well built – all hand built, fitted by coach craftsmen. Timber, all timber. It was mahogany panels on the outside and wooden frame. ... Actually they're difficult to explain because you've got to be able to realise how compact they are, you know. There was a fire, stove, you know, anthracite stove, the combustion type, the one that we had was a Doric, the anthracite stove, means you could damp it down, keep it on all night, that sort of thing. That was in that area there. We had an extension kitchen that you built on the outside. You come up the stairs there, that portion outside you built that up ... you could put some of your washing materials and things, could wash out there – basin. Used to have an outside toilet, Elsan-type chemical toilet, that was an outside toilet, which you built up.

Generally it was a bit restricted, you know, the caravan, because you'd got to take your home with you wherever you moved about. As time went on and you could tow them about, they got bigger, and the one I got after I got rid of the 20 footer was 30 feet, that had four compartments in it, you know.

More like a home ...

More at home. It had a separate kitchen. It was divided into a living room area like this and you walked through, that would be there, but the kitchen, that kitchen's there but this area when you went through here, there's a partition down the middle and there was a fold-up bed, that was another small bedroom, it folded away during the day. And when you went to the end, there was another main bedroom, which was a bed-sitting room. There was a fireplace in there too and the bed used to come out the wall. So through the day the bed went away and that was a sitting room. There was a fireplace in there and you had the fire in this end with all the kitchen, chairs and table in this end. But they were all very compact; beds fold away, cupboard space, you know, tables slide out, all these sort of ideas to give you the room through the day.

Now the modern ones, the whole side pulls out now, they pull the side out and that's another compartment. And they're 40 feet long, because they pull them behind the artic'. Ours was on a trailer with four wheels. Now they're so long they put them on an artic' unit, so they're out to 40 feet or more and the bits pull out, the side pulls out, to double the width. It's amazing what they do with them now. Even these things [his own static chalet] the showmen use now; this is purpose built. I lived in the town up there, we bought a flat, me and the wife, up in the town and once she went in the nursing home I wanted to move down here amongst people that I know and I've got everything in here that I'd got in the flat. It's just a bit smaller you know. A lot of the showmen are doing this now, coming onto sites like this with chalets or doing it with the caravan. There's caravans here, some of these people go away, you know, they go out in the summer. But this is a good site, you know, people that we know.

And at that particular time, with the family splitting up, my older brother got married and he had his own caravan and he splitted up his equipment a bit, my father. They would come together for some of the bigger fairs and then you would split up and go to the different fairs. He had to do that quite a bit, you know, he took advantage of the fact that his family was able to operate. ... Come together the bigger fairs, likes of Kirkcaldy, Aberdeen, Dundee, places like that, Glasgow.

It was the same with the other brothers. William – he travelled, William Codona travelled more round about the borders – Dumfries, Carlisle, up towards Glasgow. Edinburgh maybe, you know. That was William.[134] My father travelled north of Glasgow and up the north. He got up to further north – up in Aberdeen, Inverness, Nairn, these places. Again, that they didn't stand on each others' toes too much. They'd come together at the big fairs – likes of Kirkcaldy and Dumfries and things like that – the bigger fairs. But they had their own area. Nathaniel Codona, you know, he seemed to concentrate round about Glasgow area. He was in and around Glasgow and the surrounding – Bellshill, Barrhead, Motherwell – that sort of area. Frank,

he was about Edinburgh, Glasgow – middle part of the country.
But, they had similar rides. My father – Waltzer, Motorcycle
Speedways, Mont Blanc, Nathaniel had a Motorcycle Speedway,
Billy had a Motorcycle Speedway, they had Waltzers. They had
two or three roundabouts the same and there was a great deal
of competition, my – I'm talking about my generation now, my
father's sons, there was a few of us, actually there was about
13 cousins. My Uncle Billy had three sons, my father had three
sons, Frank Codona had two sons, Nathaniel had five sons.
So it all added up to 13 sons, and they were all in the same
business, and they were all roundabouts that they were looking
after and the competition was fierce. And this is what I said to
you; this was the driving force. The competition between the
brothers and the brothers' families pushed the standard along.

... There was a bit of friction between the brothers. There
had been from the time of the Codona Brothers. There'd always
been that bit of friction between them. They didn't always get
on. Stand on each other's toes a bit too much. But the cousins
all got on, you know, all friends with one another. It hadn't
rubbed off on us. But there was a lot of competition, you know,
somebody'd done something on the roundabout, and put a
fixture on, and put an extra one on – he put another dozen
lamps up on there – he put another two dozen lamps up. And
it was a great sight, if you went to one of the big fairs and you
saw these Codonas' machines operating on a Saturday night, in
opposition to each other, the lights going on and flashing and
the music going and all the activity. It was a great sight, you
know. You know, you went to one particular place at Ayr, Ayr
Races, the back end of the year, there were about six or seven
Codonas' roundabouts, the different brothers, all operating on
that fairground – just competition, business-wise.[135]

The important thing with the fairground job was having the
sites, you know, there was no use having equipment if there
was nowhere to put it – the Codona Brothers had a few sites
amongst them, you know, so to retain the sites they had to keep
their equipment going.

There is an association the showmen have, the Showmen's

Guild, that sort of kept an eye on the activities of showmen and if the showmen have a site which they occupy, to lease it for a fortnight; he had the rights for that particular fair and another showman couldn't take it at that time, that was within the Showmen's Guild. So they have these sites through their name, reserved, and it was very important, you see. And the Guild regulated all this and it worked quite well, actually you know. There was a period of time that you could go on a site – you couldn't go on it at the same time but you couldn't go on within a month of somebody else occupying that site. So it saved some of the sites getting abused, overproductive sort of thing, being used too much so people would lose interest in it.

It made its own calendar. The fact that you had rights of preservation for that particular site, that was a date in the calendar that that fair would be used. And a lot of the fairs were only used once or twice a year because there wasn't much point going any other time.

So what were the main venues can you remember?

There was a lot, a hell of a lot of fairs but one of the biggest fairs was Kirkcaldy, Links Market, swing of the year, round about April now.[136] Aberdeen was the May Fair in Aberdeen, St Andrews Lammas Market, Dumfries Spring Fair, there used to be a fairs at Hamilton, fairs at Falkirk, regular fairs, fairs at Trinity moor, which was an old established horse fair, there was Aikey Brae which opened on a Sunday, it was the only one in Scotland that opened on a Sunday, there was other galas, Bridge of Allan, for example, Highland games, these sort of events, Aboyne Games, Banff, Nairn Games: these were all established fairs although they were part and parcel of another activity. There was quite a lot. In between these fairs was going to what we called private business where you would go to a place and open, find a piece of land and open and advertise you're putting a fair on for no other particular reason than you'd think you're going to attract some business. That was all private business. Sometimes that worked out very well, you know. We used to go to Aberdeen in the wintertime in the thirties and opened in the middle of Aberdeen in the Guest Row, next to Marischal College.[137] We used to spend a few months in the middle of Aberdeen, that's expensive to put a show there, you know, that's the site, it was a good site, and that was up until the War started. That was private business, you know, we just went there and my father got the site and because he established that site, nobody could take it at that time, not in the Showmen's Guild. He got the use of that site every winter, you know. It was all regulated by the Guild.

... Never in a month of Sundays would you ever imagine Edinburgh or Glasgow council would let you in the middle of the street. You used to have a job in the cities, getting permission to open in an old piece of land, you need licences. Oh, there was a bit of a bias. People could object about the noise, too much noise. You only needed one or two objections, and forget about two or three hundred people wanted the fair there because one or two objections were enough to refuse your licence, you had to have a licence.

... Oh, it was hard going. Particularly in the bigger cities,

FIG. 37 Building up the 'Dodge-em' stand at the Aikey Brae Fair, Aberdeenshire, 1970s. (*Source:* National Museums Scotland)

now and again. But what happened, during the war years, when the War started, World War II, everything closed down, when you were looking for air raids, first thing you did was close all football matches, a lot of shows external to fairgrounds, thing like this closed down, you put them out of business. Then after that the next thing that happened was that you were allowed to operate during the summer months. And then you were allowed to operate with blackout covers, you didn't show any light; you can imagine a fairground with no light! That was it, you know, it was covered with all – it was candle-lit inside – nothing had to show outside. They then began to realise that people were starved of entertainment and they began to put 'stay at home holidays' which was ideal for showmen because the local authorities were looking for some entertainment. They then began to open the parks up. When I say the stay at home holidays would suit the showmen, the showmen were the people that provided the stay at home holidays, you see. So that was a sort of entrance into the thoughts of the local authorities that showpeople could do a good job here and that was the saving of our business during the war years, the fact that they realised that people needed some entertainment and stay at home holidays were very popular. Some of the best years the showmen had was during the war years. They had no competition. The only thing that was open was cinemas. People couldn't spend their money on anything else. You couldn't go on holiday, you couldn't go anywhere, so when the fair was on, 'we'll go to the fair and enjoy ourselves at the fair'. An awful lot of people as far as I was concerned, you know. From that point on I think some of the local authorities began to look more friendlily on showpeople, eventually, you know, although we didn't get doing very much until they raised the restrictions on Sunday openings and things like that. ...

And what about the – you mentioned all the brothers – what about the sisters, did they get involved in the business?

Well, they stayed in the business, the daughters until they got married and inevitably they all married that were in the business.

But was it mainly would you say it was a man's working world?

No, no. Not really, I mean women played an important part in the business, a very important part. I mean they were there, they were the financial people, they were sitting, handled the money when the ride was opened, most of the time. They looked after the kids, you know, they looked after the food and they also worked outside at night. They were on the equipment at night. A lot of the women used to operate the rides; whether the man was walking about keeping an eye on things, and didn't want to be tied in too much and the wife was sitting in the cash box operating the rides, things like that. Oh, no. ...

I saw a photo of one of these where they've got the board at the front and the platform and there's two women obviously spieling and trying to get people to go up. You know, they're wearing, I don't know ...

You're talking about the old shows. ... It's quite possible aye ... My brother Alfred married an English show-woman, Freeman, and they had a show and the daughters, the daughters used to perform in the show. I'm talking about, he got married during the war years, that was when the War started, he had this show, the Royal Dots, they called them and it was an illusion show and what they were was when you went to the show you saw little midgets dancing on top of a piano, all this was an illusion, you know, and that's where they get the Royal Dots, they were only this high, it was just done through mirrors again. Illusion, you know. But that was on until the War started. And at New-castle Town Moor was one of the biggest fairs in the country, in June. There used to be rows and rows and rows of side-shows; boxing show, circus, two or three circuses and a couple of box-ing shows. There was all these different – fat ladies, this, that and the other, cowboy show – a whole row, that was up until the War started. We had quite a number of these type of shows in Scotland. Disappeared now. Don't have them any more.

FIG. 38 John Codona's Pleasure Fairs no. 1 Dennis lorry, photographed 18 June 1962, Newcastle Town Moor. (*Photograph:* Jack Leeson. *Copyright:* National Fairground Archive, University of Sheffield)

Did the Codonas, or was it just the ghost show?

No, no. We didn't have many shows after the war years, we mostly got into the rides. The Codona Brothers didn't bother with the shows. The only one that had a show was Tommy Codona, down there with the ghost show.

Were the rides more lucrative – was that the basic idea?

Yes, yes. That's the short answer. As the rides were coming along, the younger people were interested in the rides and families. And you needed the rides to promote a carnival. You couldn't promote a fairground with just the side-shows. You needed the big rides and this was our – the brothers' idea – to promote the fairs and they needed. ...

Would you say the Codonas were the main family for machines in Scotland?

Yes. There was another family, Whites, J. White and Sons who were always quite to the fore, they had four or five round-abouts, he had two sons, operated as a company, J. White and

Sons. They were – I would say they were the main opposition people, showmen, to the Codonas, but they were always two steps behind. I'm not biased or anything like that! ... But the point I was making was because of the competition between the brothers and the standards that they set, I mean they set their own standards, it was as high as my grandfather set his standards, you know, they set their standards high. Now, anybody in our business, they had to compete with the high standards. They had to try and beat it. If they didn't get anywhere near that they were no ... So Whites were in the position that they had to keep their equipment up to the standard that the Codona family were setting and other people – Danny Taylor, Irvines, other people, you know, showpeople with one of their own roundabouts, two roundabouts, they had to keep up when they stood alongside because when they went to a fairground, and like I said, there was always a mixture, if you had three or four Codona's roundabouts there all gleaming and shiny and you had a couple of old, tatty old things, you're not going to get nothing. So they had to keep the standard up and there's no doubt that the standard of showmen's equipment overall in Scotland was higher than it was in England.

... Individual people in England had good equipment but collectively on a fairground in Scotland all the equipment was good, of a general good standard. In England you would find the three or four rides that were excellent mixed in with other equipment that wasn't very good at all. You used to see this at Newcastle, you know, you stood out a mile. We were one of these that went down to Newcastle, took rides down there, actually, we opened the eyes of a few English showmen at that time. We went down with lorries after the War, I was involved in it, we didn't have the tractions, we went down with lorries and our equipment, I had the showmen round there standing watching me erecting the equipment and when we opened up they were all looking at our lorries generating the power, wondering how did we manage to get all that stock on two lorries and they had about ten trailers. We used to do long journeys, you had to condense it, you know. They didn't do long journeys.

They could go back and forward ten mile or that, so it was just horses for courses, you see. I'll never forget that, when I was building up, erecting the machines, showmen standing around watching. They'd never seen that in their life. Wondering where it was all coming from, you know. A man said, 'You must have a small Waltzer, Gordon'. I said, 'No, it's a 50-foot machine'. 'My God'. And when I came back after I had lunch, he stopped and I took the cover off one of our lorries, the big frame on it and everything's all packed in. For example, it was a Waltzer, there was ten Waltzer cars, big, took up a bit of room. I had all them and the top of the roundabout on this one lorry. There was a Waltzer up the road there; all they had on one trailer was ten Waltzer cars. You know, that was the difference, you see; they didn't worry about having to run back and forwards, you see.

So was it your branch of the family that were the ones with the big rides and what not?

Yeah, yeah. That was the core of the family. That was the bit that become well known. They were known as Codonas, gen-erally, but there was the four branches. So people said 'You're everywhere', you see, because they thought – well, we were everywhere – but it was different branches of the family. William Codona, he was down in the Borders a lot, he travelled round. … That was Uncle William, my father's brother, William. And Nathaniel, he travelled round Glasgow a lot. We used to say he never got away from the tramlines, that was as far as he got from Glasgow. Frank Codona travelled a bit more. He travelled a bit, a bit like my father.[138] My father was the widest travelled one.

I remember you saying something about your father's … the way he dressed …

Well, you see him there [this refers to a photograph of John Codona supervising the building up of a fair in Aberdeen] He was standing on that gangway there, he's got a bowler hat on and he's got a suit on, I mean that was his working clothes! No, my father was a well-dressed man. He took a pride in his appearance latterly when he was doing business. And he was the type of man that didn't wear the same suit two days running. Probably had four or five suits that all looked the same. You know, the grey, the grey pin-stripe or the grey this or a grey that. Dark suit but same style. Always wore his bowler hat, waistcoat, gold watch and chain, you know, with the Albert and chain, and a ring, always wore a ring, gold ring with a diamond in it ... It was my father's style, you know.

... He was very particular. He would never come out unless he was properly dressed. Collar and tie. I remember when he used to have the stiff collars, you know, when I was young. But his suit was always clean – I don't know how he got away with it! Very smart man – waxed moustache. Didn't come out unless he was properly dressed. Now, Uncle Frankie was similar. He was the same, he was same style, always smartly dressed. Uncle Billy, the oldest one, he was a bit different. He'd come out with a silk scarf round his neck and I don't know whether he'd be washed or not sometimes. He wasn't dirty, but I mean he'd come out with a silk scarf round his neck and maybe no jacket on and, you know, stand around talking to somebody. That was Uncle Billy's style, you know. Uncle Nathaniel, he was some-where in between. You know, when he – Uncle Nathaniel was a wee bit stouter and he probably never looked as smart although he dressed not bad. He was the youngest. My father and Uncle Frankie were more the same style, with the moustache, waxed moustache and everything. Smart man.

Always had a whistle in his pocket, police whistle. Handiest thing in the world that; he used to come out on the ground – used to get trouble with kids sometimes, running around wild and father he blew the whistle going toot, toot, toot, toot, the kids – police whistle – were away, you know, that was it. Or, years ago, I can remember my father – when we had the Dragons, the big organ playing – I can remember my father standing underneath that extension bit, waving his hands for-ward and blowing the whistle to draw attention, you know. I was only a boy at the time, my father was down the other end. I remember the whistle then. If you heard that whistle it made you look for my father and if you were wanting something you could point at something you wanted.

You could hear it, you know. And very often he was able to blow the whistle and you'd look for him and he'd point at something, you know. Maybe somebody'd fallen off something and so they needed looking at, you know, and it was a good thing. We carried it on a wee bit on the Motorcycle Speedway there. We'd a bell in the pay box and that used to go round pretty fast, the motorbikes, you know. You'd get an occasion when somebody's kind of hanging off. And the bell would 'ding, ding' and the men that was on the platform would [look round]; 'There's somebody fallen off'. So that was the quickest way to let them know 'you'd better look out', you see. You couldn't shout – couldn't hear anybody. It was 'ding, ding' on the bell and the men would look round on their sections to go to the assistance of somebody that might be – a kid or something – might be hanging off. That was part of the job when you was in the pay box.

Sounds as though you always had a sort of fair number of people in your employment then.

Oh, aye, aye. ...

It wasn't just immediate family ...?

Oh, no, no. We needed about an average of five men on each ride. That was about a full complement, generally. Sometimes you had more than that. Sometimes you were short-handed, enough but generally five was about a full complement of staff, not counting ourselves and the managers and so on, our own family. ... We'd some of them that had been with us for a few years and they would probably leave, when we was closed up through the winter, they would leave at the back end and they would come in the spring of the year looking for jobs again, those who wanted back. Latterly, when we started to be in the Kelvin Hall, we employed all [year] they were employed. The ones that we wanted to keep. But we were lucky in as much as we had a nucleus of good men.

... They weren't showmen. They were just people that come that liked to be with the fair. A lot of them liked the life, the travelling about, just enjoyed it. The younger ones liked the aspect of wherever they were there was always lassies round about, you know. Well, we had a lot of young lads working for us. They were always smart. Our lads used to, you know, we made sure they washed their faces or looked a bit clean. And we got a few of them that took a pride in their appearance, you know. Some of them – the Smith brothers, four or five brothers Smiths, family, they all worked on the fairgrounds with different people and at one time we had three of them working for us. One young lad, Norrie, he worked with us for quite a few years. We used to go to Aberdeen in the wintertime, Christmas and New Year, he finished up – we went there that often – he finished up marrying a lassie up there, you know, so we lost him! We used to see him when we went back. But there were some good men. But we had Willie Smith who was a showman's son, who would rather work, he didn't have any business to occupy him, he worked for us as a manager. But he was a capable man, he drove the engine. He was left – he was capable – you could leave him. The same with Georgie – another one – Georgie McArdle. Although – they were with us, you know, they were always with us, but you could depend, you could leave them to build a ride up and look after it and make sure it was alright, you know. Georgie McArdle, I was apprenticed to him for a few years until the War started. When the War started everything was closed down. We had to pay everybody off – nothing for them to do, you know.

Gordon's apprenticeship started a few years before the War. Prior to this he was somewhat unusual in being left to stay with his aunt, Lizzie (the sister of his uncle Nathaniel's wife Cissie, and a former nanny for Gordon's parents, eventually to be buried alongside Codona children who had died in infancy). This was so that he could have a settled education up to the school leaving age.

FIG. 39 Lizzie O'Donnell outside the sweet shop on Union Street,
West Calder bought for her by the Codonas, *c*1930s.
(*Source:* Anne-Marie Gwynn)

Despite his settled education and the importance attached to it, Gordon left school as soon as he could, at 14, to start training for the business. This progression encapsulates some of the apparently conflicting attitudes to 'education' on the fairground. In this relatively closed community with work and family life so intertwined, the most relevant 'education', in terms of acquiring shared values and necessary social and practical skills, took place as an ongoing part of growing up. Echoes of this type of informal teaching and learning can be seen in the didactic turn of many of the anecdotes and stories in showpeople's reminiscences.

Apart from this informal learning, there were obvious types of apprenticeship: Gordon Codona mentions his mentor George McArdle and we earlier saw Jim McArdle (Snr) recalling how his great-uncle Frankie Codona became 'an uncle in every sense of the word' to his father: 'Frankie taught my father many things about being a showman, how to be a lessee and act like one. How to treat his fellow showmen as tenants, every aspect of a lessee's [business] was taught him. ...'[139] This kind of learning was highly valued. Nevertheless, even though formal schooling could often crystallise a sense of difference from the 'settled' community, value was also placed on school education, not least for its immediate practical uses but also for the wider occupational horizons it opened.[140]

I was going to ask you about how your education went when you were travelling.

[*Gordon Codona*]

Ah well, I was left behind. But my older brother, he had to soldier on.[141] He had to work – oldest son, my sister, oldest sister. There were three brothers and three sisters. And my father didn't have any education as such but he was an educated man – self-taught. He couldn't write very much or things like that but he could dictate a letter as good as anybody. That comes naturally to him because that was one of the jobs when I'd come home; 'Here, write a letter for me' and he would dictate it for me and I used to write it and it was all composed right, you know … but he made sure that we got a bit of schooling and both me and my brother were left behind. I had a younger sister went to a convent and had her education, one of the other – four of the family were left behind for bits of the time. … I was left behind with an aunt in Glasgow and Alfred, he was some time with her. … She was an aunt because her sister had married one of my uncles, Nathaniel.[142] She was a relative. My Uncle Nathaniel married a flattie – that was Cissie and that was her sister that we would be with. And she'd come into the business quite easily, you know. Two of my sisters went to a convent at Dumfries – Girvan, St Joseph's in Girvan and had their education there. But I was fortunate, I managed to go to school in Glasgow and then I moved onto St Mungo's Academy.

But that was unusual?

Just a wee bit at that time, aye. They left us behind and go on like that, you know.

I wondered if when you were at school and you were mixing with flatties as it were, if there was any sense of having come from a different background or anything like that?

Before I went to St Mungo's Academy I was at an elementary school until I was just about eleven. ... I went to school at St Margaret's elementary school. ... I used to go to school and see the lads – but I didn't mix with the children as much, or the kids as much other than when I was at school, because I was still able at that time, we used to spend a bit of time visiting. My aunt's sister was travelling at the fairground. She was Mrs Nathaniel Codona ... the aunt I was with, her sister was married to Nathaniel Codona ... and he was never far from Glasgow, so we used to spend a bit of time, and my friendship, my pals was all on the fairground, you know, we kept in contact with them that way. So I knew – I didn't have many friends, I didn't make many friends – because it was a different – we didn't have anything in common, probably that's about the best

FIG. 40 Nathaniel and Cissie Codona, *c*1930s.
(*Source:* Anne-Marie Gwynn)

FIG. 41 Nathaniel Codona's Autodrome, Kelvin Hall, Glasgow, 1946.
(*Source:* S. Thackray: *British Fairgrounds; A photographic
history* [Norwich, 1993])

way about it. And I got on not bad at school and my mother
had a notion that she was going to send me away to Dumfries
... the boys' college, St Joseph's in Dumfries. And I didn't fancy
this idea very much at all.

So the opportunity came along through the school to sit an
entrance examination for St Mungo's Academy. There was an
allocation in all the schools; each school had an allocation to
send pupils to an entrance examination for St Mungo's secondary school and the teachers picked out who they thought would
maybe have a go at this examination. And the class above me,
the twelve-year-olds, that was the class that was due for entrance,
that could sit the exam. But there wasn't enough, there wasn't
enough interested at that time, so they dropped back to the next
class and me and another lad was asked if we wanted to go,
you know. They thought we could maybe just about manage to
squeeze through. I jumped at that chance because this was a
chance for me to stay on at secondary school without going away
to Dumfries. Home from home where I was, you see. So, in the
end, I passed the exam, I probably scraped through, I don't

know, but I passed anyway and when I got to the school, into
St Mungo's, I was one of the youngest in the class, six months,
you know, before the others. But anyway, that was how I got
to St Mungo's Academy, but I made many acquaintances but
never made many friends, you know, because any chance I got
I was back to my mother and father on the fairgrounds, or my
cousins. ... I was more friendly with my Uncle Nathaniel's
boys, he had five sons and I used to relate to them quite a bit.
So that was the way it was until I left school, but I left school
when I was 14. I was supposed to stay on and I left school. I
went and seen the headmaster when I was 14 and said that my
father needs me. He just looked at me – laughed. Actually, he
knew quite a few of the showpeople because some of them had
been at the school before; he knew the name. He told me that
when I went to the school, 'Codona, you're the fairground ...'.
I said, 'Yes'. He said, 'I know one or two of your family'. And
so when I went and seen him and said 'my father needs me', he
just smiled, 'Away you go!'

But I was supposed to go on until I was 16. At that time
you could leave school when you were 14. ... It just so happened that they were at Rutherglen at the time, you know,
Rutherglen Fair, which is just next door to Glasgow. And I
rolled up there and I remember, 'What're you doing here?' my
mother said. I said, 'I've left school'. Didn't go down very well
at the time. 'Oh, we've got a new Waltzer, we've got a new
Waltzer, I've left school.' My father he wasn't worried about it
at that point; I was 14, I could leave school, you know. So he
probably thought I'd had enough then, you know, and I wasn't
interested in going into anything else, you know. I was interested in the fairground. ... This was 1934, '35. My mother
wasnae very happy, I tell you, and that was it.

... My mother, she was an English family... born in Preston.
She was an English show family. We're a right mixer that way,
I mean, my brother Alfred, he married an English girl ... my
daughter, Gail – I've only got a son and a daughter – she's
married into the Pinder's family, Pinder's Circus. They go back
I think as far as what we go back. He's got letters there and

things, old Queen Victoria command performance from the Pinder Brother's number one circus to go to Balmoral for three occasions. Queen Victoria went up to Balmoral, she had Pinder's Circus come to do a show for her kids and then for local kids. They done the pitch for three years, command performance. That was his family, 1870s, '80s or something like that with Victoria. So their family go back.

... But there's a bit of circus blood in all that lot, you know. But actually my son's married an English girl. That was another thing I was going to tell you. She's north of England. When I went down to Redcar he met an English showman's daughter and married – Cooper, well-known family down there. Actually they had quite a bit of interests up here too, Edinburgh, amusement arcades and whatever, 'Johnny', you see them about, you know. ... This is what happened. You married within, generally within the business, you know.

My father at that time, he'd stopped doing a lot of physical work. I've got a photograph of my father just doing some physical work, pretending to do it. And he had the two sons and his main operation at that particular time was site finding, looking for sites, or arranging for sites on existing fairgrounds, going to see people that were operating a fair and getting a position in for the rides, that was his main occupation.

That was on his own behalf. By this time he was on his own. We're talking about the 1930s, it would be about 1934, '35... And that was his main occupation. He spent a lot of time running about all over the country seeing – but it was quite a job; he had to go and visit people that owned a piece of land, see the man that owned it, or if it was the local authority he had to go and see them. And there was various other parts – once you'd done that you had to find out if there was any other requirements needed. Licences, for example at that time was important in Glasgow; you couldn't open – or in Scotland – you couldn't open a fair without a licence. In England you could go and get a bit of land and put your – see the landlord, whoever – and start to operate. You couldn't do that in Scotland. You had to get a bit of land and apply to the Sheriff's Court to get the licence, which – that meant seeing people and stating your case and so on. That was my father's main job at that particular time. Prior to that he was, he worked just the same as we worked, you know, dismantling, erecting and even driving the traction engines. ...

... We'd just got a new roundabout then. We'd a manager on there, a man that had been with us a few years, chap called George McArdle, he was a showman but he elected rather to work for somebody than to have his own business, and he worked for us for a good number of years, a good man, and he was a sort of a teacher for me. I served my apprenticeship under him because he travelled my father's roundabout, he travelled with my father. My brothers, one was married, he travelled with his own family with a roundabout, the other brother was single with my sister, they travelled on their own, as a unit. We had to be able to split up and divide or come together. And in my father's case, I went with my father and mother. I was only 14, you know. And Georgie McArdle was my mentor. He used to erect the roundabouts and maintain them and he worked through the day and at night and that was me learning, that was my apprenticeship, you know, and that was it. It's the same with anybody in our business; young boys and the girls, they serve their apprenticeship at home or whatever and it's a good training.

And so it would be then, two weeks and two weeks and two weeks, was that how it went, or was it a week?

No, roughly about a fortnight, yes. A Friday and Saturday of the first week, of course, you was erecting and then the full week the second week and then you would dismantle on the Monday, you didn't do much on the Sunday, we dismantled on the Monday and erect again. It used to take us two or three days to do that normally. Nowadays they do it in a day with these modern machines.

And how far would there normally be between one pitch and another?

It could be anything. It was never very short, I mean 25 or 30 miles was unusual, 40 or 50 miles, 60 miles was more the average. Or longer still, I mean we could do over 100 miles. We used to go up the north. We travelled bigger journeys on average than most people because ... when Codona Brothers split the rides up, my father didn't finish up with very many fairs, I don't know why. ... They parcelled out the fairs and my father got the short end of the straw, you know, because I know he had complaints about one of the big fairs – Ayr for example, all the Codonas were there but him. Three brothers but he wasn't there. Various other fairs; Dumfries and. ... What he did do, he had, he was all promoted, he had all his equipment on at Kirkcaldy, but he had to do that himself, you know. ... He got one of the Kirkcaldy pitches from Codona Brothers but the rest of them he sorted them out himself. That was a full time job for him was getting a run of places because if you had places, established places to go to, it was relatively easy. But if you haven't got the places to go to – that was why we would split up and that's why we were doing bigger journeys.

So you could actually be in a situation where you would finish at one place and not necessarily have a guaranteed ...

Yes, you couldn't do that, just looking for somewhere to go. In that case what happened then is what we used to call private business. It meant that rather than be closed, you'd go and get a bit of land anywhere sort of thing, and open for a weekend just to keep you going, and at the same time looking for somewhere to go. But there wasn't enough established fairs, you know, I am talking about the likes of Bridge of Allan, the regular fairs that come round same time every year; there wasn't enough of them to go round.

There was less showmen actually in the years gone by, with the big rides. But having said that, you didn't get any more fairs. There were only so many fairs. They didn't change. I mean some of them were there, we'd been going to them for 30, 40, 50 years. They were established fairs and it was difficult to establish a new fair – and you were fortunate if you found some-

where and you opened a fair for a couple of weeks and you
could go back there the next year and get a good return. The
Showmen's Guild had their own rules and regulations for that.
I mean, if a showman found a fair that hadn't been opened
before, a site that hadn't been opened before – he didn't find a
fair, he found a site, made the fair – he could open on that and
then he got protection from the Showmen's Guild for that
particular date at that particular place for the next year. So
nobody could go and occupy that stance. So that was one thing,
so if you managed to land on a site that was alright, touched
lucky, you could establish a fair. My father done a few of these,
you know, particularly in Aberdeen and up the north of Scotland.

The biggest fair in Scotland, it's round about Easter every
year, is Kirkcaldy Links market. That's what they call a starting
out fair. We used to go to Falkirk, which was Bastable's ground,
with one of our rides ... an established show firm. They had
rides. But we established a fair of our own at Dunfermline, what
I'm talking about, because we went there and found it was
alright and established a fair there.[143] So that was a continu-
ation fair that my father, well the sons actually – I don't think
it was my father at that time – sons established after the War.
And that was a regular fair; then we went to Kirkcaldy and from
Kirkcaldy we went to Aberdeen. Now Aberdeen was another
established fair that we established ourselves and we used to be
there – where we were, we established ourselves, but prior to
that, going back years, there was always a May holiday fair in
Aberdeen that went on. ... So Aberdeen was an established fair.
There was other fairs that other people went to: Whites had a
good few fairs, there was Paisley, we went to Aberdeen, we
went to Taranty Fair, which was an old market fair, only two or
three days. A couple of days but we used to fit it in. Montrose.
... Then we went down to Newcastle, which was an English
fair, and we come back up; there was always a big fair established in Glasgow at Glasgow Green for a month, that was a
long time. And there was Bridge of Allan, Inverness, Elgin,
some of the market fairs – Turriff Fair up in Aberdeen and a

few others. Then there was fairs all over – Ayr, Troon, Paisley, Dalmarnock, Dumbarton; I mean you name it there, even over near Edinburgh. ... Haddington – it wasn't a big fair, it was a small fair, it was more what they call private business. There was a few of them – Armadale, Broxburn, all these places, these were regular fairs.

... That would carry on until usually the end of October, September was the finish of the season. If you was operating in October you were doing well. We finished in October in Falkirk and that was as long as you – the weather was the trouble, you know, you got into the bad weather. March was the time that you started and you would travel during March, right through the summer; what you tried to do was in the middle of the summer holiday you'd like to have a place for three or four weeks. Going back a long time, we used to open for about four weeks at Broughty Ferry, just outside Dundee, on the Castle Green. That was a good spot – I'm going back before the War now. Things like that. But after the War you couldn't get on the Castle Green. The local authority would change their mind and say you can't have that, or somebody would build on the land and you were forever being changed. There's a few of the fairs that lasted, most of the street fairs because they don't build on the street, they leave that you know.

St Andrews for example. There's Leven ... mainly the street fairs are the ones that carry on. What's happened though in our business, all of a sudden the local authorities are looking more kindly towards the fairgrounds. They're opening them on the streets. I mean, nobody ever imagined that at the end of Princes Street there would be a fair, or in Glasgow, in the middle of – on George Square in Glasgow there would be a fairground and equipment up. This is what's happening now, and it's a good job because there's so much equipment now, the modern equipment that travels about, it's all hydraulics, it's press buttons and arms shoot out and there's not the same time required, or labour to erect them, and consequently they move quicker and they can occupy sites quicker. They're even occupying the parking places round these supermarkets, which is another innovation, which is alright. But these are sites now that's become available because the other old fairground sites on open land have been built on. This is what happens – it come and goes. There's very few – there's a fairground at Hamilton there, I think my grandfather used to go to it, the fair was on it for years and years; four years ago they decided that no more fairs on it, after all them years, and that was it, end of it, no Hamilton Fair.

Is that why your father had to be always on the go, looking out?

He was always on the go, yes, looking for sites. ... It wasn't easy to find suitable places, you know. Oh, he was always – and not only that, he was also trying to get into established sites. That was another important thing. We changed our equipment quite a bit, the rides that we had, mainly because with a different ride you could get a site, whereas somebody – the operator of the land, of the fair – if he had a similar ride, of course he wouldn't let you in and be the only one of a kind. So, my father got around to trying to get something a bit different so he could get into these spaces on the fairground. A man would make room for something that was different from what was already there.[144]

6

The Rides, the People and the Winter Ground

THE working world described by Gordon Codona was dominated by machinery – rides and transport – and, as both he and his brother Alfred (Appendix 2) describe it, it took a good spread of practical skills, the focus of professional pride, both to keep the show on the road and stay ahead of the competition.

[*Gordon Codona*]

... In the 1930s there were great changes; the rides and different things. My father had a new roundabout nearly every year, everything changing, aye, in fact all the rides – the Wall of Death, Waltzer, Noah's Ark, Speedways, Mont Blancs, Moon Rockets, Jets. ... You had to change to keep the interest going at your fairs. You changed if you thought that the opposition fellow was gaining a point or two on you, especially when you stood in different fairs side to side. And the novelty used to wear off, even on these modern rides, the novelty can wear off a bit. The only thing they don't change novelty-wise is kiddies' rides, you know. Because there's always new kids coming on! You don't have new rides, you just have new kids. It works out that way. ...

He started off – he had a Dodgem when the Codona Brothers split up. That was his share, the Dodgem and a set of Chairoplanes. And the first thing he did, he got a Wall of Death because a Wall of Death had two benefits for him; it was not too big, and it was different.[145] So he run the Wall of Death. My brother, he was only a young lad, he went round with the Wall of Death. He didn't ride the Wall of Death but he looked after it you know. We had a couple of Wall of Deaths – we had a man,

Jack Lancaster, who used to ride the Wall, and two girls ... that was my father's – a novelty, two lady riders on the motorbikes and they were good. So we had that for three or four years and then that sort of outlived its ... but he'd established sites, he'd got into somewhere, you see. And he moved on from that, he got another ride that there wasn't a lot of it, it was a Skid, a Swish, which was different at that time. ... Just a round, a big round machine, 50 feet, with the cars on it that swung back and forwards, it went round in a circle. ... As it went round, you had a pedal in the car and you could stop the car and done this. ... So he got rid of the Dodgem because everybody had a Dodgem and he couldn't get the Dodgem anywhere, so 'what's the use of this if I haven't got somewhere to get it?' So we done without a Dodgem for a good few years and we got onto the other novelty rides like the Waltzer. We got the Waltzer which was different, he got that in and Mont Blancs and God knows what else, you know, all the different – something a bit different, he was always after, so he could get it into these positions. That way he established places, you know, he got in, with the Waltzer particularly, he managed to get into a good few places – the likes of Bridge of Allan.

And were these rides made by Maxwell's?[146]

Yeah.

All of them?

Yeah.

How would that work?

Well with George Maxwell, usually the showmen went to George Maxwell. They would see something. Mind you, Maxwell went about a bit himself, you know, he'd have a look – mostly on the continent, you know, abroad. But the ideas would come from there and then they would adapt them to suit.

... What could happen – a 'for instance' – you could be abroad and go on the fairgrounds abroad, a lot of fairgrounds in Germany and France, Belgium and all these places, you know.

The rides were a bit different. You could go and see a ride there, and I know one case my father would come back and say to George Maxwell, 'I was over at so and so, there's a ride there', and he'd describe the ride. 'I'd be interested in that, George. Can you go and have a look at it?' And George Maxwell would go over and take a lot of photographs and then there would be a fair bit of discussion and if they thought that it was a feasible thing, George Maxwell would get himself busy – I think sometimes through the night! Pinched measurements with his foreman and make one. He was clever enough to see what was going on and then adapt it to the British idea. It was mostly one of the showmen that went to George Maxwell, but once he got started making the ride it was repetitive. Other showmen seen it and I think they would say, 'Who made it?', 'George Maxwell', and go to George Maxwell and that was it.

And would you chose the way it was finished, or the decoration or what not, or would ...?

You had a discussion. I'll give you an instance about that. ... The rides after the War, the Dragons, the Motors and all these big roundabouts, they had what they call an extension front, with the steps, there was a bit that came out where you walked up. And that was an extension bit – usually had four or five pillars over the steps, you know, it would come out like that from the circle. The ride was back here, this was a front. And they were like that for years and years, right from after the First – well before the First World War – right up until I changed it!

Our rides were like that. We had a Motorcycle Speedway, the Waltzer, round like this. And just after the War finished Whites had a new machine came out by Maxwell and that had what they call a paramount front. It was the same thing again, but more intricate you see. And I looked at this thing – this was on a Waltzer the same as ours – and ours was sort of the old-fashioned extension front. And it came to Glasgow Green and their ride looked ultra-modern against ours which wasn't; you know, kind of getting a wee bit old-fashioned. So I got down with a pencil and a bit of paper and I started to draw out something. I wasn't bad at drawing and I drew out, messed about and drew a design, a canopy design, pillars and so on. I thought, 'I'm gonnae change the front of the Waltzer, but I'm no gonnae do that pile of work that they've got. I want something less work but effective.' So I drew this canopy front and our old Waltzer from 1934 to we're talking about 1950; it was good looking, looked well, but it was getting a bit old-fashioned I thought, compared to this big modern thing that Whites had. So I went to George Maxwell and I showed him this drawing. I said, 'I want to put a canopy on the Waltzer, George, do the roundabout, repaint the outside of it and put this canopy on'. So I knew how to do it and I talked to them about it. He said, 'that looks alright'. Pencil drawing, you know. It was a perspective, it was under the canopy, you could see it all. He said, 'Go and see Sid'. Now Sid was his painter and decorator.[147] 'Go and see Sid, talk to Sid.' So I went and seen Sid. He said, 'Who drew that?' I said, 'I done it.' He said, 'that's alright!', which was a pat on the back to me from Sid because he was a clever man, an artist, you know. And I thought, 'that's alright, if Sid thinks that's alright, that was good', you know. He said, 'That's good – good perspective', he says. Anyway, we talked about it and went to see the joiner fellow and we discussed it all and arranged to have it done. It meant that I had to bring that part of the ride in, the outside area of it in, and they made it for us, you know.

So they done that and I remember – and I put lights on it, nobody'd had lights on the front before, I put lights on, not running lights which was a bit, a wee bit too soon for that, but I put rows of lights on the front and decorated it all, hadn't been done before. It went to Kirkcaldy and it looked well. I don't think there was a machine left with an extension front after two years! They all got rid of it. You could see it, actually people taking the fronts off. And where they didn't put a canopy on they just took the walls back, you know. I think I got a lot of work for George Maxwell. We done our rides, we done two of our own machines after that. We'd a Noah's ark we done, ... We gave it to them to do, you know.

It was my idea and that hadn't been done before. These big pillars, big rounded pillars that looked the part. But I don't know if I ever got any credit for it. I had a wee bit in a book that mentions that Gordon Codona went to Maxwell and gave him his ideas, you know.[148] Somebody noticed it.

George Maxwell was alright. You could give him the idea and he was quick to pick up on it and embellish it, you know. But a lot of the showmen went with their own ideas and he went to work on them. And I think the Codona family, all the Codona family, were pretty good at giving Maxwell wee bits of ideas, even about the construction, the manufacture, the construction of them, you know. Things that we found – little things that we found was a bit of a nuisance or maintenance-wise caused trouble. We knew more about that than Maxwell and would go back to him and say, 'Such and such gives us a bit of trouble'.

One instance was that – after I came out the army I had a bit of knowledge about engineering, I had learned a bit. Basically I did do, learned a lot about metals and things. I knew that when we come – we used to get a lot of wear on our spur pinion, didn't last very long. And I discovered that if you changed to a certain type of metal, N6, and hardened it, it was alright. So I had it done myself. ... I had this spur pinion made at an engineers and put on. I'd learned a wee bit about this and changed it round. This was what I done, got it done at an engineers. I said, 'Do one of them, make me that', and they done it and it worked out alright. That was fine, I had a pinion on there that didn't wear out. ... The central one that drives it round, big spur pinion, you know. And we got a new Waltzer. I sold the old Waltzer when I was at Redcar and I got a new one and the new one come with Maxwell's original type of spur pinion. Halfway through the summer it went. I said to Maxwell, 'For God's sake make me a new pinion, do it so and so, and so and so', you know. Told him the metal it was, the type of seal it was and so on, and how to do it, and I gave him the one that I had ... And that got me out of trouble. ...

... He built a hell of a lot of stuff for Scottish showmen.

They all bought. There were two of the English firms, Lakin in England, and Orton and sons, and Spooner was another firm; Supercar, wee Dodgem tracks. But for the round rides George Maxwell and sons built a lot. ... The Figure 8 – that came from Germany, that was a wee bit far advanced. There was no Figure 8s getting built in Britain at that time; they had to go to Germany, it had to come from Germany. Chairoplanes came from Germany at that time, they came over from Germany. Most of them were foreign built. A lot of the rides now are all foreign built. New rides, you know. But Maxwell built the bread and butter rides; the Waltzers, Noah's Ark, Speedways, Moon Rockets, things like that, a little bit of timber involved, he built a lot of those, Jet rides. He built me a Big Dipper, a Mouse – a Mad Mouse, I know that directly, you know, a ghost train, he built that for me. He built two or three of them that went to England. He was a big manufacturer of rides of a certain type and then we started to get a lot of the continental ones coming in, these fancy ones you get now, and actually he doesn't build any more rides now. He died and his son didn't carry on with the business. He had two businesses ... a lorry business where they built and decorated lorries, coach-work, along with the showmen side of it. George Maxwell, he was always interested in showmen's ... knew all the showmen, they all knew him. When he died there wasn't the same connection. His son was more interested in the lorry business, lorry cabs and decorating. And then there was the competition from the continental rides, these fancy ones. More metal than what there was wood. Maxwell was more into the joinery work, you know.

Showmen are very practical and very adaptable too, because when you're operating in our line of business you open at six o'clock at night and you're open at night and if something goes wrong you're no going to get any expert anywhere at six o'clock and seven o'clock at night. And probably you couldn't wait; by the time they arrived there it would be time to close up, so showmen had to do their own thing and be very adaptable and they could get by with a bit of string and a bit of wire and all sorts to keep the thing going, you know.

... When I was in the army I was a sergeant instructor in the Royal Engineers, and, of course, my father was in the Engineers in the First World War. I finished up operating instructing on diesel engines and pumps and so on, and that was including water pumps – these were little single-cylinder engines that drove a water pump, very important for getting water out of trenches and things. And we used to use a lot of them. But with the damp conditions round about, water and so on, they were a bit difficult to start sometimes. So, I had a fair old idea what to do with them: used to take the plug out – showmen's idea because showmen's lorries wasn't new, they was always slow to start sometimes and some of them, the old petrol one, you done what I'm talking about now; or the diesel ones, you put a torch on them, you know. But anyway, you take the plug out. So I took the plug out of this little single cylinder engine and dried the plug and got a pencil out my pocket, and I'm putting a bit of black lead on the points, across the points of the plug. There's an officer there and he said, 'What're you doing corporal?' I said, 'I'm putting some black lead on the points, sir.' 'And what's that going to do?' 'Hopefully,' I said, 'It's going to encourage the spark to jump across the points.' 'Oh aye. Okay, carry on.' So I put the plug back in and put the wire on; I was going, 'I hope this thing works now'. I gave it a couple of pulls, away it went. He said, 'That's very good. That's the sort of thing that we need in the army', he says, 'Being able to make do when you're in trouble. Where did you learn that?' 'I'm a showman, sir.' 'Oh.' I said, 'this is the sort of thing we've got to have for ourselves to keep us going, you know.' 'Well,' he said, 'I'll make sure that goes down in the code of instructions now in the course, that little tip', he says, 'that's the sort of thing we need.' ... But he was right, you know. And the other lad, he didn't know anything about that, you know, that was something that they learned, an old showman's trick. There were loads of things like that that showmen done.

I came unstuck once; we used to put these pickets in the ground, a row of them, you see, and sometimes a bit difficult to get out. And there was a sergeant there that had been instructing us and we was starting to get them out and some of the lads was having a go. He said, 'Get out the road, I'll do it, I'll do it', you see. So he started banging at this one particular picket that wouldn't come out. I opened my mouth, 'Don't you think you should try …', and he looked at me, 'Who the hell do you think you are telling me what to do'. That was that. I said no more. So I just watched him for the next ten minutes struggling with this picket here and I knew what he could do to get it out because we were knocking stakes out all the time, you know – the wee tricks that you learn. But he was trying to man-handle it straight out and it was never going to come straight out, you know. I thought, 'I'm not going to say no more', that learned me a lesson.

But there were lots and lots of things that showmen – I mean, a vehicle wouldn't start, a diesel, you put a hot flame, just a rag and a bit of flame, over the air induction and hot air would go in and give it a chance to start. All sorts of wee things. Showmen – they take a bit of stopping, you know, if there's something that needs doing, get round about it. We're not all clever, but put all the brains together and it adds up to something, you know. Very adaptable. And I think they're all proud of that initiative that they've got, you know.

The need to be flexible and adaptable is shown most closely in the stories of some of the accidents and disasters that had to be dealt with. Stories like these embody the importance that was placed on certain skills and abilities. Moreover, telling stories of how problems and accidents were overcome was a way of passing on knowledge for future use.[149]

[*Gordon Codona*]

We had one of our own lorries turn over on the road up North. One of the big lorries that held all the motorbikes inside, quite a good load. Willie Smith, he was a showman, worked for us for years as a manager, good lad, good driver, was coming along the road, and of course up the north the roads are a bit narrower and there was another bus coming. So he could see the road, so he pulls over to the edge of the road, what he thought, but there was no road underneath it. They'd tarred over, over the edge of the road and onto the grass. The road finished here but the tar went over there and he got on there and it gave way and the lorry went over on its side. And, nobody hurt, but the railings, a row of railings along the side sticking up, and the body went through them, you know. So he shouted for help and we got our own vehicles there. We had to get a recovery thing to pull the lorry up, you know. But what we were concerned about was these railings stabs going through the body, what have they done inside. But as luck would have it, where the things was packed they went through, didn't damage anything, you know, but the body was in a right mess, you know, the lorry. So that was an accident that we had.

Another one was up the north again. There was a firm called Thompsons, and they had the same thing happen. They were driving along on these – the roads were a bit narrow for big loads – and they got too near the edge and the lorry went over, and they had a caravan on the back and it went over with it. And we were at Aboyne and the message, word came through to the fairground – we were getting busy getting built up – the message came through to the fairground, 'Thompson's lorry's went off the road, down the bank' – it was down a bank – 'We'll have to go back and help'. So at that particular time I had a big six-wheel ex-army vehicle with a winch on it, and I was just unloading it at the time. So they come to me and I said, 'Well look, in about half an hour I'll be unloaded and then we'll go back with this lorry'. Now there was another showman had a four-wheel-drive ex-army thing, a Matador, with a winch, Billy Wright. So anyway, everybody else gathered up and it would probably be about four o'clockish in the afternoon. So they got these … my lorry went back and they all got on the back of mine and the other lorry and ropes and God knows what else, and we went back down the road to where this lorry was, Thompson's lorry, it was down a bank, ten or 15 feet down, off the road. The wagon was just smashed up, nobody hurt, luckily; the man in the lorry and the woman wasn't in the caravan, she was in the lorry so it wasn't so bad. And the showmen's all round about and the first thing we had to do was start picking up equipment. Somebody else come back with another vehicle, flat lorry, and we was gathering up the equipment and put some of it on my lorry and some of it on this other lorry. Plenty of hands, you know. Got all that together and 'What do we do now? Right, we need the wire ropes out now and shackles.' So they got the Matador. It was a shorter one than mine. I was blocking the road too much. So they got the Matador on with the wire rope down onto the lorry and I got my rope on at one end and we pulled this lorry – there wasn't much left of it, damaged – but we got it up straight, which was alright, on its wheels, dragged it up the bank. Plenty of sheriffs, all instructing, but the job got done, you know. We managed to get it up on the top of the road. What was left of the caravan was dragged up, put up on the top, you know. We managed to get the lorry on its wheels and couple it up behind the Matador to tow it and what was left of the caravan we towed behind my lorry. And we went back to the showground and we was in time to go to the pub and have a drink! The pubs shut at nine o'clock – that's showmen. That's how long it took us to go ten mile down the road, do all that, get it loaded up, bring it back – I think we were all thinking about getting a drink! But we was in the pub before nine o'clock.

Just because you were used to handling …

Handling stuff. Knew what to do. It just came second nature to them. I remember getting to the pub. I said, 'It's only nine o'clock! Four o'clock to nine; we're having a drink.' Everybody was quite satisfied, except the poor old bloke that's lorry's down the bank. But happy that nobody was hurt. But that was the same thing; the road gave way at the side of the lorry.

There was one or two frights with fires and things in different times, you know. But showmen are good firemen. That's another thing they're very quick with. I've seen a number of occasions where there was a fire started and they know the danger. I mean they're all enclosed together. If one's away they're all away, you know.

You've got quite a flammable combination going on …

Especially with the canvas, in them days, the canvas covers and things. And I've seen many a time somebody's vehicle's on fire round the back lighting set, and everybody runs; they don't run empty handed, there's fire-extinguishers in their hand, all acting, you know – fire out. I had a lorry go on fire with me, coming from Kirkcaldy, and it was a mistake by one of the staff. We used the lorries as generators; dynamo on the back and we run the lorries and the exhaust pipes, we used to carry them up in the air. So, this particular vehicle had an exhaust pipe with a bend on it and then a bit that was dropped on. 'Well,' I said to the man, 'take the exhaust pipe off.' So he took the exhaust pipe off, he pulled the bit out the top and didn't do the bit under-neath. Nobody knows about this, but the pipe's off. So we get on the road. And it's amazing to me but we got as far as the outskirts of Stonehaven from Kirkcaldy with that vehicle. And I'm going along and I see smoke coming out of it. And the guy's driving it and I can see – it must have just been lucky. It must have just started and smoke started coming out and my wife's at the back in the car and I pulled in and said, 'Go and stop him Katie', you know. By this time he'd noticed the smoke coming out, so he pulled over with the lorry and when we get there the lorry's on fire underneath. The exhaust pipe was pointing up onto one of the platforms and it set them on fire at the bottom – that shows the type of load that was on it. It set them on fire at the bottom. So I pulled in, jumped out the car with the extinguishers, we always had plenty of extinguishers, he was out the cab, the driver with the extinguishers. And we got over there and as soon as I had a look I thought, 'We're in trouble here', because it's burning and we can't get into it. So we're trying to get through with the fire extinguishers and somebody says, 'Get the cover off'. I said, 'Don't take the cover off, don't take the cover off', you know, the sheet that was over the lorry, 'Don't take that off'. So there was a few other showmen now on the road, they were all going to Aberdeen, so they stopped and they came on, and in the meantime the first thing Katie did she ran across to a farmhouse and got them to phone for the fire engine, just across the road from where it was. So they phoned for the fire engine and it's got to come from Stonehaven. And we're round about now and there are other showmen stopped now and we're trying to get buckets in. We're not getting nowhere, we're still burning. Even a big tanker pulled up and he had a go, he had a smashing thing, you know, so he got going with that, a big pressure one. It damped it down but it didn't put the fire out. I said, 'We've got to get down to here somehow, even when the fire engine comes'. So there was a few hands about, so I said, 'We'll have to unload the lorry', tip the stuff off, you know. And we started to take the cover off – we never got it off. As soon as we lifted it up – it went up phooph, all that was left was bits of rope. Threw it to one side. But anyway, having done that we started to lift the stuff at the side. We just hoyed it off. Didn't throw it off, it was handed off. No use breaking everything up, it was handed off till we come to the heavy stuff. Then we tipped the heavy stuff off. And it usually took about an hour or an hour and a half to load that lorry and I think in about 15 minutes it was unloaded, you know. And we got down to where the fire … and then the fire engine came. But it was a good job we got down to the bottom there because they were able to put the fire out then, you see, put it out. And I discovered then I'd got burned hands doing away with this – we manhandled it off. But there was plenty of showmen there that had stopped and helped us, you know. That was a bad one. And just one of these things, you know; the man had took the exhaust of and hadn't took the pipe off.

Now, we've got one of the big wooden platforms that holds the car on that goes round, you see, destroyed. But luckily enough the rest of it was all metal and the one above it wasn't bad, scorched a wee bit. So we get into Aberdeen. So I've got to hang on the phone now, Maxwell; 'We've had a fire on the road. One of the platforms is burned, George, one of the big platforms on the Waltzer. Have you got any sizes there?' 'Aye,

we've got the sizes. Willie'll have the sizes' – that's the foreman
– 'He'll have the sizes in his book.' So I gave him some sizes –
'That's alright, he'll have them,' I said. 'Well, we open on
Friday.' This is Tuesday night, Wednesday, you know. 'Alright.
I'll have somebody up there. I'll get one made and be up there.'
And right enough, Friday afternoon Maxwell's lorry rolls up, a
new ... and there's a bit of work in making a new platform – but
it was all there, all made, you know, ready, except that some of
the iron work had to be changed over, you know, from the old
one. And we put in on and it was open on a Friday, you know.
But that was, that was the good thing about Maxwell; if you
was in trouble, he knew exactly what was needed.

And then the fire insurance people came. I said, 'What do
we do about all these fire extinguishers now that everybody
used?' I said, 'They want refilling. At least that's ...'. 'Oh,
we're not entitled to do that.' I said, 'If it hadnae been for the
fire extinguishers,' I said, 'instead of me wanting the value of
one platform,' I said, 'there'd have been a lorry and half the
equipment of the Waltzer on there. I saved you thousands and
thousands of bloody pounds!' Oh, I had a job and finally they
turned up a few quid and managed to get some of the extinguishers topped up again. That was the insurance people! But
that was a nasty one on the road. There was a few.

It doesn't always work out like that. There was one, old
Frank Codona ..., probably a cousin of my grandfather's side
of it – he lost his arm in the War, in the First World War, called
him Wingie, Frankie Wingie Codona.[150] He was on the road
with his lorry and caravan. We could see something burning up
the road. We was in the car, me and Katie. And when we got
up there I said, 'Christ, it's Wingie. His load's ...', and we just
got there in time to help him uncouple his – his lorry was on
fire – uncouple his caravan. There wasn't a lot of showmen
there, there was only me and two or three other – a couple of
people whose cars had stopped. We pushed his caravan back
and had to stand there and watch his lorry – it was a bus, one
of these bus type of things – just burn away. ... He had side-
shows, you know, shows. He didn't have any roundabouts. ...

Shooters and all that sort of thing. Stuff that burns well, you know! ... I'm talking about the early 1950s.

The fairgrounds were dominated by the rides, but just as in the days of the geggies there was an important role played by music and performing skills to draw the punters.

... The music that you had in the fairgrounds – was that a big thing for the Codonas, the organs and that kind of thing?

[*Gordon Codona*]

Aye, it was a big thing for anybody that had roundabouts. It started off with the organs in the big roundabouts. That was the only music. I mean in those days ... there was no canned music. It was that or a band or something that sounded like a band so the organs, the fairground organs were something which was indicative of a fairground. Even now, if you hear a fairground organ playing you've got memories of a fairground. That was it until probably just at the end of the 1920s, the top of the 1930s when the canned music began to come out. Of course, there was records out, but there was no way of playing the records to amplify them if you understand what I mean. Gramophones was there but you couldn't broadcast the music until the amplifiers came out and that was at the beginning of the 1930s and we called them Panotropes. And there was a man called Moore-house who was one of the early instigators of amplified music. Whenever that came about, then you could put the records on the Panotropes as we called them and the speakers were there and that was the start of the music. Now, as soon as that started all the popular music that was on record become the music of the fairground – if it was lively; lively music, you know.

... The organs was on the way out then, definitely, because what happened with the old fairground organs was that because the music was expensive, usually it would be either paper music which was on a roll, a zig-zag roll through a keyboard, or it could be on a roller with pins on it, which was another type of organ which we used – either of those, you couldn't change the music very easily because it was expensive. So if you had a selection of music, at an odd time you'd get another new piece of music in, but most of the music was stuff that you'd heard before and you'd got fed-up listening to – we did, but I mean the customers that came along to the place, it was new to them. But on the fairground itself – I was just talking to a pal of mine just last night there, I was playing a tune on my organ and I said, 'Do you remember this, Johnny, the Valencia?' and he said, 'Aye, I remember that, it was on the organ'. I said, 'Do you have any idea how old you would be when you was listening to that music?' I said, 'It would be about before you went to school'. After that period of time the organ disappeared. But we could remember the end of that all as kids. I heard it on the organ, but I must have been a nipper you know, young, because they got rid of the organ at the turn of the '30s, you know, and I remember these tunes. I'd listened to the tunes that often then that it's instilled in my brain, as a child. But that was the trouble with the fairground organs, and then whenever the music came along on records we were able to change the music quite a bit. You could move with the times as the modern music came on; modern tunes came on, you moved the music along.

We used to have a man who used to come around the fairgrounds, he made a good business of it with all the new records that came out. He used to come round the fairgrounds with a selection of all the new records. That saved you going up the street. You could play them and buy them off him. Dick Copland was his name. He used to come round and he done it for years – sold the records and he knew the type of music that you wanted. He'd sell the records to everybody, but the trouble was that everybody had the same music. So you used to go up the street yourself and listen for something a bit different, you know. That was the amplifier – that came on and that's never left now. The quality's improved but that's the same type of music that they play now – maybe they use cassettes, tape, things like that, you know. They don't use the records now, probably use tapes, CDs or whatever, but its the same thing, the music's canned, what you might call canned music, you know. But the organ's faded out. They were big, of course. You see, these big organs was a trailer on their own, you know, and that was another disadvantage, whereas the Panotrope, as we called them, two men could lift it, you know, lift it in and out. It was just a box, whereas the organ was quite big and took up quite a lot of room, which again was a problem. Had to be worked out. So the fairground organ disappeared very quickly basically because of costs of running it and the size of it against the quality of music again that you got with tape.

And as far as drawing people onto your rides, did you rely basically on the look of the ride, or was there much in the way of ... ?

Oh, they used the mike. That was the other thing that happened; with the advent of the Panotrope, the amplifier, you got a microphone. So you were able to use a mike through the amplification system and do a bit of spieling, which happened. That was something that happened quite a bit on side-shows too. I mean, they were quick to latch onto that aspect of the amplification system – microphones. But you got going with the microphone and you either sat in the centre controlling the machine and talking through the mike and using the lights, or you had somebody else that could do a bit of spieling on the mike. ... There was a quality of spieling. ... An uncle of mine, Uncle Nathaniel, Uncle Nat, he had a Canadian working with him for a good few years and he was quite a handsome looking fellow with a wee five-a-side moustache, you know. And he, being a Canadian, when he spoke over the mike it was a bit different. The voice came over well being a bit of a Yankee drawl. He used to talk through the mike on their Speedway and he was notable, you know, because of the accent which was different from the usual Scotch. And he had a slow voice, you know, he slowed his voice down quite a bit, which is important. If you start talking too quick through a microphone, you're amplifying the quickness too, you've heard it in railway stations, haven't you. You wonder what they're saying because they're speaking too quick. He was good. My cousin Norman, he had a lot of patter. That was Billy's boy, you know, he had a good bit of patter on the microphone. There were different ones that come to your mind. We all thought we was good at it, you know!

Were you good at spieling?

Oh, aye, I used to have a go at it. We all – it was part of the job – even the women, if they were sitting in there and the microphone's there and they were getting a bit busy, they tried to draw patronage onto the ride. ... 'don't stare up the steps, step up the stairs', sort of thing. And, you know, you didn't say 'roll up' very much, 'step right forward'. And on the Speedway, 'hold tight, hold tight, we're off this time, here we go again'. And when you were going, set the speed going – 'the louder you scream, the faster we go'. All these sort of wee phrases that we used. Mind, it's a long time since we used them, mind you!

... You only heard it on the ride that you were looking at. Usually you put it into motion more when the ride was going, to create effects. Nowadays though, the effects that they use is lights. Again it's moved on a bit, you know. The lighting effects is something that comes into play when the rides go now more than – it did a bit then, we used to change the lights but not the way they do them now with the automatic light business. We used to change the colour scheme a bit to red or yellow or amber or blue, you know, as the ride was going round, change the whole ambience of the colour. But nowadays there's running lights and flashing lights and the lights do all sorts, this automatic business that they've got. ... But it's all effects isn't it. It lends atmosphere. They still use the microphones. You go on a fairground on a busy night you can listen to some of the patter. You can hear that some of them are better than others at it. But, ach, it's all part of the job.

FIG. 42 John Codona's Pleasure Fairs Waltzer, *c*1960,
Newcastle Town Moor Fair. (*Photograph:* John Gale. *Copyright:* National
Fairground Archive, University of Sheffield)

Showmen and public shared the goal of everybody having a
good time, but good times could get out of hand, often at the
showmen's expense. Nineteenth-century accounts of the fairs
are littered with stories of drink-fuelled riots often resulting in
the destruction of the showmen's property. Being able to defuse
or handle trouble remained an essential fairground skill.

Going back ... you read some of these old stories ... sometimes
showmen would set up at a place and then the roughs would
come out and create trouble. ... I wonder if that had blown
over by the time you went into it?

[*Gordon Codona*]

No, that's always been a problem. The biggest problem about
that was the drink. It was always a factor. There were places
we went to in the '30s, to go back there, that would give you
more trouble than other places. There were places that you
didn't like to go to because you knew that on a Friday night
and Saturday night the drunks would come rolling up and you
had trouble. Places like Hamilton used to be a bad place,

Larkhall, the names tell you – mining places, Larkhall, even the cities, Glasgow – some parts of Glasgow was bad to go to. We used to go to Glasgow Green, you know, and that was near Bridgton and Woodside, you know, and it was torture. There was nothing that the showman had to do about, they just come rolling up drunk. They were having a good time, but I mean the good time was probably interfering with the business; they didn't want to pay or they didn't want to get off.

In the bad places you used to get the police down. You would pay – you used to have to pay for the police to come down. They wouldn't do it for nothing. You had to get the police to get a couple of constables on the ground at some of the bad places. Other times you had to sort of look after yourself and because they had to, the showmen were able to look after themselves a bit, you know, to survive. But, as I say, some of the places you went you never heard a wrong word.

England was just as bad. I mean I went down to England and I've operated in England and it was just the same. I went to Newcastle Town Moor and I had trouble at Newcastle Town Moor on a Friday night and Saturday night with the drunks and I've had the same trouble when I went to Redcar. Busloads coming in from other outlying areas to the park, you know. You tried to avoid confrontation if you could. You tried to help them out of trouble whenever you could. Sometimes that was impossible, you know. When it got to that stage it was either deal with it yourself or close the thing up, you know. So now and again you had to deal with it yourself, so you had to forcibly take them off or throw them out or set about them or they would do that to you. And the showmen were equipped to deal with it themselves actually because they were used to it, you know. I mean they weren't frightened, you know. And very often you got … an instance was down at Newcastle Town Moor when we were down there operating, a couple of drunken blokes come on the Moor, went onto one of the rides, of course, wouldn't pay. So I gave them a run, without paying. When it stopped they wouldn't get off. The local lad went across to get the money and he got a punch in the face, you know. These two blokes – 'bring out your fighting man, we'll fight the best man you've got, bring out the best two men you've got in the fairground'. The ride's going on now, you know, so rather than stop everything, they're running on and these two guys are still on the ride, you see, and they're – 'we'll fight the best two men you've got', or whatever. They just happened to be on a Crow's ride, you see. Crow family was three, three brothers, the father, the family were doing quite well. And one of the sons, George Crow was about six foot two. And eventually word gets to George, 'A bit of trouble at the Twist there, you'd better go and have a look George'. And he goes over, 'Come on, now. You'll have to get off, you can't sit on there'. 'We'll fight the two best two men you've got here.' He said, 'We don't need two men. I'll do. Only me then.' Bang, bang, bang, bang, bang – 'Take them two men away.' That was it, you know. He knew what he was doing. Bang, bang, bang, he said there was three hits. One each on them two and one when they hit the ground. That was it.

But that – you got this, them people didn't – they were looking for trouble, you know. Larkhall was a terrible place. Used to go there on a Friday night and Saturday. But that wasn't always the case, you know, other places you went to you never had no trouble at all. It's not changed very much. What they've done now in a lot of the fairgrounds, we put a fence round about, which gives you a bit more control. They've got security men. A nephew of mine, he runs – named Charlie Horne – he runs a few fairs and he says since they put the fence up and security men at the gate, if they have too much to drink, they don't get in. So that saves a lot of trouble.

Strathclyde Park over at Hamilton there opened up and they were having a lot of trouble. I know the Taylor boys well, and I said the same thing, I said, 'You know, when I put the building up I was having trouble, but when I put the building up at Redcar, I didn't have any more trouble, I could control it, shut the doors'. You know. And I said to them at Strathclyde Park, 'You know, if you'd fence this place in you'd save yourself a lot of trouble'. And they did do, you know, made a difference, turned them away. You see it's psychological I think, can't go anywhere. I had that as soon as I put the building up. Not only that, you can see them around the enclosure. A couple of times I had occasion to shut the doors and call the police. When the police came down, 'Where are they?' I said, 'They're there, there and there'. They can't run away, you know. So they realised that eventually but it's not a good business that. We don't look for trouble, the showmen, you know. I mean trouble's a loss of business. You're losing money when you've got trouble. We don't look for that at all. It's there.

It's the drink. It's endemic to the type of business. Not only that but they're a menace to themselves. If they come on with too much drink they can injure themselves, injure other people. And the trouble now is that in our line of business if an accident happens, not through the fault of the operator but through the fault of the customer, the drunken customer, the Health and Safety come down and close you up. I mean, they do, they come down and until they find out what's happened and ninety-nine times out of a hundred it's people acting silly. If they will come on and sit down, nothing will happen to them, but they come on to be clever, they want to show off. They'd do tricks on the ride, ends up getting hurt. Trying to jump on when it's going, trying to jump off when it's going. All these silly things. So, it's the same with the football crowds I suppose, it's just endemic. You get the nutcases but we're trying to control it a bit better. Now that we've got these – fencing it in and security men, which we didn't always have, you can stop it happening, which is the main thing. Prevent it, rather than cure it, you know.

... There was this fair at Hamilton. I told you Hamilton was a bad place to go to. And they were having trouble there with fighting men come down, some of the locals would come down and they were giving trouble on the show ground. And the showmen were a wee bit outnumbered, you know, at that stage. So they sent word out to two or three fairgrounds round about and got some help, some other showmen came in. And it's coming up for the Saturday night now and these other showmen had come round the fairground. It was one of the showmen's jobs to go round the ground with a bit of chalk and the troublemakers ... where they was giving trouble got a wee chalk mark on their shoulder, unbeknownst to them, you know. Went round there, done that for half an hour, got a lot of them marked, and shut the gate, so they can't run away with the gate. ... So the showmen set about them. They said they never had any trouble at Hamilton after that, you know. That was it. That was the only way to survive because they were taking a fair bit away from them, you see. Now if they had a wee chalk mark on the shoulder, they tapped them on the shoulder, when they turned round they got chinned.

I had an uncle that was like that. My mother's brother, he was five foot five high and six feet six wide, you know, and that was his favourite when he had trouble; tap them on the shoulder, 'Now you shouldn't do that ...', when they turned round. He used to move about that far, you know, and as they turned round he went like [bumps them], said, 'What are you doing down there, why d'you fell down there?' But that was it. That was when he was having trouble. ... But you had to do it so that nobody knew you'd done anything. He had it off to an art – he didn't do anything, the man just collapsed there, you know.

It's no as bad as that now but it gets bad at times. The danger now – they've got knives and things. In them days it was just a punch on the nose, you know, nowadays we're actually getting showmen killed. Not even on the fairground, just because they're from the fair, you know. There was a lad, a showman that I knew his father, got a knife going to help somebody at Redcar, just coming out of a club. They come out of a club and Walter was having a wee bit of an argument and they walked away from it, and as he was walking away one of the lads that he was with got pulled back, you know, and so he run back, actually he was a rugby player – he played for Carlisle rugby club, you know, well known – and he run back and challenged them when he run back – they pulled a knife and killed him. The guy got five years for it, apparently. And that was just because he run back. He was a showman and I think they sort of picked on him a wee bit in the club, you know. Another lad at Ayr, McIndoe, he was out at Ayr with a few of his friends at Ayr and one guy fancied his coat, he'd a fancy coat on, you know. And they wanted his coat off him. Anyway, they didn't want trouble, so they ran away. 'Come on, get away, we'll get away out the road.' So they ran away but split up a wee bit and one of them, person called McIndoe, ran the wrong way and he couldn't get out, he was in a dead end. They jumped on him, three of them, put a knife in him, killed him. ... Terrible thing. But I mean that's the difference, you know, knives, you find them now.

... But we've got to contend with it, you know. It's one of the bad sides of the business. There was a lad on here last summer was threatened with a bottle, you know, kind of took a charge at him and jabbed him with a bottle, but he – didn't do him a lot of damage but it's done him damage. He managed to deflect the blow a bit of the broken bottle, but he's got shingles now, you know, the after effects of the trauma of it, you know. ... A fellow looking for trouble, you know, the trouble was there for him. You get these instances every now and again. ... But there's other businesses where they have the same trouble I suppose. ... It can happen to you just if you're going for a night out.

Travelling took up six or seven months of the year. For the five or six months that remained, a good winter ground was essential. The ground near Glasgow owned by John Codona's Pleasure Fairs [JCPF] for three decades played an important role in the success of the firm as a base for maintenance and repair that carried on over the winter. Like many other sites across Scotland – including the Fun City – it was also a temporary community for the families who wintered there.

[*Gordon Codona*]

Years ago, I was a little boy, we opened on this piece of land at Riddrie. On this land there was a garage and a cottage-style house on it and there was a garage there and a bit of land at the back and we opened on there and apparently these people in the house took a notion to me, about two or three years of age, you see. They said to my mother, 'Leave him behind when

you go away'. She said, 'No way!' Anyway, through this bit of
a connection my father always used to stop at the garage when
he was coming by and he was travelling, he would stop and
put petrol in the car. More or less kept in contact with these
people, friendly with people, the 1930s. Anyway, so he stopped
at the garage one day to get some petrol and the old man says,
'We're selling up, Mr Codona. We're selling the land and
retiring.' My father – he knew the place, you know – he said,
'I'd be interested in this'. At that particular time we spent our
winter down at Oatlands at somebody else's premises and we'd
been looking for somewhere and this came out the blue. My
father said, 'I'll be interested. I'll buy it off you.' Discussed the
price – my father bought it. And, it would be about 1942 – it
was '42 because I just went into the army that year. The year
before we'd been in at Oatlands. And the house was there which
was an attraction to my father because at this particular time
he hadn't been too well and he moved into the house. And this
yard was ideal, it was big enough for all we wanted and it had
lock-ups on it which they'd let out, and if we wanted, when the
let finished, we used them ourselves, you know. We only kept a
couple for other people that had been there a long time and we
used them ourselves. I built a couple of sheds round there.[151]
And that was our winter quarters and it was ideal. It was on the
north side of Glasgow, on the way out, just at Barlinnie Prison,
that was on the way out. We always travelled from Glasgow
out; we didn't have to go through to Glasgow – it was on the
way out, you see ... ideal. And the trams and the buses passed
the door, there was a whole row of shops – every kind of shop
you needed was there just outside the door for people for
winter quarters for ourselves and for anybody that was on the
... that wintered there – you know. It was an excellent ground.

I remember coming home from leave and they were digging
the road up outside and my father had got them and instead of
taking all this tarrage out the way, dumped it down inside on our
land. Some of it was tarred over but some of it needed surfacing.
And my father was doing a bit at a time and this was a good
opportunity he thought for – use this tar that they were taking

away. When I came back off my leave my father said, 'Will you
spread that tar!' I was a young fellow so I said, 'Aye, I'll
spread it'. But it had been laying a bit too long, you know, and
I remember it was hard work, checking through it, but when it
was laid out it was alright. ... Chucking all these heaps of tar –
that was a good leave that! I was young and fit, you know.
Anyway, as time went on and we gradually got the surface on,
and we used the tar, it was ideal; it hardened down and covered
the muck up. But there was a bit at the back that sloped down
and we wasn't able to use because it was below the ground
level maybe four or five feet, three or four feet. And, I'm married by now, round about the 1950s, and they're digging up the
crossing stones on the tramlines – the trams used to pass there.
Going to take them up the road. So I see these lorries, these
tippers, loaded up with the things. I see these big granite sets
they used to have on the tramlines; digging them up to get the
lines up. I said to the fellow, 'What are you doing with the sets?'
'Oh, we're taking them away and tipping them', you know. I
said, 'Why don't you tip them in here?' 'Oh, that would be
great.' ... 'He said, 'You better have a word with the gaffer, the
man in charge'. So I went over to him and I said, 'Look, I could
use these sets. ... Why take them away. I'll have them off you.'
'Oh, that's fine. That'll save us a big trip Mr Codona, we can
do it with half a dozen lorries. We can bring one lorry in at a
time, you know. Fair enough.' So they done that and I had
a reckon up and I think I reckon I had about 10,000 tons
of sets. They were heavy, you know. We filled all the back of
the ground up. And at night – they had a 'dozer and rollers and
things there, you know – and to the guy that come on with his
'dozer I said, 'Look, can you give them a wee shove and level
them off a bit, you know'. 'Aye, I'll do that.' Give him the price
of a drink and we levelled all these sets off at the back. The yard
was twice the size after that. We could use it; it was too soft
before, you see.

There was a barrage balloon on this during the war years,
on this site. They used it for a barrage balloon and they had a
shelter built up, brick shelter, and they had another shelter for

the barrage balloon staff, and we had a smaller one, and a concrete ring with hooks on it. We used to pull the balloon down and anchor it. That was it. And we used to go round this concrete ring to turn the vehicles on it because it was a bit soft at the back. So by the time I done all this with the ground we got some fair old use out of it. And that was it. It didn't cost very much either.

I went away in 1960 but they still used it until my brother went away to Aberdeen. He opened up the amusement park at Aberdeen, he didn't need that anymore and the town had been at us for quite a while, threatening us with compulsory purchase because they wanted this land. Actually, they couldn't take it by compulsory purchase, basically, because we used it for accommodation in the wintertime. But they threatened that and at that time, you see, when shows are – where are they going to go, the shows? Another piece of land; so they showed us various sites in and around Glasgow, none of them was as good. You couldn't get another one as good for what we had. It was impossible; house and everything and all this, there was even the garage, the pumps was there for petrol if you wanted it, you know. Actually, we did clean them out and could store some petrol in them. And when he went to Aberdeen, he then got in touch with the town and said, 'Look, I'm prepared to sell the land now', you know. I think it was in about '72, when he went.

... So when he went to Aberdeen and opened up in Aberdeen, I think it was '72 or '73 ... what he done, he went up to Aberdeen and he had enough land, he put chalets and some of his caravans, and my mother had a chalet, double chalet. So he had two or three chalets up there, there was room for them. As time went on he used the land and he went into houses in Aberdeen, just a progression, same as I done in Redcar. But, aye, it was a good few years. It was a good buy, my father done a good bit of work there. But the people that was on there – we used to have a few showpeople on it in winter and everybody that was on it, they all said there'll never be another ground as good as Riddrie for a winter ground, you know.

7
Family and the
Fairground Community

WORKING on the fairgrounds is a way of life involving family, friendship and community and a strong sense of identity of what it means to be part of that community. This is true of many occupations, but is greatly strengthened for showpeople by the travelling. There was, however, as in any business, a great deal of competition and rivalry, so that while being a 'showman' was a positive identity, encompassing prized skills and values, it also had to accommodate some of the conflicts and tensions within the show community. Not all showmen were the same: being a good showman could mean being able to manage other showmen, while for those being managed, it could mean trying to get one over on the manager. As Alfred Codona put it:

> [what] Alfred Codona's rules for running a good fair include
> [is] to remember that showmen are fickle people and if you
> show them any weakness they will take advantage. They know
> their rights and being in competition with one another like to
> try and fiddle an advantage for themselves and, if the lessee can,
> control that in a firm, fair manner with the object in mind of
> trying to present an attractive fair as possible.[152]

Nevertheless, despite the competition, show families relied on the travelling fairground community more than any local ties. This is changing as more families settle, and when I asked Cathy Macintosh if there was any sense of separation between showpeople and the rest of the public, she initially said no, but went on to explain:

... but the showpeople are very, very clannish.

Still?

I think so. Families are clannish – well, you can see because Gordon now, he's my cousin, but we're still very close, you know, sometimes you don't get that closeness in a lot of people. We are a – any relations, they're close relations – I'm an only child and with the result, all my cousins, touch wood, I could go to any of them and that's it. I don't know about anyone else, but in our family that's how it is. We're a very close family, on both sides. But I don't know, I don't know if everybody else is like that. Our children are very close, you know, it's, I don't know, maybe the Italian bit coming out in us.

That would make sense, yeah. I think it's also if you're all in the same business as well.

Well you talk the same language.

Yeah. And even if you're competing with each other you're ...

You're still of the same ...

It's a friendly rivalry ...

It is a friendly ... but it is, you talk, I don't know, you talk a different language, I don't know, you just talk different. The men talk about lorries and what have you; it's all lorries. Well, anyone settled would talk about plumbing or electricity. There's a lot of our family, their children have gone into law, and doctors. My aunt's son, he's a lawyer, he's a QC, I think. And, you know, they've gone into university and made something ...

I was going to ask, because Gordon was ... saying that from your grandpa William's branch of the family, there was 13 cousins. Two generations, a couple of generations after that, and I was thinking, well that's not leaving a lot of space, you've only got Scotland, you've got 13 cousins, you know ...

I don't know how many cousins I had at one time. Now, I'm beginning to worry because I'm one of the old ones and you think, oh, to heck, there aren't many of us left.

I suppose that must have forced some of them out of the business because there wouldn't have been space for them in a way …

Well, there was a lot wanted to go further. It didn't really force them out but they wanted their own niche in life I think, they wanted to be lawyers or they wanted to be different things, you know, they just wanted their own space. This is what happens. You see, they weren't so well educated years ago. As the years have gone on, they discovered that they had to go to school and then they had do this and that and they decided that, 'Well, I can make a living outside the business'. And, touch wood, some of them did very well.

Despite the rivalries and competition that were an inherent part of the life, for Gordon Codona the community of showpeople was 'a marvellous community'.

And was there a sense of a difference … you kind of hinted at that when you said that the Scottish showmen's rides were a higher standard. Was there a sense of difference between Scotland and England, do you think?

[*Gordon Codona*]

Us within the business could see it at the time. Not every – a lot of showmen in England had good equipment, you know.

But I mean, was it like a separate world?

No, no. No. No, they mixed – we used to have different functions, showmen's functions in the wintertime, fellowships and things like that. Ladies' nights they called them and they had them in England, we had them in Scotland. We just used to interchange. Scottish showmen would go down to England and go to their functions. So we had football matches. We had international football matches between Scotland and England. The showmen had three or four football teams that we used to play in the wintertime. We used to get games against some of the clubs, you know, the Glasgow clubs, Edinburgh clubs. They were good teams, good fun, it was just something to do and we used to have our dances with the football matches and the international game was a great occasion, Scotland playing England. … We went down to Crystal Palace's ground. I was involved in one of the teams, not playing – the committee, and we went down to London for one international to play the English showmen and we had special plane from Glasgow to play in London because that many went down. And at the front of the plane there was a boy with a steam engine – 'Steam Engine' at the time was the Scottish showmen's football team. … That was after the War. Great support. … One of the Codonas played in the football team, you know. Two of them, actually. … Bit of rivalry, plenty of rivalry, you know, there was, but that was alright. Oh, they mixed quite well.

Actually, I don't think there's a community anywhere that you could go into a place and nearly know everybody there, you know, in Scotland. If we go to England you don't know everybody, but there's half the people there know who you are, they know of you. I mean I went down to England, the north of England, to Redcar in 1960 and my wife's father was – although he travelled in Scotland latterly – he originally came from Sunderland, O'Brian, and he come from Sunderland and my wife had one or two relations down there. But having said that, when I went down I mean people knew of me. It wasn't strange to them, you know. I went to the functions and things down there and you just joined in until they knew you. … I don't think there's a community anywhere – even if you go all the way down to London – wherever you went, you know. The Guild itself caused that, the Showmen's Guild of Great Britain used to have functions themselves with different sections. There was a Scottish section, a Welsh section, a North of England section of the Guild, you know, they each had their own section, but it was all part of the one thing. And they used to have an annual dinner and each section had a dinner, and the different sections used to come for the functions in the wintertime, so it was a good, good community, a marvellous community actually.

It's thinned out a wee bit now because so many showmen have settled down. Sometimes the only chance they get now is to go to some of these functions, but there's not so many of them now. Also, it's the people who have settled down have become involved a bit more in the community where they are, you know, the different static sites, and it's been the cause of showmen marrying outside the business now. Obviously they're meeting people outwith the business and there's more people now marrying outside the business than ever before – which is not a bad thing. Although, there was a time when you never, ever married outside, it was unusual. They did marry, you'd get one or two but that was an unusual thing. And if a man married outside the business, the wife obviously had to come into the business.

Was that hard for the wives?

Aye, it could be hard for some of them, yeah. They always got a bit of help from the other women, you know. They realised that. You don't get it the other way round, that the man would leave the business, you know. It didn't happen that way, you know, because they didn't know any other business.

And what about the daughters going out the business?

Oh, that happens quite a bit, aye. The daughters are, quite a few of them, marrying out the business. And the other thing that's happening now is a lot of the families, now, they're upgrading their education. There's quite a lot of them going to university now. We've got show families now who've got sons and daughters now that are lawyers and doctors and who have university degrees, which was never … 20 years ago that didn't happen because they never got the time to spend getting educated. My granddaughter she's at college in Aberdeen, you know. I've got another, my cousin's son, he's turning out to be a lawyer. He's going to Canada for a year to carry on his education. He's at university in Edinburgh. I mean this is the sort of thing that's happening that didn't happen before, you know. He won a bursary thing at university to go to Canada for a year as part of his lawyer, his legal stuff, you know. It's a good thing, you know. The way the business was prior to that, they didn't get the opportunity. I was fortunate, and some of our family; I was left behind to go to school. That didn't always happen.

The fairground had its share of characters and I asked Gordon about some of those he remembered from his travelling days. His recollections are full of a sense of community and fellowship, together with an appreciation of colleagues as good showmen, a status to be proud of and worthy of respect.

[*Gordon Codona*]

Auld Subi we called her. ... She was of gypsy origin and she used to tell the tale, that was doing fortune-telling.[153] We called it telling the tale. And she used to go round fairgrounds with a – she had a small trailer caravan ... she finished up in my time with a Romany caravan, decked out Romany inside of course, the outside appearance wasn't your original Romany caravan, you know, not in my memory. Could have been before that. She was an elderly woman when I was young. ... When she was slanging, doing her business, she'd sit outside on her steps ... with a scarf round her head and earrings and the usual sort of gypsy garb, a long gown thing on, you know, that was old Subi.

And would she mainly work in Scotland or all over?

Mostly Scotland as far as I know. She was a character. Everybody knew old Subi, you know. You always – she was on her own, just lived on her own, but if she needed any help to move her caravan or anything like that, there was always plenty of showmen round about to help her, you know. She was that type of person, an elderly woman; you kind of kept an eye on her, you know, see if she was alright. She was an old character.

And I think you said that when she died they made a fire of her ...

Yes, that was the idea, which was the custom; the caravan was burned when they died, you know. I think in her case she didn't have any relatives that anybody was aware of.

And then you mentioned Phelps ...

Phelps – he was Welsh. ... He had a show that he'd built himself.[154] It was a model in a lorry, big enough to go inside a lorry. He was one of the few showmen in them days, I'm talking about just prior to the last World War, the Second World War, that had a new vehicle, it was a brand-new lorry. And he had this model, it was a mining show inside and you walked up into the lorry and you walked round. And it was a cut-away of a Welsh mine. When I say cut-away, it was sliced right through the tunnels, if you follow what I mean, you know, you have a mining tunnel underground and it showed you the overhead workings and then it showed you a section through the work-ings, showing you the – little models of men, all working models, working away in the tunnels, with little bogeys going through the tunnels. It was really a marvellous working model. And only somebody that had made it could maintain it and keep it going, you know, it was one of those types of models. It was quite big. It was always an interesting thing for anybody and it was well made and the models of men digging away and cutting away in the shafts of the mine, there was overhead pit workings with the lifts going up and down, all these, and the bogeys running through the tunnels in the pit, models of the coal. It really was an excellent model and he travelled with this, him and his wife, Phelps.

And was he a showman ...?

Oh, no. He was an honorary member of the Guild. He was a showman in as much as he carried on his business and he lived in a caravan the same as anybody else ... he'd come into the business with this model. He found out that it could be exhib-ited, which it was, it was a good model. He didn't only come to Scotland. He went down into England too. It was a well received model; very intricate. ... In fact there wasn't any other sort of things like that I'm aware of; there may have been somewhere, but not on the circuit in Scotland. His was the only model like that, you know. And it was a thing that you couldn't dismantle. This was why it was built in this lorry. It had to stay as it was. ...

And did he do well with it, do you think?

Well, he got a living out of it. It was different. Yes, I would say that in a mining community he would do very well. You know, wherever. He done alright, I must say, he done alright, it was a different type of thing altogether. It probably didn't have the appearance on the outside to entice you in; it's a model of a mining village. Some people would look at that and say, 'What do I want to look at that for', but once they got inside they were amazed at what it really was. He was quite a well-known man. He didn't travel after the War though. He sort of finished up during the war years. I'm talking about the 1930s, late '20s and '30s, mostly through the 1930s, my memories of him with his show. But it was always well received.

And then the other character we talked about was Dare-devil Peg ...

Dare-devil Peggy was the high diver. In those days, as an attraction for the fairground, the lessee or the man that was promoting the fair would hire the likes of Dare-devil Peggy, which was the common one, because he had a 70-foot tower, square tower that he climbed up to the top of and he dived from the top of that into a tank of water that was about four foot deep. It was a tank that was made up, it was not very big actually. It was quite a hair-raising thing to see him climbing up the 75-foot, 70-foot tower, you know. It was only a square ladder frame, stayed, and he got on the top of that and at night he used to dive in flames. He'd go on the top of that with a sack round him and they used to light the fire, light the water – put some petrol or something like that on top of the water and put a match to that. And he used to dive at night from the top of the tower into the water. Because whenever he hit the water the splash was enough to put the fire out, you know, hopefully!

... He went all over. Different people – we ourselves didn't only have him, he was all over. Different people at different fairs. ... I know that we had him at Aberdeen and he was in Glasgow, Edinburgh, wherever there was a decent sized fair on. Edinburgh was one place, Meadowbank – he was there.[155] But various – the bigger fairs. Actually I would say the bigger fairs because they had to be. To pay him you had to – you couldn't have a little small fair, it had to be something quite big so that you could afford to pay. ... I mean I wasn't involved in paying him at that time. But he was somebody you had to consider a wee bit in them days, to pay him, you know, for the duration of the fair because he used to perform every night the fair was open, sometimes twice on a day that you was open in the afternoon; but he was, at that time, he was an expensive prop for the fair.

... There wasn't very many that you could hire because you had to have somebody that was up a bit, that people could see from round about. You couldn't put them in a building. It had to be an open-air attraction on a fairground. I remember my father one time had a – I think the Lad-Ringos or something they called them. It was a high frame and on it there was a long ladder with revolving wheels at each end of it and these artists went up on that and they done acrobatics while the wheel was going round; the main circle was going round and the wheels at the end was going round, and they were doing all sorts of tricks and things on the end of the ladder and things, you know. If you can envisage a pedestal with a long arm and at the end of the arm was two circular frames with the ladders fixed, and things on it, you know, frames, and they went into the frames and they were doing tricks as the whole lot was going round. It was a good act. I'm sure they called it the Lad-Ringos at the time. That was a bit of a novelty that hadn't been seen. I think that set my father back a few quid, you know.

... We only had it once and I only seen it once – I didn't see

anybody else with it. It was a good novelty. These were the sort
of things – an aerial act of some kind and anything like that,
that people could see, you know, stand around and watch, look
up and watch. You couldn't put nothing in a show because that
was taking people away from the fairground. It had to be where
they could visibly stand there and look at it.

... Powsey was another man who was a high diver. ... The
thing about Peggy of course, he only had one leg, by the way. I
forgot to mention that. That's why they called him Peggy, you
know. He had one leg and it was quite clever to see him go up
this ladder on one leg, you know, because he'd got to pull himself up with his arms. ... He was, he was well built. He took a
wee bit longer to get to the top of the 70-foot frame, ladder.
That was part of the act, watching him climbing up with one
leg.

... And then you mentioned a couple of lads with shooters ...

Aye ... they were a couple of Jewish lads and when they finished
at a fair they used to bundle their show up, tie it in a bundle
and then put all their other gear in hampers and then they got
a carrier to come and take it away. That was how they travelled about. They had a shooting stall, you know, but it wasn't
very elaborate, but they had the gift of the gab ... you know.
They were always very well dressed. You know, they wasn't
your typical showman; they were always well dressed because
they wasn't doing any dirty work – they didn't have any lorries
to muck about with or anything like that. They just came to
work and opened their stall and they wrapped it up when they
finished and got a carrier to come and take it away to the next
place – up in a lorry and away it went. ... They were quite
characters too, everybody knew them. They were an asset to
the business; they were well presented and polite, you know,
very good-looking.

*And were there any particular showmen outside the Codona
family, any particular characters that stick out in your mind?*

Oh, there were a lot of them, aye. Oh, some of the older show-men – there was old Bill Bastable, he was a character in his own way. He used to walk about with his walking stick and I only remember him as an elderly man, Bill Bastable, a bit of a gammy leg, he walked about with his walking stick; but he used his walking stick to good effect pointing to this and pointing to that, you know, and he didn't drive because of his leg. But I've heard stories of when he'd be chauffeured about in his car, who-ever was driving his car, they'd always be getting instructions to hurry up and 'shoot man, shoot, shoot' to overtake some-body, this was his ... to overtake – 'Shoot, shoot', you know. That was his type, you know, that was old Bill.

Another man that I always thought was a good showman was a man called Danny Taylor. He was a Kirkcaldy man and he travelled about. He had roundabouts and he had quite a big family. But he presented his fair with a bit of showmanship. He would run a night when a mystery man was walking about on the fairground and lots of carnival nights when you threw streamers about and things like that, you know. It could be a bit of a pain in the neck with the streamers round about your equipment, but he used to do all this; give carnival hats out, carnival nights. Full of ideas like this. Most other showmen didn't seem to do it and he'd have the mystery man walking about. If you found the mystery man you probably got a ten bob note, you know, if you found out who the mystery man was. Everybody was going, 'Are you the mystery man? Are you the mystery man?' Even if he was the mystery man, he could say 'No', you know! Somebody got a ten bob note anyway that night. All these wee sorts of gags and things on the roundabouts and a proper carnival night with the flags and streamers and things. He used to promote nights like that on his fairground. His equipment wasn't bad, you know, but he depended a lot on his family, his three or four sons. He was a good promotions man, Danny Taylor.

But there was quite a few types of characters in the business. ... There was – the names come into my mind – you know Cathy that you saw, Solly's father Tommy Mac, he was Tommy

Macintosh, that's Solly's father, he was a smallish man but a great footballer, you know. He was a footballer family, the same as what Solly was. They were into the football clubs that we had at one time. That was a great thing amongst showmen. There were four or five football leagues in Scotland and they used to compete with one another. They had a wee league, the top of the league and they had club competition; there was an Irish football club the Thistles, the Carnival Celtic, the Borders football club. And the showmen all played football and now and again they would have games with some of the juniors' clubs in different places that they went to. You know, they were good enough to have a game of football with some of the local teams. It was a good thing, you know, it promoted the show-men amongst the locals. There was quite a good interest in football. They had an international game too between Scotland and England. It was quite a big event and that was a collection of footballers from all the different football clubs. England had, they more or less sorted them out in counties. There was a Yorkshire section of the Showmen's Guild, they had a football team, there was a Lancashire section of the Showmen's Guild, they had a football team, the London section had a football team and so on, like that, Notts and Derby and so on, Wales – they all had a football team. In Scotland we didn't have a section as such, it was all the one section, the Scottish section. We had three or four football teams within that section. The result was that the teams used to travel from Scotland down into England and vice versa to play each other at football. It was a social event at the same time. It was the wintertime of course. Nothing went on in the summer because everybody was too busy, you know, at their job. It was only a wintertime thing when people had settled down for the winter that the football matches and the functions and all these sorts of things carried on. But they were great social events. You went down, had a football match and that night there was a dinner and dance, you know, and everybody went home the next day on the buses. It was a good couple of days outing. We went across to Dublin just after the War with the Hearts football club. But that was a bit different. We decided – we couldn't go by bus – we hired a plane. There was such a big interest in the Hearts team, flying them over to play a football team in Bray [near Dublin] that we filled the plane up. We had to get another plane. There was two planes. A lot of these people went and they'd never flown before, just after the war years.

... It was a novelty. It was that big a novelty, I'd flown a couple of times at this particular period, and I remember getting on the plane and 95 per cent of them on the plane had never been on one before. We took off – it was one of these DC3s, you know, good planes – it took off, and when it took off and you undone your seatbelts I just got up. And there was a chorus of, 'Sit down, sit down', 'Don't stand up, don't stand up'. We were flying now, you see. They didn't know. 'Sit down Gordon, sit down, don't stand up.' Rock the plane, you know! But that was a novelty for them there, you know. That was a big under-taking for a football club at that time. But everybody enjoyed a winter break. I think they shoved a few professional footballers in their team to make sure that they won, you know! But any-way, that was some of the antics that we got up to. But that was a good night out in Ireland. The funny thing was we had quite a few showmen with us – Kellys, O'Brians and one or two names like that – and I remember some of the Irish saying, 'You've got more Irish people in Scotland than what we've got over here'.

Cathy mentioned about storytellers and said that your Uncles William and Nat were both very good storytellers, you know, that you could ...

Uncle Billy, aye. You could listen to him all night. He could tell a good tale. My father wasn't bad either, you know. But Uncle Billy was funny, you know, you could get in a group with him and he'd stand there in the middle of a collection of men on a fairground talking and he'd have them all laughing, you know. I remember one occasion, he had a ride, a Moon Rocket and during the war years – they were doing very well – he was down

at Carlisle and they were talking there on a Sunday. They'd been
open on a Saturday night, they'd been very busy on a Saturday
night and this Moon Rocket had done quite well, the men were
standing around talking about it the next day and one man said
to Uncle Billy there, 'I wish I had a penny for everybody that
had been on that Moon Rocket last night, Billy'. Billy said,
'That's alright, I got a tanner for everybody that was on it', he
says! That was him, that was Uncle Billy, very quick like that,
you know, had an answer right away. But that's the sort of thing
you heard as you was going on talking about the business.

... There was quite a few quick-witted and funny people in
the business. And there was one or two in our family, in amongst
the Codona family. They weren't the only ones, but they were
quite quick-witted in their talk. The one that I mentioned there,
Norman, that was Uncle Billy's son, he was quick-witted, he
was funny; he could get up and do a turn. He could sing you a
song and tell you a few jokes and all this. Uncle Nathaniel had
a couple of sons and they were the same. You could listen to
them talking. My brother, oldest brother, Billy, he was a good
talker. But through the family, there was a bit of wit going
through the family. Must have come from the old shows.

... They'd done a bit of acting when they were younger,
stand up in front of an audience probably, which is something.
But there were notable fellows. There was a man in the business,
a fellow called Herbie Knowles. Now, he was well known as a
card player, playing cards. Now, he was an expert; he was only
self-taught, I mean he wasn't a man that had been away anywhere. He played cards and he knew how to handle cards. And
he could memorise the cards. The people around wouldn't play
cards with him, you know. Used to play bridge a lot. That was
one of the games, contract bridge, that the showmen used to
play; stand round a diesel barrel on its end, that was the card
table, and four of them would stand there and play bridge. And
he got that nobody would play with him because he would
memorise everybody's hand, what everybody had in their hand.
And this is quite true. And he was full of tricks, card tricks,
you know, sleight of hand and all this kind of thing. 'Pick out a

card', and you'd hold the card and put it away and he would tell you what card you had, all these sort of simple little tricks that the guys get paid for doing nowadays. I remember my son, we had a ride, a ghost train, when I was in Redcar. It went up to the Kelvin Hall and my son, he'd be in his teens then, he was up there looking after it and I went up there to see him. And he's talking to the stall just beside the ghost train. Herbie Knowles had got this stall and he shouted over, 'Aye, you've got your dad up now, Gordon'. So we went over and apparently at a quiet time this Herbie had been showing my son Gordon card tricks. He started talking to him and showing him card tricks and Gordon said to me, 'Dad, do you know that man that shouted?' I said, 'That's Herbie Knowles'. He said, 'I wouldn't like to play cards with him,' he says. Herbie was a character. Everybody knew Herbie Knowles. If you were going to play cards with Herbie Knowles you better tie one hand behind your back, you know! He wasn't a cheat, he just could memorise all the cards, you know.

People like that, you know, these were characters that come to your mind at times. We always had, somewhere about there was a good painter or a good joiner, electrician amongst the showmen. Billy Testo was an electrician, you know, he was a good electrician and anybody that'd got a wee bit of a problem with a dynamo or a motor, 'Go and have a word with Billy Testo'. He was well known as a man that had an ability as an electrician. There were other lads in the business that were good mechanics, that knew quite a bit about lorries and things, and so on. And you went to these people for advice if you needed it, you know, and they were always willing to give you it. Some of them went into business a bit, repairing lorries for other people, they would do repairs for them. The Paris family was like that, they were pretty good as mechanics, they went into a bit of repair business but, ach, I can't remember them all.

Do you remember the Stewarts with their boxing booths?

Aye, well, very well, Johnny Stewart – the family of Stewarts; there was Johnny Stewart, Stobo Stewart, Spider Stewart, that was their nicknames, with their boxing shows. But Johnny Stewart travelled up here. The last of his sons lives over in Glasgow just now, Douglas Stewart and his wife Rosie. … The other man was Paterson, he had a boxing show too. Johnny Stewart, the family was well known in Scotland and England, you know, and he had a good quality, he had a good show, it was a well presented show. He had three or four good boxers with him usually. He used to throw the gloves out for some-body, a local to go three rounds with one of his men. They went on until the boxing control people – you had to have a licence to fight and that stopped the boxing show because you couldn't promote boxing, you couldn't have a boxer in your show and have an amateur coming up to fight him. So that cut that down. …

And was it just a show front type of affair?

A big show front, a stage on it, you know. And the boxers used to come out there. They usually had a couple of punchballs on the outside where the employed boxers would demonstrate their punchball antics, and then whoever promoted it, usually Johnny Stewart or one of his sons would do a bit of spieling to get them interested. They'd introduce the boxers. He'd say who they were and where they'd come from and what weight they were and he'd say, 'We're looking for some of the local lads that fancies going three rounds with him', you know, 'and if you last three rounds you'll get X number of pounds', you know, 'for the three rounds' and 'Who have we got here?' He would have to sort of match them up if somebody said 'I'll have a go', you know – he would match them up with one of his men, weight for weight sort of thing, roughly, so that it wasn't a wee man against a big man sort of thing, sort the weight out a wee bit. And he had everybody up on the stage until he had four fighters, he had to have four opponents for them. And then they would go inside and then he would start, he'd have them on the stage and then he'd start to get the customers in. Roll them up and get them in and fill the show up while these other guys was on parade for a while, to encourage the punters. And then

he would go inside and get them ready and if the show was
filled up he would get in the ring and introduce the fight. And
usually it was a bit one-sided, you know, but now and again
you'd get a decent lad in who'd maybe he'd handled himself
before with boxing amongst the customers. And if he got a
good fight that's what he wanted, you know. He didn't want a
one-sided fight, he wanted somebody to go in there and stand
up and have a decent fight. But his own boxers were a bit easy
on the customers, you know, if they found they were mugs they
didn't brutalise them, but they had to make sure they didn't
last three rounds of course! But you seen an odd good fight
now and again with the local lads. He let it be known then that
the man had lasted the three rounds, you just lasted the three
rounds with all your teeth, in other words don't chuck it before
the fighting finished. And when that was over they came out
again and then they would start all over again, looking for
another show, you see, to get as many shows as you can out
of the night.

But that was old Johnny Stewart; he had a nice big show
front, boxers painted on it, you know, and well lit up. All the
Stewarts, their shows was well presented. The two of them at
Newcastle Town Moor – Stobo Stewart, Spider Stewart, that
was their nicknames – they were all the same quality, very good.
They've disappeared from the fairground. I think there was
one down at Newcastle a few years ago, but I don't know what
happened to that one now. I think they take a chance when they
operate now, if they do operate, unless they've got some other
fighters; sometimes I think what they're doing now, they've got
their own boxer and they promote a fight and they get a professional boxer in and then they put him on now, the odd time,
but that can only be done at a big fair.[156]

*... And, what would you say – to be considered as a proper
showman in the business – did you have to have come from a
generation of showmen or ...?*

To get in the Showmen's Guild you had to be the son or
daughter of a showman, in other words somebody who was

already in the Guild. You were the son or daughter ... the first generation probably they must have come in from somewhere. To get in the Showmen's Guild that was a ... it was a closed shop you know. The Showmen's Guild was a closed shop, one of the first ones. You couldn't get in the Showmen's Guild unless you were the son or daughter of a showman.

... If you were a showman you had to be in the Guild. You couldn't carry on your business without being in the Guild. That was it. It was a closed shop; you had to be in the Showmen's Guild, like the dockers. You couldn't be a docker unless you was the son of a docker, exactly the same thing. And the Showmen's Guild had its own rules and regulations, very strictly controlled. And it was well controlled, you know. And they regularised fairs so that people wasn't jumping on top of one another at fairs. The fairs was regulated; there was a timescale for the fairs in a town, for example. You couldn't go a month either side of an established fair. ... So you don't get too much. You couldn't go on another showman's site. You couldn't take his site on a fair. You was restricted. You couldn't say, 'I'm going to go to this fair', and say to the promoter of the fair, the lessee, 'I'll give you an extra fiver if I stand there'. You couldn't do that. You wasn't allowed to do that, you know, it was well regulated. ... A daughter could marry a man outside the business, which happened sometimes, he could come into the business. So he was able to join the Guild and then he could carry on at that. The sons, of course, the sons just carried on in the normal way. If they married outside the business and the wife came in, she didn't have to be a member of the Showmen's Guild, but I mean she was then classified as a travelling show person. So that was the regulation there. It regulated itself and there was no way – you couldn't get in.

It's not the same now, by the way. What do they call it now? Discrimination! It had to happen with everything, whenever they brought the law out about discrimination and so on a few years ago. I mean you cannae have a closed shop now in a union. You probably know that. Well that was it. That's the same thing that affected the Showmen's Guild, the union;

although they called it a guild, it was a union. They had to abide by the law and the law said you couldn't discriminate. So I mean that opened the doors. They've still got to be voted in, of course, which is one restriction that you get. But the net result of that is that we've got a lot of people in the Guild now, travelling now, that haven't got a big background of history. I would say 60 or 70 per cent of the showmen now travelling have got a good history in the business and maybe 25 per cent now haven't got that history. They can still be good showmen. I mean they can still do the job alright, you know.

8

Travelling and Settling

CODONAS from different branches of the family still travel
the fairgrounds, but many have followed the trend towards
settling. Codona-run static sites, amusement arcades and leisure
centres can be found across Scotland and the North of England.

Having travelled since he left school, latterly as a director of
John Codona's Pleasure Fairs with his brother Alfred, Gordon
Codona decided to start a settled business of his own in 1960.

*Coming up to date, how is the business – has it got more
difficult?*

[*Gordon Codona*]

There's always been, there's always been problems in the business. One of the biggest problems in the business is sites. One
of the things that's helped us now is what we could call the
street fairs and things like that which has helped quite a bit.
One of the biggest problems we get now – I mean, I'm retired,
I finished up with an amusement park at Redcar and I sold that
– one of the biggest problems now is the cost of the equipment
you've got to use now. There's still some of the traditional rides
going about like the Waltzers and Dodgems – Dodgems will never
die out, you make your own fun and the Waltzers are seemingly
very popular – some of the rides were gradually fading away,
the traditional rides, because these new rides were coming in
that are so expensive and to buy these new rides you've got to
have a run of fairs, what we were talking about, places where
you can take them. And now we're getting showmen now who

to keep in business they go to Dubai, Hong Kong, Spain. Instead of when we used to think, 'if we go to Nairn, well, it's a long way away', they're shipping the stuff abroad now, they're going abroad. They're going all over the world. There was a fair on in Hong Kong, last winter there, and they go to Dubai, the Middle East, they go anywhere.

Do the Codonas do that?

Oh aye. A second cousin, my cousin's son, Raymond Codona, he does quite a bit of it. He promotes the fair in the SEC in the wintertime in Glasgow, but, aye, they do that.

And do you think they've still got the same ... sons going into the business?

Yes. ... They do. That's still carrying on that way. But what we're getting now though is we're getting quite a few showmen settled down. I mean I settled. In 1960 I was in business – John Codona's Pleasure Fairs. My older brother he came out. ... His family was growing up and so he wanted to be on his own. The same thing happened with me with my family. I'd been looking to settle down and I didn't like this no operating on Sunday. I'd had a case of being in England, I was in the forces and I'd seen the war years while I was in England with the forces, been over to some of the fairs and seen them open on Sundays and I got a taste of England and I came to Redcar. It was an amicable break-up with my brother, you know. I'd just decided I wanted to go on my own and fair enough. So we split up the equipment and I went down to England and that basically was because you could open on a Sunday, it was open seven days a week and conditions were a wee bit easier down there. There was no licenses like you had in Scotland and it was a good move for me eventually. But it wasn't a good move to start with. I had got down onto a seaside and I saw it in its best conditions and when I started to operate we was blinded with sand because I hadn't realised.

... It was open land when I first went there in 1960, a big car park, it was part of a car park and the town fenced it in.

They were looking for an amusement park, they wanted it – this was the attraction: usually you were fighting against the council to get established somewhere. In this case it was the council that wanted one, you know. But they were particular what they wanted because they'd had a man there the year before to open up an amusement park. But all he done was opened up a fairground, you know, with lorries and diesel vans and stuff all over the place and they didn't want that, that's not what they wanted. ... They advertised the place and they were looking for offers; there was seven, eight, nine people who put in offers for it. And they looked at what I wanted to do and they had me down there and talked to them and I showed them some photographs of the stuff that we had. They were very much interested in the equipment because they'd had a real sickener with the guy before. And I knew who they were talking about and his stuff was, his equipment was terrible, you know. So I talked to them and showed them that they weren't being – but before they would commit themselves they wanted to see the equipment. I said, 'Well, if you come to Kirkcaldy', this was Easter time, I said, 'You'll see most of our equipment operating'. So they thought that was a good idea before they decided anything. They jumped in two cars and eight of them came up at Easter, holiday time. They came up to Kirkcaldy, they were delighted with what they saw; all our equipment was up, it was all well presented at that time with the lorries and I took them in the caravan. The caravan was there, and Katie, and I introduced them to the wife, you know, and they had a cup of coffee and sat there and we talked about things. I said, 'Well, has it been a wasted journey?' They said, 'Oh, no'. They said, 'We're delighted with what we've seen. We can see what you're like', you know. I said, 'Well that's what you'll get. You can see what you'll get'. And that was it. That was the clincher. They went back and I took a lease on the place, with some options, you know.

When I saw the site it was just earth, gravel, you know, hard gravel. And they put an eight-foot wall round about and enclosed what I wanted. And I built up there and got open and the wind started to blow and then the sand started to come in, which I'd never experienced. All of a sudden I'm operating in a desert! Could never get rid of the sand. And sand and grease, oil, is a good grinding compound and you were listening to it happen. And it would blow in over the land. So I thought, 'What can I do here?' So the first thing I done then was got – I arranged for a contractor to come and, after we'd built up, to tarmac all round about everything over the ground, to see if that would help it, it would maybe blow over. It made it better underfoot, but I mean it didn't stop the sand blowing underneath and everything, you see. That was the first year. The second year – the business wasn't all that good the first year – but I'd arranged to put a Dipper up – Big Dipper. George Maxwell was making it. He'd made one already and I'd seen it, you know. I thought that's something that we need – an amusement park's got to have something like that, you know, memories of Fun City. And, well, we put the Big Dipper up. So that was a help. But the sand was still – the sand was going to be the killer because it was getting in everywhere, knocking hell out of the equipment. Dodgem cars was getting full of sand; it was hard work. The wind was nasty. So I'm thinking, 'I'm not going to stay here doing this all of my of life'. And I decided that there was only one thing to do – and not only that, the other thing that happened was, where the site was I discovered that the coaches was at the front of me, on the town side. And everybody came out of the coaches and turned their back on me, walked away. Coaches was important. And when it rained on the site, everybody ran away to the town. It was right on the beach side, you know, they went towards town which was at that end. And I thought, 'Well, I'd better keep the people here', and the only way to keep the people was to provide shelter, you know. So I started making some enquiries, talked to my son about it, you know, started making some enquiries about a building. And I got busy with my pencil and paper again and scaled out what I thought – the size of it. I'm working from scratch now, I can't look at something and say, 'That's what's been done before', you know. This is all new. I was the first one to do this – put a building up for amusement equipment. It hadn't been done before. People had put stuff in a building, you know, but nobody had ever started and said, 'I'm putting a building up built for that purpose'. So I've got to get the sizes, rough sizes, scale it out and figure out what I need. I done all that and went to one of the steel erectors, talked to them, got prices and I went to the town. This is the third summer now, I'm into the third summer. I went to the town and started to talk to them. As it happened, it wasn't so bad. I knew a few of the councillors by this time. They wasn't all happy but there was a few of them on my side. I said, 'I want to put a building up'. 'Oh that's great.' 'Put everything in – indoor amusements.' 'That's fine.' 'But I don't want to put the building up where I am.' 'Ah ... oh,' I said, 'There's no way I'm putting a building up there where every-body ...', I explained to them, you know. I said, 'If I put the building up, the building's got to come right forward and the buses can park at the back'. I said, 'I want to be nearer the town, not further away'. About three hundred feet we're talk-ing about, you know. And, oh, long, big discussions. I was adamant. I said, 'Look, if you say no to this, that's the finish of me'. I said, 'I can't do it – sand'. The result was they realised that sand was a big problem, you know. 'Can't do it,' I said, 'It's impossible – can't keep going.' Anyway, with a bit of help from one or two of the councillors it was alright. They agreed that I'd move the site, which was important, from there to there, and then I'd put the building up there and the buses was there. And thank God for that; they've got to walk past me now, or through me. If anybody wants to run away from the fair they've got to run through me to get into town, you know! Now, they done that and that made all the difference. It cost me a lot of money. Mind you, I took a big step at the particular time because after I'd been there a couple of years and it wasn't as it might have been, I was taking a big gamble spending all that money on a building. Mind you, the building went up with nuts and bolts; I said to my son Gordon, 'If this doesn't work out, I'll have the bloody nuts and bolts – we'll have this build-ing ...!' Anyway, it worked out fine in that as soon as we put the building up, we got the shelter, the equipment was protected;

when it rained they didn't run away, they run in, peoples round about, they ran in.

What equipment did you have?

That's it there. You've got a Dodgem, you've got some ghost train, there's another ride there that I'd taken out the idea ... [looking at photos] ... that's the ghost train. Used to bring this up to the Kelvin Hall. It's a big ghost train, it goes inside and comes out again, it's a double-decker.

So you were able to take things in and out of this building?

Oh, aye. Oh, aye, it had big doors on it, yeah, at the back.

... And did you operate all the wee side things, and all the rest of it, or did you just parcel it out?

No, I operated all the rides, the kiddies' rides, the amusement arcade. These side-stalls they operated themselves. Actually, the manager that was with me, he had some stalls and two or three of the people that worked for me, they had the benefit of the stalls that was there and it wasn't very many actually. But it suited them that they worked for me and they had that. They had families too, you see. The girl that come in there and operated the bingo, which we didn't operate; there was somebody there that operated the snack bar, we rented out the snack bar. There used to be a ride on here, Motorcycle Speedway, I took that out and put the cars in. But these were the kiddies' rides; there was quite a bit of kiddies' stuff. ... We operated the amusement arcade. That was an important part of the job. ... All the family worked with me.

... It was a good move for me basically, but, I mean, a big jump, jumping away from an established business, which it was; John Codona's Pleasure Fairs was quite viable, you know, and doing away quite well. And it was a big step into the unknown. It was a new place; I couldn't look at last year's information. It was hard going for five years.

I finished up selling the place. But while I was there we branched into amusement arcades in the winter. Closing down wasn't good before I went to the Kelvin Hall, one or two years before I done that. The equipment that I had was alright, but I was competing against other people that had the same stuff and you had to tender for the Kelvin Hall and it wasn't worth my while to compete against the people that was up here because I had the journey to do before. But in the wintertime I got into amusement arcades in Middlesbrough. I opened a couple there which was good for business because it run all the year round and my son was interested in that side of it too. … then I extended the building – I had the Big Dipper outside and it gradually lost its novelty, so I got the chance to sell that and when I sold that I extended the building by another 100 feet, 150 feet. And when I had done that I could put more equipment in; I put the ghost train in with a view that that was something I could use when I went to the Kelvin Hall … Gordon [speaker's son] would be about 16 and he was born in 1949 … [it was] 1966 maybe.

And how many years did you do that for?

About seven years in the Kelvin Hall. The tender was getting higher and higher every year, so it began to …

Who was the lessee, or did you deal directly?

Local authority. … They were hard to deal with. They wanted their pound of flesh.

They probably thought it was a … I remember going when I was young, going to the Kelvin Hall and it was always packed.

Oh, good for the winter. Good business for us with the ghost train. It was a novelty. They hadn't seen it before. It was in for seven years, right on the trot. … My son went up there and used to look after it, and then Gail went with him and when Gordon got married, Gordon's wife went with him with the ghost train. Oh, they enjoyed it – great for them, you know. But at that particular time I had a couple of amusement arcades going in Middlesbrough, which is near Redcar. I finished up quite alright, you know. But Gordon was more interested in the amusements

arcades and I got the chance to sell the park and me and the
wife was ready for a bit less – a very intensive thing to look after
an amusement park, work intensive, you know, there was a lot
of things to do and there was simpler things that you could do,
without that. ... And Health and Safety and all these other
things coming into it a bit hard on you. And you required a big
staff in the summertime, lot of part-time staff. We decided to sell
and we moved back here. Gordon's still down there with his
wife still operating, but not on the amusement side.

I sold it before I came up here, '87. I decided, 'Why are we
down here', for about a year, 'Why are we down here looking
for a house? Gordon's in Newcastle, Gail's up here, we don't
need to be here now. We've sold the park.' It was getting on my
nerves being in the park because it wasn't getting run the right
way. It was deteriorating before my eyes!

Gordon Codona's brother, Alfred, ran John Codona's Pleasure
Fairs with Gordon until 1960 when Gordon left for Redcar.
Alfred's son Barry travelled with his family until 1970, when
they settled in Aberdeen, taking over the beachfront amusement
park. Codonas had been appearing in Aberdeen since the nineteenth century and Alfred claimed in one interview that they
presented the first set of gallopers to be seen in the city, presumably sometime around 1900.[157] 'Codona Brothers' promoted
fairs in the 1920s and Alfred's father John made regular appearances in the city from the early 1930s. By the time he took over
the amusement park in 1970 the traditional summer holiday
business had dwindled. Interviewed in 1977, Alfred recalled:

[Alfred Codona]

When the Glasgow Fair came along you had a million people
spreading out and very often the working people with the most
money were the folk who came farthest to Aberdeen. People
came in large numbers just after the 1914-18 War. ... The
beaches were very crowded. ... I suppose the big days of the
Glasgow Fair ended in the mid-1960s and after that the Fair

seemed to coincide with horrible weather. Of course the beach is still very busy with Scottish trades holiday people as well as those from farther afield. Nevertheless, the main trade at Aberdeen Beach is provided by Aberdonians themselves; they really like coming to the beach and to the funfair and, I believe, if it wasn't for them and the fact that unemployment is less here than in other places, then our business wouldn't be viable.[158]

As this trend continued, the business was expanded and developed to cater for a more local clientele. Alfred's sons, Alan and Barry, carried on the family businesses after their father's death, overseeing a further substantial programme of expansion in the late 1990s.

[*Barry Codona*]

... I haven't really taken a lot of interest in the history to be honest, but I know from conversations over the years there was always a family of Codonas in Glasgow, we used to call them the Vinegar Hill Codonas, which was an area of Glasgow and we always knew that, basically, all the Codonas that we come across in the UK we could attach to the family tree somewhere along the line, but what we called the Vinegar Hill mob. There was definitely quite a lot of Codonas in that area that weren't in the same business as ourselves, maybe they were at one time, I don't know, but you just knew, you'd read in the papers about ... whatever it was, you'd read about the odd Codona from that area, some story or whatever, and we couldn't associate them with any of our family.

My mother and father, I think it would be probably late 1960s, took a trip to the States. There were relations of my fathers, not Codonas, I think it was a grandmother on my father's side, the name was Broughton, and she had relatives of her family over there. But while they were over, they were driving somewhere in California and at the side of the road they saw a filling station with the name Codona and they decided to stop and the family were delighted to see them and try and make acquaintance. And there was some link, but it come from the circus side of the family. That's about as much as I can remember about it.

I was born in 1952 and at that time my father was still travelling. We were generally based in Glasgow. We had winter accommodation on a piece of ground in the east end of Glasgow called Riddrie, Croft Road, and we had sort of winter, well, premises there. My grandmother actually had a house on the bit of land and that was a sort of winter base and we had accommodation there with sort of sheds and I wouldn't say a building, but between a shed and a building, where we done all our maintenance and painting. And we were there from sort of mid-October through until about mid-March every year and we actually attended the Kelvin Hall in Glasgow, the fairground which opened there over the Christmas holidays. But we were generally based there right until the time we moved up to Aberdeen.

We had Waltzers, Dodgems, what they called a Ben Hur … a type of Speedway, a set of Jets and later on, about 1968 or something like that, a Twist ride. I travelled. I was quite fortunate, well, when I think I was about ten, nine or ten, which was about '61 or something like that, I went to boarding school which was quite privileged really for travellers. Before that we used to sort of, we went to school in Glasgow from sort of October to mid-March and that was the time the season set off, which was slightly premature before the start of the Easter holidays, then we went to Dunfermline and Kirkcaldy and when we got to Aberdeen that was more or less the start of the Easter term and we went to school, well I went to school with other kids on the fairground, we went to school at Aberdeen for three weeks, then we went to school in Inverness for a fortnight, Elgin for a fortnight, which took you up to the beginning of June. And then we had a prolonged summer holiday, because by that time we were starting sort of two-day fairs and things – Taranty, Turriff show, places like that. We didn't then go back to school until probably mid-September, when we were actually back in Inverness, the first town we were at for a couple of weeks. It was bad enough, you know, moving school every other week.

You couldn't get an education at all really, but it was better than nothing I suppose. At least you learned to read and write and that's all most of the parents were looking for in those days. I was fortunate because when I was ten I managed to get away to boarding school, go down to Dumfries – St Joseph's college. My brother also went there as well and probably you could count like a handful of other fairground children. I left there about 1966, '67 I think, and my father took on the amusement park in Aberdeen in 1970 – I think I was about 17 then – but still maintained the travelling fairground link, still operated the travelling fairgrounds probably three or four years after that and then handed the business over to my cousin John Codona. That was Billy's son, my father's brother.

I think the travelling life is a marvellous life when you were young. You know, I'm a young lad moving from town to town, different girls in every port sort of thing, which was great fun. Great as a teenager and as a young man, but an extremely hard existence as you got older. And I think my father recognised that. He'd had an eye out for quite a few years and had a few opportunities of taking over permanent amusement parks which offered a far more civilised lifestyle. At that time he never had any notion of moving into houses to live or anything like that, but at least your caravan would be settled and you had electric and toilets and running water, etcetera, which we didn't, we didn't necessarily have in the normal way of life. So when the opportunity came up to take over the amusement park in Aberdeen, he didn't hesitate really.

Admittedly, there had always been an amusement park in Aberdeen, which was run by a family called the Croll's; they were from somewhere in south Wales. They always actually operated, the family operated two amusement parks; one in Porthcawl, that's in south Wales anyway, and one in Aberdeen, and the town council decided to build a new amusement park in Aberdeen and Croll's lease was due to expire by about 1969 or something like that, so they advertised the site which came to let my father have the opportunity and basically the family's operated there ever since.

It was just a vacant site. It was basically just across the road from where the previous amusement park had been, but essentially the council agreed to basically tarmac an area, put a wall round it, my father put up a building which actually housed three rides, which was Waltzers and Twist the first year and then he put another half a dozen rides outside. There was two or three of the rides from the old amusement park that my father purchased.

It was very successful from the minute the gates opened, to be honest. We in fact opened in 1970 and you had the start of the oil boom in Aberdeen where you had a tremendous increase in the local wealth. And Aberdeen's a very prosperous city as you know, and a lot of money going about, etcetera, etcetera, and so the business came from the local population and the beach was pretty successful in Aberdeen, through the town centre, that boomed. But at the same time, that was the start of your foreign package deals and what have you. The holiday business drastically went downhill. But it was far more – I think it done a lot better than what it had done in the previous years before my father took over the site. I think it was mostly down to the local prosperity.

We've ran a fairly static course, I mean, we've plodded away quite nicely. We also have, as well as the amusement park in Aberdeen, we also took over what was initially a snack bar. There was a snack bar on the beach, a fairly big snack bar, 5000 square feet or something like that which had previously been run by the council as a milk bar if you like, run very poorly as councils tended to run things in those days and it had actually lain empty for about eight to ten years. And at the time my father took over the amusement park – my father had always had a travelling fair that visited Aberdeen, straight after Kirk-caldy Links Market every year, and he'd always made a very good job of running that. So, I think, to be honest, when the council actually advertised the new amusement park to let, they were pretty hopeful that my father would come in and make them an offer, through their association with him running the travelling fairground and also running that very well. So, when

my father spoke to the council about taking on the new amusement park, it became fairly clear that as far as the council were
concerned, he was the only man who could do it, and my father
insisted, he asked for a good deal as far as tarmacadam areas,
putting up walls and things – he managed to get the council to
do that. He also insisted on taking over this snack bar, cafeteria
– it was called the Holiday Inn – as an amusement arcade. And
he said he wouldn't be interested in taking over the amusement
park unless they let the Holiday Inn building to him as well.[159]
So that really was a gold mine, you know, from day one, and
helped develop the amusement park as the years went on. The
business just ran from 1970 probably until the mid '90s, when
we sort of looked at what else was happening in terms of the
company and decided that the amusement park could do a – by
the time the '90s come around, the holiday trade was totally
gone, there was not tourists coming. What you had was the oil
industry was creating for the town a lot of prosperity; accommodation – hotels and things become on a par, cost wise, with
the likes of London and these places and there was no possi-
bility of holidaymakers coming to Aberdeen. Even a bed and
breakfast was 30 or 40 pounds a night, and there was no way
that people would pay that. People were going abroad. So the
holiday trade had totally gone and the business was really
surviving purely on the local population. The only holidaymakers really would be people from other parts of the UK, up
here to live and work, and they would have visitors coming up
to visit them for a couple of weeks. That was really the only
visitors we were ever seeing. So we started looking into making
the firm more suited towards an all year round trade with the
local population and to then develop the amusement park into
more of a family entertainment centre; we incorporated ten-pin
bowling, bar, children's fun play area and things like that. And
basically that's what it is now, to be honest.

*So, you'd gone into this business, and is your brother in ... are
you kind of running it together or ...?*

Well, not at the moment. Basically, before we started developing it as a family entertainment centre I actually left the business in the early '80s, it would be about 1982, and we ... diversified into the pub business in the city centre and bought a business which was 'Mr G's' ... an established business – it had a lounge bar, a la carte restaurant, nightclub, and I worked at that business for about seven years; and actually at that time we also built another one called Mr G's Inverness. In 1989 I think it was, I ... had a heart attack at the age of 35, so we decided that I would come out of the nightclub business, which was a stressful business, and I went back to work in the business down on the beach. It was actually my baby, as well as being a family entertainment centre which was built in the amusement park. And I done that, and seven or eight years ago, basically a lot to do with the family situation – because I'm the youngest of the family and married late, whereas my brother married quite young, so my children are eight and ten and brother's children are in their thirties – so there didn't seem a natural progression in the partnership, and we decided to split the businesses up ... my brother basically took over the amusement park and I took over Codona's Holiday Inn, the amusement arcades, and I actually developed that into what is now known as the Board-walk ... basically an amusement arcade but it's got a kids area in it. But unfortunately last year I had another heart attack, so I decided to sell that and ... I'm not doing very much now. I've still got an arcade up in Inverness. We built a nightclub and bar up there on the top floor and there was a shop unit, which we run as an amusement arcade, and then we sold the bar and night club but kept the amusement arcade. At the moment my business interests are purely just the amusement arcade in Inverness.

The amusement arcade business must have changed quite a lot since you've been in it, with the new video games and what not ...

Not really. I would say it did change, yes, I mean video games became very popular and profitable to run, but I would say they've had their hey-day now and it's really, you had the stage where fruit machines took a lot of money in arcades as well, but we're getting back, I would say, to more like amusement arcades getting more like what it was 30 years ago; penny machines, etcetera. As long as you determine what you specify an amusement arcade as; you know, in town centres now you have what to most people look like amusement arcades, but they're probably termed in the industry as adult gaming centres, where they only have fruit machines. Whereas, in terms of amusement, arcades are coming back more with novelty games, as they were 30 years ago, not a lot of fruit machines in them. The one at Inverness, although it's a town centre seaside resort … the nature of Inverness with tourism, it generally operates more as a sort of beach-front amusement arcade would operate.

I think basically a lot of amusement arcades had it very easy for a long time. So, initially the amusement arcades down on the beach generally all incorporated novelty games and they also had prize bingo in them, and then all of a sudden the video boom basically just took off and it was very easy. The bingo side of it and the novelty games, they were always hard work; they had to be well run and giving away prizes, etcetera, and buying stock in … the amusement machines, with the actual construction of them, there was lots of moving parts and things, there was a lot of maintenance. All of a sudden video games – it was dead easy. Fill a place with video games – people were fighting to play them. So the novelty aspect went out the window, prize bingo went out the window because they were hard work. Just, basically, anywhere you could get a license to operate an amusement arcade, these video games were so successful that it was easy money, really, and the novelty side of the thing just disappeared. Now, all of a sudden, the popularity of the video games decreased, and the manufacturers were having to try and work at alternatives to try and build the business back up, to attract a wider variety of client than those that just played the video games.[160]

I suppose maybe with people having computers at home and stuff, that's probably changed it, you know, because they can play all these games on their computers …

They can, and to a degree the amusement arcade industry they combat that by building bigger, better arcade games – the driving machines with the moving feet and all that kind of thing, but that only had a novelty value really. And like you say, people can play games on the internet now against other people as well, and with broadband or whatever, it doesn't really cost them anything.

And so what do you see as being the future of the business?

Very much, like I say, back to the family amusement arcades. We're very much back to where it was 30 years ago – novelty games – I mean even things like arm-wrestling machines, punch-balls, things like that, that were popular 30 years ago. But there's a fair bit of maintenance to them, a fair bit of hassle in operating them or what have you – people pulling balls off springs and things like that. I think we're definitely moving back now to being a fun family business rather than either completely catering for gamblers or completely catering for teenagers who want to play video, space invader type of games. I suppose really it's made it an awful lot healthier. …

The business you're in, you're dealing with the public all the time – has that been a difficult aspect of it?

Not really, no.

Because I think in the past … in the fairgrounds it could be a problem …

There's always plenty of undesirables about, and if you're looking for – every town's got layabouts or thugs or what have you. Certainly with amusement arcades there is the attraction of somewhere they can just walk into … certainly the potential's there. Certainly any arcade that's not well run will have major problems. But it's not something that's ever caused us a problem or couldn't get on top of it.

And do you think the show community has changed over the years that you've been in it?

I don't know that the community's changed, except that it's got an awful lot smaller. Around the early '70s – I'm not sure of the date, it was before we moved to Aberdeen – at one time, up until the early '60s, you couldn't actually … an amusement arcade, or fruit machine, or any kind of game, couldn't pay out cash. A machine could only pay out tokens and round about – sometime during the '60s, mid-'60s, '66 – the government changed the law, where machines could pay out cash, and that was when the amusement arcades began to really flourish; and whereas in places like Blackpool there might be two or three amusement arcades, basically every shop on the sea-front become an amusement arcade. And they made good money. So the people that took on most of these amusement arcades were virtually all fairground people and travelling showmen that had looked for an opportunity to better themselves and come out of the travelling fairground business to operate in one town. I think most of them probably started off still living in a caravan somewhere, but over the years that's changed and half of the fairground fraternity are now what we called settled-down travellers, that have moved into the amusement arcades. Probably – I wouldn't say initially they moved into the amusement arcades; sort of next generation then moved into the – probably the natural progression for a lot of families, as we did, was things like bars and nightclubs and, you know, probably a certain percentage of that have now moved into other normal, run of the mill businesses. I would say through that natural progression that the fairground – I don't have specifics on it, how many people there are in the Showmen's Guild now – but that certainly had a major impact on the number of people travelling. I think a lot of things influenced that as well; I think schooling's been a major thing. There's no way you can travel the fairgrounds for eight months a year and give your children an education. I think another thing that's happened – a lot of the fairground fraternity now, although they're still travelling to some degree, they're generally, their main residence would be a caravan based in Glasgow, but they take another smaller caravan out and do a few of the fairs. There's also been – maybe more short-term, over the last ten, fifteen years – the rides on the fairground have had to be a lot more sophisticated to generate enough income to sustain them. The smaller rides, older rides, even the Dodgems to some degree have not become viable, and the only rides that are really making money at the fairs are your huge rides that are two or three hundred thousand pounds cost. So the amount of opposition means that the rich have got richer, but poorer for the smaller operator that used to operate your small fairground hooplas and things like that, they tend to be disappearing and there's just a few of the big rides going about. There's certainly not as many fairs now as what there used to be. Any sizeable village would attract a fairground once a year at one time. The big fairs prosper fairly well, but the smaller fairgrounds are disappearing.

That's a very outside view. I'm not really involved in travelling type of business now. Just I have an outside view, that's the way it's going.

So is there less of a sense of a fairground community as a result of that, because it seems as though it was very strong at one point?

I wouldn't say it was less of a community. There's no question if you're counting the amount of caravans that are parked in the winter round Glasgow now, it's nothing like it was 30 years ago. But probably as a community, although half of us are now living in houses, we still feel part of that, that we're part of the Showmen's Guild and we're travellers is what we call wirselves.

And do you think … I've spoken with other people that are probably about the same age as you and they were saying when they were growing up there was still a certain amount of prejudice against the travelling showmen?

I don't think that exists now to be honest. But it's certainly something that was evident. I think there was the same situation, because I think most of the travelling people always felt that they were a touch smarter than what we call 'flatties' and the flatties felt exactly the same. And I remember when I first moved up to Aberdeen permanently, I was only a young lad of 17, 18, and I felt it a little bit, you know, going out to a – well it wasn't a disco then, it was a dance hall and meeting people and chatting up girls … and some of them … looked down their nose at you because you lived in a caravan. And I suppose that wasn't fair, because we don't live in caravans, but I don't see any sign of that being the case nowadays. … I think people are more open with their views now than what they were years ago.

And did you have a strong sense of being part of the Codona family, that heritage?

I've definitely got a lot of pride, absolutely. I think there was – well, I was quite lucky to a degree. The family were all – although there were a lot of people that looked down on you, travelling people and something like gypsies or what have you – we were always quite fortunate, most of the people that knew us had a very good opinion of us. You know, we always had a good reputation; we come to a town, went on a site, my father was particular about cleaning a site before we left, no rubbish was left behind, the rent was always paid, the suppliers were always paid, and people that knew us always thought very highly of us and I suppose I enjoyed the benefit of that. I think it was only the people that didn't know us that put two and two together and formed the wrong opinion of us. I always had tremendous pride in the Codona name. I must admit I have seen examples of people in our business, maybe kids that went to school with us, and were embarrassed to say where they come from. You know, they didn't like the other kids to know that they were from the fairground, etcetera. I'm not saying that was the case with the majority of them but there were definitely occasions where – I'm not saying that they would refuse to say where they were from, but they would try to keep the thing low-key. But I certainly never thought that. I always had a very strong sense of – I was proud to be a Codona. I certainly had no fears of where I was from.

And do you think your kids are going to go into the business? Are they showing any interest?

Had I not sold my involvement down at the beach I think there'd probably be a 50-50 chance. Certainly, they can do what they want to do. I'd encourage them whatever it is, but given my situation – I'm not involved, only up in Inverness – I don't see the potential for any of my kids working up there. I think more likely that they'll progress in their own careers. I don't know – it's hard to say – I suppose if they failed in making anything in life, then it's always an option for them. But I'm 52 and I've had some heart trouble and, as far as I'm concerned, I don't intend to develop anything in the business again now in the fairground field.

And did you ever feel that you wanted to do anything else, or did it just ...?

To be quite honest about it – I don't knock it but I wasn't really encouraged, as I don't think any of the children were. ... I was very much encouraged to come into the business. I was sent to boarding school, which suggests otherwise, you know, that I might be given the opportunity; but at the same time, when I was about 14½ I was wheeked out of boarding school to work in the business. So I can't really say I was given the opportunity, to be honest. I think regardless of how well I'd done at school or whatever opportunity I'd been given, I think I would have still come back to the business because it's something that I enjoyed very much. As I say, I don't think I was given the opportunity, but I think given the choice, at the end of the day I'd have been in the business anyway.

Justin Codona is the great-grandson of Nathaniel Codona, one of the four 'Codona Brothers', and married to the great-grand-daughter of William Codona, another of the four. His grand-father Cecil was one of five brothers – with John, Nathaniel, Raymond and William – who, like John Codona's brothers and then his four sons, formed themselves into a firm.

[Justin Codona]

They had their own firm and when it broke up, you know, they split all the rides between them. But I don't know what happened – if it was when Nathaniel senior died or whatever, then they split the firm. I can't quite remember what that story was, but I know they split all the rides. They had property in Paisley and stuff like that. They split it all and I know that Johnny, that was the other brother, that was the fifth brother, and I know that my grandfather Cecil and his brother Johnny, there was a Dodgem ride and I think it was the same one that they had in the family, there was only one Dodgem ride, so they had to split it between them. You know, they split so many cars, and they tossed a coin for the pay box, as we called it. You know, they took so many parts each and made a whole one each kind of thing.

You could put sections in them and make them bigger or take sections out and make them smaller. But they ... whatever way they split the firm up, they got this Dodgem and they had to split it between them. So they took half each, you know, they sorted out who was getting what and they must have obviously completed it to get the thing operational again. I can't remember exactly what else – I know there was Chairoplanes, they were a popular ride at the time, there was a Speedway, and, you know, the other brothers, it all got split between them. That's going back a while. The fairs that they run, they must have split them as well. I remember being told the story a few times, you know, but you just, over the years, you forget, you know.

When the firm was broken up Justin's grandfather Cecil had Dodgems and children's rides that he travelled Central Scotland with until he died in 1955, when Justin's father was 13.

[Justin Codona]

He was in it all his life then basically. He actually carried on travelling from then. They carried on with the business with his mother. She was a Robertson and there was a few brothers of those and they kind of kept the business running, you know, helped them ... I reckon it was until – he carried on just travelling, up until he died in '94.

He was a keen footballer, you know, he used to play in the showmen's teams. The English showmen play the Scottish showmen. They used to do that every year and he was the star player for Scotland, you know. ... It used to be in years gone by it was, you know, more of a bigger deal than what it is now. But I know he was the – they actually stopped doing it for a while in the '60s and the first year they actually held it again I know my father played and they actually beat the English showmen seven-nil, and my father scored four of the goals. He was one of the top footballers. I think he actually said that he'd been offered trials here and there. One was with Raith Rovers, but there was never any time to pursue that sort of thing. Not like it is now where, you know, where it would be a lot of money involved or anything. It never went down that alley, you know.

So when you were growing up and travelling, how did that affect your going to school and things like that?

Well I used to – obviously we was in Glasgow all winter, so I was at school all winter, and basically at the start of the season and the end of the season we were at more places where we'd be there for two or three weeks. I used to go to different schools at different places, you know. ... It is quite uncomfortable. Like the stranger on the block sort of thing. We used to go to the start off at East Kilbride, you know, and I used to go to school there and that, and I can remember I didn't look forward to it, you know.

And do you think there was prejudice against the showmen almost, you know, the community, maybe it was because you were travelling or something. ... Did you encounter any of that?

Yeah, we did get a fair – you know, 'gypsies' and so on. You know, yes, there is quite a lot of that.

And do you think that's still the case?

Aye, you know, from certain members of the public. You know
– if they've got a problem with you, then that's the first thing
that comes out.

I was always in it. We've actually got a Waltzer ride now and
also ... some kid's stuff as well, and that did belong to my father.
I can just remember with the Waltzers. I mean it's the same thing
as they've got now ... helping to set up, pack up. I was probably
helping out from when I was about ten or eleven years old. I
started helping out then, and then as I got a wee bit older even
more so ... collecting the money on the rides, and maybe you'll
know on the Waltzers you've got to push the carriages round
and things like that. When I was old enough I was doing that.

And how has the business changed since you've been in it?

I wouldn't say it's changed an awful lot. Obviously in terms of
the equipment and stuff, we've got a lot better equipment now.
You know, we're more in line with the European showmen and
stuff. They was miles ahead of us at one point in terms of the
equipment but we're catching up now. I've still got the Waltzer
and I've got a kiddies' buggy track. That's like a continental
children's ride. That's the two ones that I run.

And what are the main venues in your calendar?

Main venues – I suppose between June, July and August
there's a lot of events – gala days and so on. We do two or
three through in West Lothian round that way, a lot of gala
days, Saturday gala days ... mainly the events rather than the
fairs coming to town, private business as we call it ... a bit of
both, but obviously if there was an event that's usually better
business than just the private business.

I stick to central Scotland. Basically I always did, we don't
even really go up north. As far north as Dundee, you know,
that's about it. As far south as Lanarkshire and Ayrshire. The
season usually finishes the back of the Guy Fawkes, the fifth of
November. And that's us, you know, next week [i.e. end of
March] starting off again.

And what do you do over the winter?

Well, I always do a bit of maintenance in my spare time, but I work, you know, driving for an oil company, and that tides me over.

And do you go to the same places year after year, or does it ...?

More or less, give or take one or two new ones or some that, you know, the sites have changed or whatever. But there's a nucleus of a run that we do, where ... over the years I suppose it hasn't changed a lot.

... It's the same probably in any business; there's a lot of red tape these days, you know, licensing and councils, you know. It can be difficult. I was talking to my cousin tonight, you know, he had a licence in for a fair and the police was making representations to the council, you know – 'that lot, they bring a hooligan element' and all this. But I mean we don't arrive in a town and bring them with us; they're their own people. You know, we find a lot of that; it's easier to get rid of us than to police the actual, the local problems – to address the local problems if you like. I think it's just the joys of dealing with the public. I suppose it's the same in any business that deals with the public, you know.

Do you think public behaviour's got better or worse, or is it just the same over the years? That's 20 years I suppose that you've been in the business.

I think probably in some ways. I don't know if it's got better, I think it's more controlled now, if you like. You know, a lot of sites have got their own security and that, stewards on a lot more of the fairs now, where in years gone by we didn't have that kind of thing, the stewards on a lot of them, fixed business what have you. It's probably more controlled, not so much better behaviour.

And I've seen that you now get funfairs setting up in supermarket car parks and stuff like that ...

Yes, aye, that's starting to get more common. I've done one or two. Like you say, in the shopping centres and things like that there is. It's not so much the council bringing them in, it's more the showmen trying to target and securing them sites. I've opened one or two of them myself. I think not last summer but the summer before, I was at Cameron Toll. ... I'm trying to think what other ones round Edinburgh – I've been open in Craig-millar before as well, next to the Quicksave, I've been up there, and you know Niddrie. Sometimes in the poorer areas you get a better spending punter if you like. I think you find that quite a lot.

Most of the time we're on site. You're not having to com-mute. But yeah, for security reasons, you've got to stay and look after the equipment as well. But you're finding more and more now, a lot of the showmen are buying houses and com-muting, settling down but still being in the business. Like you say, running it from home.

And have you got kids?

Yeah, two small kids.

So you don't know whether or not they're going to go into the business yet?

No. I wouldn't be able to say right at the minute, but they seem keen enough.

Would you want them to go in?

Yes and no. I'd like them to – we're trying to keep them in school, you know, so they don't miss any. Like, when I was younger, there was a lot of weeks missed and things like that. What I want to do is give them the chance so they don't miss any and give them the chance so if they want to go down that road, they're able to. Basically, I didn't have the chance to do anything else. I was into this and that was it. At the time I was fine, but now I'm older, you know, you're thinking you should have done a bit more education-wise and maybe have went into something else, but now it's like, well, it's the only thing you know. If you're having a good spell then it's the greatest thing. If you're going through a tough patch, then it's like, you know, 'I could do with getting out of this'. Up and down. It can be the greatest thing in the world and then obviously the worst habit in the world as well, you know!

FIG. 43 Justin Codona (right) in front of the pay box of his 'Starchaser' Waltzer, waiting for business to start on a rainy Polbeth Gala Week Saturday afternoon, 2004. Although they involve a lot of work for two day's worth of business, such Gala days across West Lothian and Central Scotland are a mainstay of Justin Codona's business. Polbeth – which he organises – is preceded by Whitburn and Armadale Galas (organised by Nathaniel Codona) and is followed by Lesmahagow. (*Source:* Frank Bruce)

APPENDIX I

Biographical Notes for Harriet,
William and Adelaide Codona,
John W. Cardownie and Francesco Cardoni

HARRIET Codona, William Codona and John W. Cardownie were, as far as we can tell, all children of John Codona [1]. William and John – as well as William's wife Adelaide – had successful performing careers. Like another of John's probable children Harry – whose daughter Harriette is given in Perez Calvo 2007, 115 as a niece of William – Adelaide and John travelled to the United States where they enjoyed continued success.

Harriet, William and Adelaide

Harriet was born in Scotland in 1848, the daughter of John Codona – probably John [1] in a first marriage – and Elizabeth Hart who married in North Leith in 1830 (noted above). She was living in Sheffield in 1861 at the time of the census with her mother Elizabeth, at which point both were 'dressmakers'). She married Spanish trapeze artist Francisco Rizarelli in 1865. She may well have been the equestrienne Madame Rizarelli who appeared with the Rizarelli brothers (Francisco and Domingo) Circus in the 1870s and '80s; she may also have been the Miss Codona who had appeared in the Circo Price in Madrid in 1862 alongside her 'brother', presumably William, and in several seasons as Signorita/Mdlle Cardoni with Hengler's Circus from 1861 to 1864 (the year before Harriet married) across the United Kingdom in an equestrian act that included dancing on horseback. Several references (see above) suggest an ongoing relationship between the Codona and the Rizarelli families from the 1860s to the 1880s.

William's parents were also John and Elizabeth (Elizabeth Codona, c1814-79, is named on William's gravestone). According to the 1871 census, Adelaide was born in c1846 in Champagne, France. The earliest references to either performing are possibly those for Mdlle Cardoni with Hengler's Circus, if this was not Harriet. The 1862 appearance of Signorita Cardoni alongside her 'brother' Signor Codona could have been her with her husband William, since family legend – very obscurely – hints at a teenage pregnancy with one of the Codona family in the winter of 1859, and in 1862 they were both still teenagers (see above). The earliest billing of Signor Cardoni is not until 1867 when he appeared in MacFarland's Circus in Dundee 'in his illustrations of natural character on horseback'. The next two years or so were spent overseas, for in 1870 they advertised as follows in *The Era* (14 August 1870):

> Notice to circus proprietors. Mr and Madame Cardoni will conclude a successful engagement of two years at the Cirque Parisien France, on the 9th September, and will be happy to arrange with proprietors after that date for the following performance – Madame Cardoni. First class bare-back Trick act Rider, and Mr Cardoni. Back and Forward Trick-Act Rider. Number of Scene acts. All letters addressed to the Cirque Parisien, Cambria, up to the 25th, after to the town of Arras, in the North of France.

Thereafter, they appeared as man and wife mainly with Charles Adams' Circus across the north of England until William's death in 1873. After this, Madame Codona continued to appear with Adams' Circus until 1877, when, based in Birmingham, she placed another notice in *The Era* (25 March 1877): 'Madame Codona will shortly be at liberty to take an engagement in England and Abroad, as a first-class Bare back trick-act rider, with own horse ….' At some point after this, she travelled to the United States and in 1879 toured with 'The Great London Circus', part of a 'monster combination' of three shows that visited dozens of towns across the States. Then she continued to appear with major North American circuses, as well as making trips to the United Kingdom and Europe. Her last appearance seems to have been in 1888, by which time she was in her forties and possibly ready to retire.

Chronological references

- William Codona, born 1844 (his birth certificate gives place of birth as Accrington, Lancashire).
- Adelaide Codona (own family name unknown), born Champagne, France, c1846 (details taken from 1871 census, see below).
- Harriet Codona, born 1848.
- *Liverpool Mercury*, 19 January 1861, Mdlle Cardoni with Hengler's.
- *The Era*, 5 January 1862, Mdlle Cardoni with Pinder's Circus in Dundee.
- Miss Codona is noted with the Spanish Circo Price with her brother in *Badajoz* in March 1862 (Angel Suarez Munoz and Sergio Suarez Ramirez, 'Teatro, parateatro y prensa en el Badajoz del siglo XIX', *Revista de estudios extremenos*, vol. 57, no. 2 [2001], 760-1).
- *Liverpool Mercury*, 18 October 1862, Mdlle Cardoni noted with Hengler's.
- *Caledonian Mercury*, 28 February 1863, Mdlle Cardoni with Hengler's, Edinburgh (appearances noted until May; see also *The Scotsman*, 27 March 1863, 1 April 1863, 25 April 1863 and *The Edinburgh Weekly Review*, 14 March 1863, which notes 'Madll. Cardoni in one of her pleasing graceful Acts').
- *Glasgow Herald*, 1 July 1863, Mdlle Cardoni with Hengler's (noted until October).
- *Liverpool Mercury*, 10 November 1863, Mdlle Cardoni with Hengler's (noted until December).
- *Caledonian Mercury*, 18 February 1864, Mdlle Cardoni with Hengler's (noted until April; see also *The Scotsman*, 5 March 1864, 12 March 1864, 3 May 1864).
- *The Belfast Newsletter*, 2 May 1864, Mdlle Cardoni with

Hengler's (noted until June). The issue of 13 June 1864 notes: 'The characteristic dances of Poland, Spain and Italy by Mdlle Cardoni on horseback are incomparatively artictic [*sic*]', and a week later 'Mdlle Cardoni danced very prettily as the Highland Lassie'.

– *Glasgow Herald*, 13 July 1864, Mdlle Cardoni with Hengler's (noted until August).

– *The Era*, 7 July 1867, MacFarland's Circus, Dundee, 'Signor Cardoni in his illustrations of natural character on horseback'.

– *The Era*, 26 July 1868, 'Wanted to complete the brothers Risserellas and Co.'s Circus for America. First class male and female equestrians (a family preferred) with their own horse; ... For particulars Mr J. Emont, Care of Madame Codona, 5 Victoria Street, Scarborough, Yorkshire'.

– *The Era*, 14 August 1870, notice to circus proprietors regarding the return of Mr and Madame Cardoni from a two-year engagement at the Cirque Parisien France (see above).

– *The Era*, 13 November 1870, with Adams' Circus, Carlisle – 'Mdlle Rizarelli and Signorita Codona ...'.

– *The Era*, 25 December 1870, with Adams' Circus, Carlisle – 'Signor Codona took his benefit ...'.

– In France, *c*1871. William and Adelaide Codona's appearances in France and then Spain *c*1873 are suggested by two census entries. The 1871 census listing for Caroline Street, Wigan, has equestrian William Codona, 25 (his birth certificate is for 1845), lodger, born Accrington, Lancashire, and his equestrian wife Adelaide Codona, 25, born Champagne, France, as well as son, Louis Phillip Codona, one, born in Lyons. The 1881 York census record has Louis Codona aged ten, born in France, and Eliza Codona, seven, born in Spain – though William may have already been dead before she was born. That Louis is William's son is further confirmed by a record of the death in 1900 in York of Cecil Phillippe Codona, son of Louis, who we are told is 'buried with his grandfather'. Cecil Phillippe's name appears on William's gravestone. [I am indebted to Joy Cann of York City Archives for searching out York material on William Codona, and to the late John Turner for references to Adams' Circus.]

- *The Era*, 14 May 1871, with Adams' Circus, Bolton, as Signor and Signorita Codona.
- *The Era*, 25 May 1873, with Adams' Circus, Bradford. The issue of 8 June 1873 notes 'Madame Codona's daring performances'.
- *York Gazette*, 1 July 1873, with Adams' Circus in York (a substantial, elaborate timber theatre), billed as 'Mr W. Cadona, England's Peerless Somersault Rider', with wife Madame Cadona, 'the accomplished Equestrian, from the Principal Continental Cirques: and late of Metz and Strasburg'.
- *York Gazette*, 18 October 1873, describes a benefit for William Codona's wife and reveals that William Codona was brother-in-law of Charles Adams.
- 13 October 1873, William Codona dies.
- *The Derby Mercury*, 2 June 1875, advert for Adams' Circus puffs the 'Great success of Signoretta Cadona, the most daring equestrienne in Europe'.
- *The Era*, 20 June 1875, with Adams' Circus in Derby.
- *York Gazette*, 31 July 1875, with Adams's Circus in York as Signorita Codono.
- *The Era*, 30 January 1876, with Adams' Circus in Bradford as 'Mdll. Cadona'.
- *The Era*, 6 February 1876, with Adams' Circus in Leeds.
- *The Era*, 11 February 1877, with Adams' Circus in Leeds.
- *The Era*, 25 March 1877, notice of Madame Codona's availability to take engagements (see above).
- 1879, tours the United States with 'The Great London Circus'. The full itinerary can be found at <http://www.circushistory.org/Routes/CB1876.htm> and traced through notices in the North American press.
- *Liverpool Mercury*, 2 December 1880, with Hengler's Circus, billed as 'Madame Cardoni. America's Greatest Lady Equestrian: her first appearance in Liverpool'.
- 'Mlle Cardoni' is noted in Madrid in 1882, appearing with the Rizarelli family and trick equestrienne Miss Liria at the new Summer Circus and Racetrack by *La Illustracion Española y Americana*, num. XXVI, 15 July 1882, 19, with a portrait on

page 32. The similarity of this portrait with that on an undated poster for 'Adelaide Cordona Queen of the ring', appearing with Adam Forepaugh's American Circus (a copy is held by the John and Mable Ringling Museum of Art Circus Museum), certainly suggests that they were the same person. However, this is hard to square with the billing of Adelaide Cordona with Sells Circus in Iowa only a month earlier (*Waterloo Courier* [Iowa], 14 June 1882). Perhaps this was a case of Harriet Rizarelli reverting to her maiden name, or some other relative.

– 1884, Mlle Adelaide Cordona/Senorita Adelaide Cordona was appearing with the Sells Brothers four-ring circus on a seven-month tour of the American mid-west (two bills for this are in Sayers, 1981, 13-14). Other appearances with American circuses between 1879-1886 are listed in Slout 2005 at:
<http://www.circushistory.org/Olympians/OlympiansC2.htm>

– *Morning Oregonian*, 21 July 1888, with Sells Brothers, Portland.

John W. Cardownie

The obituary of John W. Cardownie – 'Death of an Aberdonian in America' (*The Aberdeen Weekly Journal*, 16 May 1900) – provides a valuable summary of his life:

An expert in the step dances of Scotland, England and Ireland. … As a dancer he attained distinction along with his wife Tina Jamieson – a well-known vocalist – and his three daughters. He toured throughout the Kingdom as well as abroad, the 'Cardownie family' being favourites on the music hall stage. … Nearly four years ago … Mr Cardownie left Aberdeen. He then went to America accompanied by his daughter Louise. Mrs Cardownie took up residence in Liverpool, where her son … is in business. … Mr Cardownie … the son of a travelling showman and was left in Aberdeen practically as 'nobody's child', had an eventful career and practically 'dragged himself out of the gutter'.

Clues about the 'travelling showman' are given in his death

certificate and the report of his accidental death in New Haven in *The Music Hall and Theatre Review* (11 May 1900), which show him as having an Italian father (Spanish, according to the *New Haven Evening Register*, 26 April 1900), but this does not fit the Scottish records. Twenty-year old John Cardona is listed as marrying his wife Christina in Aberdeen in 1877 when both were working in a flax-mill. His parents are here given as John [1] (circus performer) and Louisa. The problem is that the John given as the father of John died in 1884, when John was adult, contradicting a statement in the New Haven report that J. W. Cardownie's father died when he was a young boy. Maybe this was an uncle or relative looking after the orphan. Francis Cardownie [2], *c*1790-1859, probably the brother of John [1], is a candidate for the biological father since he died when J. W. Cardownie was very young. He appears to have taken the 'Cardownie' form of the family name, and might well have been born on the continent.

[John W.'s] performing career had begun by 1877. In the *Aberdeen Weekly Journal*, 24 July 1877, he is among the prize list at Aberdeen Highland games for the Sailor's Hornpipe (in costume). Two months later he was billed at McFarlands Grand Music Hall, Aberdeen: 'For this night only, Mr J. Cardownie, champion Sand Dancer, will appear.' For the 1878 birth of his daughter Isabella, he is listed as 'professional dancer' and thereafter there are regular appearances noted in music hall, at soirees and competitions, including some with Mrs Cardownie, mainly around Aberdeen. He was still semi-professional in 1881 when the census has them in Aberdeen, John a traveller for a tea company and with two children, Louisa (11 months) and Isabella (aged two). The year 1887 seems to have been the turning point; he begins to be noted in *The Era*, mainly across Scotland. In December he was billed as 'champion all-round dancer of the World' in the winter show at Edinburgh's Waverley Market (*The Scotsman*, 9 December 1887 – his Scottish career can be followed in detail in the digital archives of *The Scotsman*). After 1890 he began to travel more widely across the United Kingdom. By 1892 he puffed himself as:

Mr J. W. Cardownie, the unbeaten All round dancer of the world. New show a tremendous success. Splendid Stage Apparatus, Gorgeous Costumes, Swift changes, Brilliant Music, Marvellous dancing and the only performer in this line on the British stage. Returns everywhere at big increase of Salary and still going up. This week, Alhambra Stockport; next week, Victoria, Bolton. Agent, Warner.

From 1894 he started promoting a troupe of dancers, advertising in Liverpool for 'a girl from twelve upwards ... to Join Cardownie Troupe' (*Liverpool Mercury*, 23 October 1894). The Cardownie Troupe prospered: 'Their dancing the absolute Rage of London ... no vacancies 'till '96' (*The Era*, 6 April 1895). Several years of touring the UK follow (with summers spent still competing on the Scottish dance circuit) until 1899, when *The Era*'s 'Music Hall Gossip' noted that the Cardownie Troupe 'sail for America where they open on Proctors [Vaudeville] circuit on April 10th' (*The Era*, 23 March 1899 – he had already visited New York in 1893 for a Highland dancing competition).

The American tour was a success: 'Cardownie dancers ... greatest hit ever in America. Four months tour such a success that they have rebooked on seven Vaudeville circuits' (*The Era*, 23 September 1899). By early 1900 'The Cardownie Troupe of International dancers are the top-liners at Tony Pastors [the main vaudeville circuit]' ('American Music Halls', in *The Era*, 27 January 1900). Their success was cut short a few months later by J. W. Cardownie's death in a boating accident in New Haven in April 1900, by which point the 'Cardownie Troupe' – consisting of of J. W. Cardownie, his sister Louisa, Miss Phoebe Carlo and Jessie Bowman – was described as being well known in vaudeville throughout the United States, billed as 'Europe's Premier international Dance Team'.[161]

After their father's death, the three daughters continued on the stage: 'The three Cardownie sisters make their first appearance since their recent sad bereavement, and their dances prove as popular as ever' ('American Vaudeville', *The Era*, 16 June 1900).

Francesco Cardoni

Born around 1893, puppeteer Francesco Cardoni began his performing career at the age of ten. He moved from Naples to Rome
around 1918 where he performed his Pulcinella shows with
glove-puppets at a stand in the Borghese gardens in Rome until
he was in his eighties. This particular puppet tradition is generally seen as being the direct model for the Punch and Judy glove-
puppet shows made popular across Britain from the end of the
eighteenth century and performed by several Scottish Codonas.
Even in the absence of conclusive evidence of a family connection, this linked tradition combined with his name makes a case
for including a brief biographical sketch of this Italian showman – effectively the same as the first of the Codonas to come
to Scotland ('Cardoni' is the name given by Pat Feeney who
worked with the family in the 1820s, and who said they were
the first to bring Punch and Judy to Glasgow. 'Francisco Codoni'
is the name used in one of the earliest British records, for the
christening of his son Guillemus, 4 September 1804, St Peters
RC, Lancaster. Whether he was from a performing dynasty is
unknown, but given his early start it seems highly likely, not
least because his skills were not quickly acquired. 'Manipulating
the puppets –, a bright student can learn that in two or three
months', he told an interviewer in 1953, 'but then there is the
co-ordination of voice and action. One must be able to handle
a cast of ten figures – each with a different personality, distinct
voice. One must bring them on stage, give their pieces, take them
off, bring them back on and remember which voice was whose.
It takes for ever' ('US Finances Puppet Show for Italians', syndi-
cated Associated Press feature in the *Zanewille Signal*, 10 May
1953. Most of the biographical details are from this and also
kindly supplied by puppet historian and performer Bruno
Leone.)

He claimed to have performed in 'public squares and before
most of the now uncrowned heads of Europe', but at the time
of this interview he was working for the Mutual Security Agency,
financed by the United States. His job was to show movie shorts

and give a puppet show presenting America's view on the world. This was welcome well-paid work: 'We were almost on the rocks, finished. What with movies, radio ... modern life.' None of his three daughters wanted to go into the business, but in 1953 he had a student, Giuseppe Pio (possibly Pino), and was also master to Carlo Piantadosi, who still performs in Rome (see Alessandra Litta Modignani, *Dizionario Biografico e Bibliografia dei burattinai, marionettisti e pupari della tradizione italiana* [Bologna, 1985], page 53 for Cardoni and 108 for Piantadosi). Francesco Cardoni died in Rome in 1977.

APPENDIX 2

Alfred Codona

ALFRED Codona was Gordon's older brother. His third-person memoir of working in his father's business, John Codona's Pleasure Fairs [JCPF], starts during the traction-engine era.

[*Alfred Codona*]

One of his earliest memories is going to school at Aberdeen when five years old. It was Codona's first visit to Aberdeen, or at least John Codona's first at the end of 1920. He had just started school in Edinburgh a few weeks before and they suddenly decided to move to Aberdeen to open over Christmas and New Year, at the Gallowgate on the site now occupied by Greyfriars House. It was quite an open space and there would be five or six roundabouts there and the school actually adjoined the ground. The school was known as the Middle School. John Codona's wagon was actually parked right outside the railings of the school, so that at playtime Alfred's play piece only had to be passed through the railings – it was most convenient. The fair was open in Aberdeen for several weeks, until after the New Year when the rides were pulled down and the family spent the rest of the winter on open fairground at Pittodrie at the rear of the [Aberdeen Football Club] stand. They didn't start out again until the beginning of March, so Alfred and his sister continued to attend the Middle School, going to school by tramcar from Pittodrie. At the start of the season the Codona family moved to Perth, before going on to Kirkcaldy, and then on to Alloa, Kilmarnock and into Ayrshire for a while.

When Alfred was seven years old he was first left with people at Livingston, then a village, just out of Edinburgh where he spent eight or nine months with these people, where he attended the local school. He always remembered playing football with a chap who was eventually to be a notable football player called Tommy Walker, who played for Hearts and Scotland and eventually became manager of Hearts. The seven-year-olds played football on a small piece of ground next to the coal pit at Livingston. Alfred did go back home for a couple of years and attended school at various places that the fair visited. When he was eleven years old he was left in Glasgow to finish his education at Elementary School that he left at 14. When he left his last school in Glasgow, the next place he went to rejoin the family was strangely enough the Gallowgate in Aberdeen, on the same piece of ground that they were on when he started school nine years before. The fair at the Gallowgate hadn't carried on every year, but they were back that year for the Christmas and New Year fair. By this time Alfred was ready for work, which until recently he has been doing ever since, and again they left Aberdeen this time going to winter in Glasgow. Alfred, being big for his age, obtained a driving licence by saying he was 17; one only had to say what one's age was in that day, no proof was necessary. He started to drive on an old solid tyred motor vehicle that they had to pull John Codona's caravan. He was promoted from this when he was 15 to driving a traction engine. He had had various shots of driving the engines previously, usually with his father in attendance. The first time on his own was in Dumfries, Alfred was 15½, and he was sent off on the journey from Dumfries to Carlisle fully in charge of this traction engine. With three trailers at the back it was actually the Wall of Death he was towing. He eventually became a very experienced driver. As time went on he gained experience of fairground matters. In the same year as his first journey [he was] in charge of the engine and road train.

In 1930 John Codona obtained one of the first Noah's Ark machines which he christened the Jungle Ride. Alfred was left in charge of the Jungle Ride, getting it built up and pulled down;

he was gaining experience as an engine driver. Arthur Pepper, an experienced engine driver, started work for John Codona; for the next two or three years Alfred had nothing to do with the engines as they had a very good and experienced man in Arthur Pepper. Alfred went back to driving a motor lorry; in between times though, he moved an engine here and there when necessary. They had three roundabouts by this time and three traction engines. In 1932 John Codona again found a site in Aberdeen to open for Christmas and New Year. This time the ground was in an area known as the Guest Row on a site facing the Marischal College, part of which is now used by Marks & Spencer store. They continued to open on that ground until the outbreak of the Second World War in 1939.

Business came to a halt with the outbreak of the War; the Codona's were in Fife. John Codona obtained permission to pull his equipment on to a piece of ground in Stirling which was used as a showground called the Goosecroft, but they were only allowed to operate in a limited way taking precautions to ensure the blackout. By completely covering in the Motorcycle Speedway they were able to open on every weekend right through the winter of 1939-40; it was completely blacked out with no light showing anywhere. It had a big black screen cover right round the whole roundabout and shading lighting inside. The famous firm of Speedings of Sunderland, who supplied showmen throughout the country with canvas and tilts, came to Stirling and measured up the rides before manufacturing the black-out screens for the Motorcycle Speedway and the Waltzer.

The Codonas operated sometimes quite largely at different places using this system at some places. The country was zoned into different areas. On the East were restricted areas where the showmen were not allowed to use any form of lighting. They could only open there in the summer months during the hours of daylight which would mean a 10.30pm close in June, 10pm in July as time went on being restricted to an 8pm close.

During the War it was a different way of carrying out business, it was very difficult getting people to help because many people, indeed many showpeople, were in the services. Alfred

Codona was given an exempt occupation on a threshing mill in Ayrshire, simply because of his experience with traction engines. Agriculture was a very important part of the war effort as the country could not import food.

John Codona was still active on the fairground at that time and indeed still running the business. Alfred found the farm experience different, things were difficult for everybody in wartime, but one redeeming feature for showmen was that people could not get away on holiday so most town's promoted holiday at home events where a fairground could operate as an added attraction. It was difficult for the showmen to operate and equipment available was limited; indeed there were not many showmen available to operate, many were on active service and business had to stop, but to some extent some managed.

Alfred worked on the threshing mill and at weekends tried to do something in the fair business. There was a time between April and August when things were at a standstill as far as threshing was concerned and Alfred used this to get away and do something toward the holiday at home fairs.

Glasgow Green was probably the most well known holiday at home fair (the predecessor of the present day fair). Leith Links, Riverside Park, Dundee were other fairs that Alfred Codona's family attended in wartime.

As the War progressed, the Codonas [John] kept some of their equipment at Cumbernauld behind a little garage there, where it was safely and securely parked, as the man who owned the garage also had his house there and allowed the family to park there. In 1943 the John Codona's Pleasure Fairs [JCPF] premises at Riddrie were acquired; it became their home and base for the next 29 years. The ground had previous to this lain empty for many years; Alfred remembers it as he actually attended school at Riddrie. It was open ground and there was a little filling station at the front of it when Alfred was a small boy; there was a house attached to the filling station.

First of all John Codona had gained use of the Riddrie ground to park some of his lorries as they did a bit of contracting with their lorries in Glasgow in 1941. Because of that, he found out that the people who owned it were getting on in years and wanted to dispose of it. John Codona took the opportunity and acquired it. There were nearly three acres of ground where the family of John Codona remained until 1972.

The John Codona lorries used for contracting in 1941 carried sand bags as there was a big rush on barricading hospital doors and windows, so lorries were required for moving the sand bags which weighed ½ cwt each. The Codonas carted the sandbags from a quarry at Kirkintilloch to various hospitals around the city. This work helped fill in some months. They went on to carrying cement from the docks out to the new defence installations at Inchinnon and this carried them through the winter. This work came to an end as the country became better organised and there was a better supply of contractors and government assistance became readily available; the showmen were only filling in during the emergency.

... As the War ended things got more or less back to something like normal. There was a special system of fuel rationing for showmen's vehicles during the War. One applied to the local fuel officer – every area had its own fuel-rationing officer – for enough petrol coupons to take you to the next fair/place, and at each place you had to get the coupons for the next journey. ... It worked well as they were able to contract fuel, as this was a very valuable commodity in keeping the country going and meeting the needs of the War.

Fuel needed for generating on the fairground was not rationed. It was a different fuel called gas oil, a diesel fuel, but it could not be used for road purposes. The steam engines went off the road at more or less the start of the War. John Codona last used his engines in 1942, 1943 at the latest, then they lay in the yard at Riddrie until they were sold off one by one mainly for scrap. One is still around in preservation; the other two were broken up for scrap. Using the gas oil for generating, the authorities realised abuse could be made by using it for road purposes. A regulation was taken out stating that gas oil could only be used for generating purposes in a vehicle that was immobilised. To get over this a separate tank had to be used and a red dye was put in the generating fuel tank, and if one was found, during one of the frequent spot checks, with red diesel in your tank while on the road, you were in trouble.

The fairground business was treated with some importance by the government during the War as a ration for timber, steel and other commodities required to keep in business was provided for maintenance of fairground equipment. They were able to get what the showpeople called a 'licence' for these commodities. The Guild Central Office in London handled these licenses. Despite this, one had to make do and mend and use all the ingenuity of the showman to keep going. New equipment could not be bought; generators were at a premium as all electric generators were required for war purposes.

During the War John Codona was in the throes of transferring the diesel power from steam; a period of transition. Showmen knew all about traction engines, but they had to learn about diesel engines. Things such as fuel system air locks, when the fuel was not getting the pump and one had to get the air out, caused problems. The knack of bleeding the system had to be acquired. Other new problems arose. One had to decide what was the best diesel engine to suit his purpose. It became clear that the Gardener Engine was ideal. It was originally designed as a stationary engine, and of course the main purpose of an engine in fairground use is to generate power rather than to transport goods on the road.

The showpeople had to find places to acquire lorries that were second hand but had some life left in them. John Codona and others got help in that direction from a firm at Linlithgow (a firm of hauliers); even in wartime they spent time helping the showmen.

Food rationing applied to the showpeople the same as everyone else, but at some places they may have got over the odds as they were only in town for a short while and would not be continually coming back expecting more.

The Codonas experienced one or two air raids in Glasgow, which was rather alarming, but there were no injuries to the family or their equipment.

By the end of the War there were no new roundabouts, timber was in very short supply, and as timber was the basic material in all roundabouts this caused difficulties.

Lang Wheels of London designed and built a Dodgem track which was almost completely built of metal – metal uprights and top structure – the only place they had timber was under the floor plates and the buffer round the sides. It was very hot and heavy and not the easiest of rides to maintain, but John Codona had one built. Supercar later did a better job of building an alloy Dodgem which was far lighter and easier to handle. When the iron Dodgem was ordered, Billy and Alfred were pretty much in charge of JCPF.

John was still alive; he had suffered a heart attack in 1943 and from then on he was semi-retired, leaving Billy and Alfred to run the business.

Gordon was still a little young at that time; he had also been in the forces from the age of 18 until the end of the War. Gordon Codona was a staff sergeant in the Royal Engineers because of his ability in the training HQ in Ripon where he lectured on diesel engines and pumps, etcetera. He never went overseas, although he was on a draft to go. At the last minute he was recalled to Ripon, having got as far as the railway station. To do the job he had to have some outstanding ability.

Alfred Codona actually volunteered for the services. He registered aged 23 at Stirling, which meant that he would have certainly went into Argyle and Sutherland Highlanders. People were beginning to relate stories of the previous War [World War I], where the Argyles had served in the trenches. A friend of Alfred's had gone to the Argyles and had quickly found himself in France with the BEF [British Expeditionary Force] where he suffered the Normandy evacuation.

At that time Alfred volunteered for the RAF as that line appealed to him, although he realised that the evacuation may not be enough to get him far. At the medical he passed, but was warned if the army called him up first he would have to go. This was not encouraging, remembering his friends experiences with the BEF. It was at this point that the opportunity arose of the exempt occupation of threshing where the firm had three small Foden steam engines for Alfred to look after. The fact that the threshing business was slow at the same time as the fairground business was busiest, was an extra bonus for both parties; it meant the threshing people had one less wage to pay.

Towards the end of Alfred's second year threshing, he began to suffer with severe indigestion. [This was] possibly activated by the rich food that the farm people fed the threshing mill people, giving them huge helpings which, although being worked off, caused enough problems to take Alfred to see the doctor. [The doctor] sent him to Glasgow where a duodenal ulcer was diagnosed. [He] asked if Alfred was in the army; when he replied 'no', the doctor told him that the army would have nothing to do with him as long as he had his ulcer.

At this point Alfred decided to leave the threshing business. He had medical certificates, but thought that if the army came looking for him he would refer them to the medical man he had seen in Glasgow. By this time Alfred was married and had started a family on his own.

The traction engine was a 'brute of a thing'; many showmen were experienced in their workings. Tales were often told on the fairgrounds of accidents and engines falling through bridges, etcetera. Listening to these stories helped Alfred Codona on one occasion when he had a breakdown with one of the engines. Alfred was 18 years old at the time; he was with a chap who was also a showman, a little older than Alfred, and was employed by John Codona. Alfred came across him one day while driving a motor-lorry; the engine had stopped just out of Inverkeithing. Alfred stopped to find out what was wrong, George McArdle replied that a connecting rod on the engine had been bent. The connecting rod connects crankshaft to the piston and what could happen with traction engines is if you got water that had added chemicals or too much water, instead of steam rising in the cylinder, water would pass into the cylinder and water had a hydraulic action which when the piston went in it came to a dead stop and bent the connecting rod. Alfred had heard a story about someone who had had this happen on the road and they had taken the rod out and straightened it at the side of the road. George McArdle was afraid he was going to be stuck there for the night, but Alfred decided to take the connecting rod out. Traction engines had very little encasement apart from inside the boiler and the cylinders, so the connecting rod was accessible and one could remove the connecting rod in 15-20 minutes. They removed the rod and meanwhile one of Alfred's uncles passed by in his engine. Alfred stopped him and asked for a couple of shovels full of his bright fire. The engine was travelling and the fire would have been bright. Alfred now had two or three men round, he quickly got some bricks and put the fire in between them. He took the extension chimney from the canopy of the engine and placed it on top of the improvised furnace to give the fire draught. They had no bellows, but this got the fire bright. The connecting rod was then put into the fire, and while it was heating George was put to fetch one of the long blocks used for putting under the centre of the ride for packing, which was in good sturdy condition and level on the top. It was long enough for the connecting rod to slide on. Alfred instructed George to put the rod flat on the block, warning that if it was not straight it would twist and not fair on the crank and wouldn't be a cross head. It had to be straightened and kept true; one end was a fork where the cross head pin went through and the other was a straight block where the bearing went over. George McArdle said that it could not be done, but Alfred said, 'We won't do anything if we won't try'. Meanwhile the connecting rod was getting very hot in the fire. It had to be red hot. George was instructed to get the sledge hammer and told that he was only going to get one shot at straightening the rod. It could only be hit once by the hammer as any more would twist it off the true. Eventually everyone was apprehensively in position and George was instructed to hit his rod which was being held on the wooden block. It was almost perfect and after waiting some time for the metal to cool it was refitted and after one and a half hours they were all ready for the road again. This is an example of the ingenuity of the travelling showman. The engine in question was '*The*

Supremacy'. It was en route to Kirkcaldy Links Market and they managed to get there before dark and got the centre set before taking the connecting rod to local engineers who straightened it properly and put it back into the engine. The passing uncle was Nathaniel Codona in the engine, *'The Margaret'*, which was being driven by a big chap called Bert.

Alfred was very pleased with his emergency repair; he was only a young man but had listened to others stories of how [to] get by: 'This was how one got experience of how to table jobs because other peoples problems were always things that you could learn from.' The traction engine was a 'horrible, thing'. They used to drive the power from the traction engine, 'on the belt'.

One would have a man that could probably steer the engine and he was capable of keeping it steamed up while it was stationary, driving the engine while it was lighting. He kept the water in the boiler and the engine was governed so that he did not have to control anything. There were safety valves also so it was safe.

The biggest trouble was if you had someone new, 'driving the lights'; one didn't always get the same coal wherever you went, some coal 'clinkered' and got on to the fire bars. This was when the coal went to red-hot ash which settled, not letting air through.

Alfred Codona would be dressed in his Sunday best on Saturday night sitting in the pay booth taking the money for the machine. The engine would be pumping away at the side. He remembers one night like this in Aberdeen; at 8 o'clock he switched the machine on and he noticed the lights go down a little. He sent one of the attendants across to the engine to see what was up. He came back saying that the engine was 'not steaming'. There was no one else to sit in the pay box so he had to close the machine, lock the money away and go to the engine. The water in the boiler was away down at the bottom of the gauge. When it gets towards the bottom [there is] a fusible plug above the fireplace on a T.E. [traction engine] that is filled with lead and the water on the top usually keeps the lead from melting, but when the water gets down to this stage the fusible plug is not getting water on the top, the lead melts and the steam comes through and puts the fire out. This cannot happen as this means a big job. This is called dropping the plug. Anyway he opened the fire door and it is piled up with coal right to the door with coal 'all smoke and no steam, no heat!' Off came his good jacket [and] he asked for the shovel and shovelled the 'clinker' out of the fire by putting some of the fire to one side, disposing of the 'clinker', and [putting] some of the good fire back once the air is seen to be getting through. It was a big long shovel with a steel handle and he had to painstakingly take the fire out one shovel at a time and throw it out of the engine, then take it back again, then he had to sit and wait for the steam to get back up and, before leaving the man to drive the lights again, warn him not to put too much coal on the fire. He returned to the machine dirty and half an hour's premium time business lost.

At some country places that the Codonas visited, they could not get 'steam coal' (this was smokeless coal) and they had to use the kind of stuff used to burn in houses; this would cause lots of black smoke sooted up inside the tubes from the fire box through to where the chimney went up. Through the front end of an engine is the boiler which is a series of tubes which takes the smoke out in the smoke box then up the chimney. When the tubes get sooted, this impedes the draught (as in clinker). In order to remedy this, the door at the front of the smoke box opened. A long rod that has a 'tube brush' on it is pushed through the tubes. Again one usually has one's good clothes on and as the tube brush is pulled out all the soot comes out and covers you. For some reason the men were not allowed to do this; they were considered slow so therefore Alfred usually did this himself and again one went back to the pay box with the Sunday suit filthy.

These two stories would have happened while Alfred was travelling the Mont Blanc after Arthur Pepper had left Codona's and Alfred had this kind of job to do as well as drive the engine on the road [the *Fearless*].

Alfred would have been about 24 and now quite experienced

by the time that the Second World War broke. All of a sudden the diesel engine came along, the first diesel engine that John Codona had had a generating set built by Fowler of Leeds. This was a portable set that could drive a couple of machines. It was a big diesel engine that was put on one of the trucks for transportation; it only needed starting up and away it went and one could forget about it.

The T.E. needed coal, water taken to it, you had to have spare water tanks to keep you going for the day, depending on the water supply you had on the fairground. 'Water Dandys' used to be used which were basically two wheels with a barrel on it. You had a man called 'The Dandy Man' who would go to the well, fill it up, take it back to the engine, fill the tanks in the engine, and at a big fair like Kirkcaldy or Glasgow Green there might have been one or two stand pipe taps there and all of the Dandy Men would be queuing up and fighting with one another to get to the tap for water. They then had to pull the dandy through the crowded fairground. After the pubs came out at night they would receive all sorts of abuse while doing this, trying to delay and sabotage their route back to the engine. The coming of diesel put a stop to this.

The Wilmot family initially used an old petrol engine. Alfred Codona caught on this and put a generator under the back of one of their petrol lorries. The petrol engine was governed, but the diesel engine opened up new possibilities and life changed completely. A lot of work was got rid of when the steam engines were got rid of; it was hard work getting power and propulsion from a steam engine.

The most difficult journeys by steam engine were from places where one set off with a poor quality of coal. The art of getting a traction engine 'along the road' was to keep the water and the steam up. The driving was elementary, levers were pulled and the type of care given to driving any vehicle was taken. One had to be careful on steep inclines, one had to know the lower gear in order to negotiate steep hills both up and down. When going down hill one had also to make sure that there was plenty water in the boiler in order not to expose the lead fusible plug when the water shifted. Another thing one had to do on some of the well known very steep hills was to take the trailers down one at a time in order that control of the loads could be maintained and so that the wheels didn't lose their traction on wet or greasy roads. It was a far different thing from sitting in the cab of a lorry with your feet on the pedals. There were various pieces of road where it was not at all easy to drive a traction engine. The road between Hawick and Selkirk was not good, being very hilly. Forfar to Dundee in days of old was also very bad, particularly at Powrie Brae as you go into Dundee where there were twists and bends, and when towing three trailers and waiting for traffic, coupled with the fact that one could not keep into the side of the road. One had to keep the engine out to make sure that the final trailer did not end up in the ditch. The driver had to direct the steersman to keep a good road position. If one could get on to the road and average between six or seven miles per hour, that's including stoppages for water, you were getting along well. Every ten miles or so one would need to stop for water, but the engine itself could achieve ten, or if a Burrell, twelve miles per hour, but with 20 minutes needed to stop and fill the water tank at a burn or something like that it all took time. If you could average covering six miles in an hour you were getting along fine.

If you set out with a poor quality of coal, then every time you stopped for water you would have to clean the fire and take 'clinkers' out. Sometimes the coal would not provide a lot of heat, making it difficult to get a good head of steam, especially if it was a heavy road like the road from Aberdeen to Inverness, as one was just out of Aberdeen and one had to negotiate the Tyrebagger hill at Blackburn which was a good long climb before falling ground, then a big pull out of Huntly before going down into Keith. These are 'sore' roads where you have maybe two miles of climbing, although not too steep it was heavy going and would use steam and water. In order to ensure good coal the Codonas would send word ahead to the suppliers.

The suppliers would get to know when the fair was coming

and order in coal for them. Fife had a lot of good coal. 'Cowie Joe' was good, it came from the pit at Cowie. Blairhall had a good pit, producing good steam coal, which like all good steam coal glistened, didn't produce a lot of smoke, didn't silt the tubes up and burned to almost nothing, leaving minimal ash, and didn't clinker. When the War started the quality of coal available to the showmen declined. Half of it became ash, making it liable to clinker.

Many of the old watering stops are not available now with the construction of new roads. If one had not been on a road before, they would contact another showman that had in order to find out the watering stops. When Alfred travels nowadays he often thinks of picking up water at places that he passes. From Aberdeen heading for Glasgow, the first watering stop was nine miles out of Aberdeen at Cammachamore; that would take you through Stonehaven, when you would get up out of the town and stop beside the railway four miles from Laurencekirk. Taranty at Brechin was another water lift, taking you through Forfar just past Glamis where at each side of the road were two ponds where more water could be obtained. One had to be careful that the pipe that sucked up the water did not get right to the bottom of the pond or burn. One way of doing this was to take the shovel from the engine and lay it gently under the end of the pipe so as not to stir up silt and therefore provide a lift of clean water. In some places it was possible to get dirty water and this would cause the engine to prime as the water would get into the cylinder causing a hydraulic effect giving a risk of the connecting rod bending or even breaking. The next stop for water after Glamis was through Couper Angus on a piece of straight road which was a good place to lift water, then going into Perth through Burreltown. The lifting places were known more by sight than by name. Sometimes there were no watering places by the side of the road and one would have to uncouple the engine and take it up a farm road. When short of water it would not be the only time that Alfred has driven an engine into a farmyard with steam blowing everywhere out of the exhaust and put the pipe in the trough and incurred the wrath of the farmer. They soon settled when told that if the engine did not get water it would explode!

The Fowler diesel generator was an orthodox six-cylinder diesel engine with a generator on the end of it. It was a great innovation. The Codonas did not know much about diesel at first and worried about what to do if anything went wrong as they were used to the open construction of steam engines and the diesel engines workings were totally encased. They had to learn with experience of things going wrong and trying to fix it for themselves. Listening to others' experiences helped, asking contractors, garages, building up knowledge with experience.

The Codona family had many good friends in the contracting world they could go to for advice. Callanders of Forfar, William and Alec, were agents for Gardener engine parts and knew Alfred well – they were most helpful. Their mechanics were also helpful.

Eventually a similar expertise was gained in diesels to that of steam power. They could do most jobs themselves, although understandably experts were still called in for major jobs like line boring cylinders. Forbes in Aberdeen did a lot of work not only for the Codonas, but for the whole of the North of Scotland.

By the end of the War John Codona's Pleasure Fairs [JCPF] was fully equipped with diesel engined vehicles [and had dispensed with] steam entirely.

Direct shaft drive was the chosen source of generating power by JCPF by that time, having come along with diesel power. They learned how to adapt all the different lorries for this, adapting driving shafts; each make of lorry had a different driving system of connecting shafts up. Basically the shaft was uncoupled from the back end of the lorry and lifted it up to another shaft that went into the generator; it was a simple as that but you had to avoid various pipes and tubes and cross members, etcetera.

JCPF usually had two vehicles on a ride and both had generators so in the event of a breakdown minimal time would be lost in coupling up the spare lorry for generating. They did have breakdowns including bearings going, crankshafts breaking and various things that could not be mended immediately but causing little inconvenience. The lorries were usually parked side by side. Sometimes both lorries would generate, one driving the ride, the other driving the lighting.

In the event of a breakdown a lot of the lighting could be shut down in order for the bulk of the power to be used to drive the machine.

The diesel were very reliable, they were kept well serviced; the Codonas knew when they had to be reconditioned and it was done. In general they were very hard-wearing with a lot of life in them. JCPF carried a stock of spares for them, including injectors, filters, fuel pumps, etc. Tyres actually caused more problems. New tyres could never really be justified on the fairground because the fair lorries didn't do sufficient mileage on the road to justify the expense of a brand new tyre. A second-hand one that was sound in the casing would be enough to keep going because they didn't do enough miles to wear the tread out. They did have the odd puncture. Regulations changed and you could not have a tyre that had any blemish or was low in tread. When the showmen had to comply with these regulations much of their trouble with tyres disappeared.

When one bought a second-hand lorry it usually had good tyres on it as the contractor would keep his vehicles well 'shoed'. If this was the case, the tyres would do the showmen for years who only did around 1200 miles per year. JCPF once pulled on to the ground in Aberdeen [and] a representative from the Old Webster Tyre Company called and asked for Alfred, enquiring as to who supplied JCPF with tyres. He looked around at the large amount of lorries thinking he was on to a bean feast.

On being told that tyres usually came from scrapyards as the lorries only did 1200 miles per year, his face immediately fell as he realised that they weren't covering enough miles to wear tyres out. Alfred immediately asked him if he had good second-hand tyres for sale!

John Codona died in 1948, Billy Codona died in 1952 and Alfred at 37 was running JCPF.

Alfred's wife Emily was in the side-show business; her maiden name was Freeman. Her father had a model colliery business which Alfred remembers as a child. Another similar show was travelled in the north of Scotland by the Phelps family. The show consisted of a working model with many moving parts, picks, shovels, pulleys, winches, hoists and lamps. They moved on to have various other illusions and side-show attractions. They travelled widely as most side-show people did, as once people had seen the show they did not go back to see the same thing; so they travelled the whole country including England and after ten or so years would have to change their attraction. Alfred and Emily met when they were on the same fairground but their courtship lasted eight years because they were so far apart most of the time. The Freemans would be in England when the Codonas were in the North of Scotland, so opportunities for courting were few and far between. They were married in Glasgow in April 1941; the Freeman's were in London when the War started and as the bombing became worse moved back up to Scotland. They arrived back in Glasgow in the backend of 1940 and it was then that the wedding was arranged for April 1941.

John Codona died in the house at Riddrie in 1948. He had the house done up when he moved in, in 1943; latterly he was pretty much confined to Glasgow, he couldn't get about much because of his heart condition. For the last six years of his life he was not very well. He was 56 when he had his first heart attack.

In 1960 Gordon Codona saw the opportunity of a place at Redcar; he wasn't thinking entirely of himself as he discussed the opportunity of getting established on a static site. He negotiated it entirely for himself which was unusual as Alfred had previously seen to this side of things for JCPF. But Alfred was delighted for him to have a go at Redcar on his own, as their families were growing up and as this happens complications arise – it had happened with the Codona brothers in the previous generation – so Gordon went to Redcar on his own. The JCPF equipment was split up and Gordon left JCPF in 1960, leaving Alfred with the travelling business. Alfred gave Gordon the Jets to Redcar for his first year as an added attraction for him, coming back to Alfred at the end of August. Alfred still had the Dodgem and Speedway.

From 1946 JCPF had operated something, sometimes two or three rides in the Kelvin Hall each winter. It was let under competitive offer basis.

All of the rides used to run off a current of 110V DC which was a safe current. If one put their hand on the terminals only a slight shock was received. Of course, the fair generators produced 110V DC. When they went to the Kelvin Hall they went on to the town power. Then a motor was used which was 440V 3 phrase. The motor was then coupled on to a 110 V generator. This method was also used at Arbroath when the Jets went there as they too came off town power.

In 1963 the Cyclone Twist was purchased to add to the Supercar Dodgem and Jets and 1962 Maxwell Waltzer. In 1966 the ex-White's Motorcycle Speedway was acquired from Jackie Hammond. In 1968 the Old Aberdeen Amusement Park was put on to a year lease because the town wanted to improve it. JCPF answered the city's advert and were eventually successful in acquiring the let, subject to them putting up the buildings, and JCPF eventually settled in Aberdeen opening in 1970. They did go back to the Kelvin Hall until 1972 before finding out that they had enough to do in Aberdeen without this annual trek down to Glasgow. It got to the stage that they didn't really have the right equipment for moving. They became static and confined the bulk of their activity to the Aberdeen park extending it twice since taking over.

JCPF presented their Jets at Nottingham Goose Fair on one occasion. They were given the opportunity of occupying one of John Farran's sites there. The Jets did very well, too well actually as the following year John Farran's son-in-law Charles Thurston acquired a set of Lang Wheels Jets and that was the end of JCPF going to Nottingham on Farran's ground.

JCPF were given Jack Hoadley's position at Newcastle along with the Jets; they also had his position at Hull until Hoadleys acquired the first Hall and Fowlie Twist. He had the first one to appear in Britain and wanted his position at Hull back.

Alfred took the Jets to Hull, while Paddy travelled the Dodgem in Scotland and John Codona was with the firm by this time after selling the Moon Rocket. John managed the travelling fairgrounds once Alfred settled in Aberdeen.

Alfred Codona's rules for running a good fair include to remember that showmen are fickle people and if you show them any weakness they will take advantage. They know their rights and, being in competition with one another, like to try and fiddle an advantage for themselves and, if the lessee can, control that in a firm, fair manner with the object in mind of trying to present an attractive fair as possible.

The lessee should strive to avoid untidiness by not having spare vehicles and caravans higgledy-piggledy lying around as though they had fallen from the sky, but try to set them in some sort of order. It wasn't always easy to get people to comply as many tried excuses; this requires firmness. Usually this approach eventually led to compliance. When the showmen accepted that they had to do things Alfred's way then he was able to present a good fair. He eventually got the name of 'If he says it, that's it!', and he found out that was the only way to do it. He had to have his mind made up exactly what he wanted to do before going out to set a fair and not let any arguments that would arise distract him from this. One has to know what you are doing for a start.

Alfred was never happy with the thought of leaving the stress of running travelling fairs to his sons; he managed to do it, but being at the mercy of other showmen who are looking to live and to live well being achieved by fair means or foul in some cases, is not a good heritage to leave to one's family … it is possibly one of the reasons that the JCPF Ltd settled in Aberdeen.

Alfred was also involved in the Showmen's Guild regulations and was well versed in their rules and regulations, therefore it was not easy for someone to pull the wool over his eyes because he knew more than them. 'At the same time one has to be fair and see the other fellow's point of view' … that is also important.

CODONA FAMILY TREE

THIS partial tree (pages 256-57) connects those mentioned in the book born before 1914. Follow the vertical line going from below a name to trace the history of his marriages(s) and children in chronological order. A horizontal line going to the right from this vertical indicates a child, and = indicates a marriage (note: in cases like William [1] a marriage may be followed by children, then another marriage and more children). To find a mother and father, follow the horizontal line to the left and take the vertical up. The numbers in square brackets indicate the order in which the named individual appears in the text.

Frank [1] (c1760-d. c1836/7 or 1849 – see note 19)
= married Helen Lamb (c1765-1846) before 1802?
— Frank [2] (c1790-1859)
— William [1] (c1804-77)
  = married Maria Charlton in 1826
  — William [2] (c1840-84)
    = married Mary Kerr/Carr in 1862
    — William [3] (1863-1931)
      = married Mary Ann Kennedy in 1879
      — Catherine (c1880-1951)
        = married Albert Biddall (c1894-1947) in 1924
      — Beatrice (c1882-1955)
      — William [5] (1884-1948)
      — John [4] (1886-1948)
        = married Florence May Broughton
      — Frank [5] (1890-1936)
      — Nathaniel (1892-1949)
      — Rebecca (1901-?)
        = married Harry Paulo
    — Frank [4] (1870-1938)
      = married Phoebe O'Brian before 1891
      — Hannah
    — Thomas (1876-1944)
    — John [2] (c1883)
      = married Selina Pinder (b. 1889) in 1909
  = married Margaret McKellar (c1826-99) in 1849
  — Henry [1] (1859-1923)
    = married Helen Barr in 1878 (d. 1893)
    — William [4] (b. 1880)
    — Henry [2] (b. 1884)
      = married Laura Caddick (b. c1890) in 1908
    = married Martha Freeman in 1894
    — John [3] (1895-1964)
  — Frank [3] (c1866-1927)
    = married Janet McKelvie in 1887
— John [1] (see below)

John [1] (c1806-84, son of Frank [1] see above)
(see Appendix 1)
 = probably married Elizabeth Hart in 1830
── Harry
      = married Amelia Lawrence before 1863
      ── Harriette (c1871-c1892)
          = married Frank Brown in 1891
      = married Lizzie Marcellus in 1873
── William (1844-73)
      = married Adelaide (b. c1846) by 1871
      └──Eduardo Codona (1859-1934)
── Harriet (1848- ?)
      = married Francisco Rizarelli in 1865
 = married Louisa Lightfoot (c1825-d. after 1891)
          before 1853
 └── Elijah (b. c1853)

NOTES TO CHAPTERS

1. Such reports of the fair were an annual staple of the Glasgow press, part of a mid-nineteenth century journalistic trend for picaresque accounts of popular entertainments. The Scottish fairs also featured in poems, chapbooks, ballads, prints, paintings and essays (see Morris 1999, 89-109). *Glasgow Constitutional*, 16 July 1836. The original 'Hottentot Venus' was South African showgirl Saartjie Baartman who died in 1815.

2. *Glasgow Constitutional*, 16 July 1836. The article continues: 'In this same booth we observe another of the fair familiar faces – that of Hughie Watson. Hughie is connected with our boyish recollections too. We have seen him play Mouse in the Gentle Shepherd fifteen years ago. We laughed much heartier then ever we shall do at any such thing again. ... The "wild beasts" we see, have honoured us at this time with a visit. The collection of rare animals is at all times a treat and we are happy to see so many young Masters and Misses entering this set of booths. ... There is the usual number of giants and giantesses, fat boys, dwarfs, pigs, &c. &c., that generally visit us during the Fair. Those who are inclined to see these things, should not expect too much for their money. But shall we visit any of them? If we do not enter one, at least, it would be ungracious. If we could manage to get into any one by a back entrance, we would not hesitate a moment. Ah, here is one; and we have been fortunate – just in time to see the performance commenced. ...'

3. Telephone interview with Jim McArdle (Snr), 4 July 2008. Jack House, 'Codona; the royal family of the fairground', two-part feature in the *Evening News*, 1 and 2 December 1954.

4. The interviewees are direct descendants of William Codona [3] and a grand-daughter of his brother Frank.

5. Sanger, 1926, chs IX-X.

6. For his analysis of how this theme appears in interviews with Australian showpeople, see Danaher, 2001, 77-85.

7. For the sense of difference felt by Irish tinkers, see Court, 1985, 1-8. For theatre performers, my thinking was shaped by having interviewed a number of variety theatre performers, in particular Dave Hunter, who stressed camaraderie amongst 'pros', but also the need for 'closeness' with his audiences (see Bruce, 1996). All three groups have strong traditions of using distinct varieties of narrative for passing on knowledge, maintaining group identity and negotiating problems. For analysis of this in the case of non-show travellers, see Shaw, 2007, 28-48. His conclusions could very largely apply to the showground tradition.

8. Dancer John Cardownie's successful music hall career lasted more than 20 years. 'Ventriloquist, Illusionist, Humourist, Guide, Stage Manager' Louis Cardoni (probably the son of circus equestrians William and Adelaide Codona) had a short career. In *The Era*, 11 January 1896, he advertised for work in his 'Twentieth week of Tour with Kingston Diorama'. He had left the business by the time he emigrated to Canada in the early 1900s.

9. Telephone conversation with Jim McArdle (Snr), 2 July 2008, and typescript account 'A Showman's contribution to the war effort', made by his son Jim (Jnr). Michael McArdle went on to build up his business, taking over as lessee in mining towns like Whitburn and Fauldhouse around Edinburgh. These had been Nathaniel Codona's pitches before the War, but according to Jim he gave these up because they were too rough: the Codonas had become too upper class; Michael had worked down the mines and could 'communicate with all classes'.

10. *Glasgow Constitutional*, 15 July 1837. See note 19 for an alternative date of death for this Frank Codona.

11. '"Old Malabar" (By an old play-goer)', *North British Daily Mail*, c1871, an interview with showman and juggler Patrick Feeney pasted into a Mitchell Library Glasgow cuttings book, 'The dark side of Glasgow', 17-19; 'Baby Farming', cuttings from the *North British Daily Mail,* December 1870 to August 1871, G914.443DAR (445033). The Bartley Minch he mentions

apparently joined forces with Mr Cardona at one Glasgow Fair around this time; according to Robert Alison's *The Anecdotage of Glasgow*, 'Minch and Cardona had a monopoly of the Olympic', 1892, book IV. The earliest evidence of the familiar Punch and Judy glove-puppets appearing on the streets of London is for 1785. For Punch in Glasgow, see MacGilp, 2008, 30-2. For the debated connection between the Italian Pulcinella and British Punch puppet traditions, see Byrom, 1983 and the more recent summary in Speaight, 1995, pp 200-6. See Appendix 1 for a biography of Italian Pulcinella performer Francesco Cardoni.

12. 'Most Beautiful girl with the circus', *The Fort Wayne Sentinel [Indiana]*, 8 July 1910 – a promotional article for the appearance of 'La Belle Victoria' with the Barnum and Bailey Circus.

13. See Appendix 1 for William and Adelaide Codona taking the name Cardoni and variants. *The Winnipeg Free Press*, 1 December 1951, has this filler: 'Iron-jawed Jesus Cordona, a circus aerialist, lost three front teeth a week ago. Now he's unemployed. Cordona, 20, earned his living by hanging from a trapeze by his teeth. He does an act with his sister Ramona, and his brother Francisco.' I have been unable to find out more about these Cordonas. 'Cardoni's Fantoccini' are noted in London in the 1850s (see below).

14. Whiteley, 1981, 22.

15. Modignani and Mantovani, 2002, 74 gives the family tree of the Cardona family. See Appendix 1 for Francesco Cardoni. Any shared ancestry is unknown, but both had roots in Naples where Cardoni was the name of one of several powerful Spanish landowning families that had settled in Naples during the sixteenth and seventeenth centuries when it was under Spanish rule (see Giannone, 1742, 738). Perhaps this was the source of the confusion over Spanish or Italian origins.

16. These are for the 1877 marriage of John Cardona, son of John Codona [1], whose name is also given as Cardona on this document; also, the 1893 birth certificate of James Johnstone Cardona and the 1899 death certificate of Mary Kerr/Carr given as wife of William Cardona.

17. The first Frank's grandson William has both Codona and Cardownie (or possibly Cardowna) on his 1884 death certificate and Cardownie is the name given on his great-grandson William's birth certificate. According to Mrs Janet Cardownie, who heard the story by chance from a work colleague, the name Cardownie was formally adopted by her husband's ancestors – either Frank [3] or William [2] – after a family row. It seems to have been only this Frank's descendants, who were not showpeople, who kept to this name in Scotland, and it may have something to do with the fact that having been listed as an adolescent in the 1881 census as a comedian, by the time of his marriage in 1887 he was an ostler, subsequently served in the army, and ended his career as a hawker. His 1927 death certificate gives both names: Codona and Cardownie. See below, however, for performing Cardownies in the United States.

18. *Glasgow Constitutional*, 14 July 1838. 'Our old friends, Mumford and Codoni' are also noted four years later (*Glasgow Constitutional*, 13 July 1842).

19. William [3] in 'Death of William Codona at Tranent', *Edinburgh Evening News*, 11 August 1931, and John [3] in 'One-man band's Farewell', *Edinburgh Evening News*, 30 October 1946. Family traditions are unreliable and John does talk of himself elsewhere as a great-grandson, but it seems that there were two Franks: a great-great grandfather who died c1837 as mentioned above, and the Francis Cardownie who died in 1859 being the great-grandfather. However, the 1841 Birmingham census has an entry for showman Francis Codony, aged 81, and Leonora – perhaps a variant of Helen – Codony, aged 76, both born overseas. This Francis died in Birmingham in 1849. It may be that he was the well-known figure described in the *Glasgow Constitutional*, and a disappearance down south meant he was taken to have died. Alternatively, he could have been the father of Frank [1], feasible if he was indeed around 100 years old when he died around 1837. Pat Feeney's statement in 1871 that two of the sons of the Cardoni who died in c1837 (or 1849) were alive and one was dead, exactly fits the death certificates of Francis (c1790-1859), William

(c1802-77) and John (c1806-84), suggesting three brothers.

20. For Italian migration, see Sponza, 1988, especially 38-40, 62-74 and ch. 6, 163-94. For the highly organised world of the street musicians, see Zucchi, 1999.

21. For Italian peripatetic entertainers from the sixteenth to eighteenth centuries, see 'Carnival and Popular Entertainers' in Richards and Richards, 1990, 15-31. As they note, this is a field 'comparatively little examined by theatre historians, first because it has apparently left only few and scattered traces, and second because theatre history has traditionally been concerned much more with... the "great" tradition ...', 16. For the prolific Italian puppet tradition, see Byrom, 1983. For Millar and Purvis, see MacGilp, 2008.

22. The *Edinburgh Advertiser* for 12 September 1786 has two adverts, the first for 'the last week of performing horsemanship ... on one two and three horses at the circular riding school in Dr Hope's Park, adjoining the Physical Gardens, Leith Walk, by nine capital performers not to be equalled in Europe, from Mr Jones Equestrian Amphitheatre, London, under the direction of Mr Parker'. Two columns away, on the same page, more circus-style entertainment is offered by a company probably linked with Jones and Parker, since they were involved at various points with the brother of one of the performers, Mr Rickets the clown. Billed as 'Les Varietes Amusantes' at the back of the Black Bull Inn, Pleasance, the 'great variety of new performances ... under the inspection of Monsieur Dubois' includes 'the much admired Ombres Impalpable' (probably shadow puppets), the balloon song by Mons. Dubois, slack rope vaulting, the peasant of the Alps with the wooden shoe dance and egg hornpipe, rope-dancing by the celebrated 'Little Little Devil' performing new feats on the rope with a table and chair, as well as 'the child of promise, only 17 months old', Mr Ricketts the clown, and a pantomime.

23. Speaight, 1990, 129-41.

24. Tobin, 1968, 46-54

25. Highfill, Burnin and Langham, 1993.

26. The certificate for the marriage on 12 May 1890 of Frank Brown and Enriqueta Codona gives her parents as Enrique

Codona and Amelia Lawrence (my thanks to César Ortega for this). This Enrique was Harry Codona and details of his and his wife Amelia's career, as well as the Codona-Brown connection in North America, are given below. See also 'Marriages celebrated at St John's church, Buenos Aires, 1888-1900', 12 March 1890, which includes Frank Brown, 31, born England, marrying Harriette Codona, 19, born USA (this can be found at <http://www.argbrit.org>). She was described as an 'outstanding' artist in an acrobatic show directed by her husband in Argentina (see Perez Calvo, 2007, 115).

27. *Glasgow Free Press*, 16 July 1823. Mr Brown was probably the 'equestrian and equilibrist' noted in John Turner, 1995, 15. 'Codoni' is billed again with J. Brown, his wife and also a P. Brown at his Olympic Circus for the fair of 1826 in 'a commodious New Circus, which will be fitted up with unusual . elegance and splendour' at the foot of the Saltmarket (*Glasgow Herald*, 7 July 1826). Members of Brown's company appear to have been in Scotland in 1817; two Mr Brown's had appeared billed as 'clown to the rope' and 'principal Rider at Astley's Amphitheatre', alongside 'Mr Wilson on tightrope' in a circus performance in Edinburgh's Pantheon Theatre in 1817 (*Caledonian Mercury*, 20 October 1817).

28. The register of baptisms, marriages and deaths for Pittenweem (St John's) Episcopal Church (1799-1854). The early records for Codonas in Scotland are puzzling: first is the old parish record (OPR) for the marriage of Joan Codone to David Gilchrist in Edinburgh, 30 June 1823, in which the father is described as a deceased cabinetmaker; then a month later comes the OPR for Francis Codone marrying Elizabeth Buchanan in Glasgow, 20 July 1823. Two years later, however, is the Pittenweem Baptism where the parents are given as Francis Cadone and Maria Charlton; and a year later the OPR for William Codony marrying Maria Charlton in Edinburgh, 15 March 1826. Maiden names are not generally given in episcopal records, suggesting that they were not married. Possibly two Franks [1 and 2] are involved in 1823 and 25. Similarly, two Maria Charltons may have been involved in the 1825 and 26 records. In the 1826 record Maria is listed as 'daughter of the

late Walter Charleton Performer Ireland' and several Charltons were involved in the circus over the century, including a later Maria Charlton said to have been 'one of the finest horse-women in Europe' (see John Turner, 1995).

29. 'The old fairs at Pittenweem', *East of Fife Record*, 10 August 1908.

30. See 'Anster Fair', stanzas LXII-LXVI, canto II, in Scott and Lindsay, 1989, 29-30.

31. *The Life of Billy Purvis the extraordinary, witty and comical showman*, Newcastle, 1981, (facsimile of 1875 edition), 93-5, quoting in turn from J. P. Robson, *Life and adventures of Billy Purvis*, 1849.

32. 'The Biters Bit', *The Edinburgh Advertiser*, 23 September 1828, taken from the *Glasgow Chronicle*. The story also appeared in the *Caledonian Mercury*, 18 September 1828, *The Belfast Newsletter*, 19 September 1828, and *The Morning Chronicle*, 19 September 1828.

33. 'Fraud on the public', *Paisley Advertiser*, 13 September 1828. The description of the fair appears in the issue of 16 August 1828.

34. For the history of the travelling fairgrounds, see Toulmin, 2003. For the Glasgow Fair, see Burnett, 1999, 31-7 and King, 1987, 157-62.

35. Miller, 1849, 85-6.

36. Anderson, 1910, 12, quoting from William Buchanan's *Glimpses of olden days in Aberdeen*, Aberdeen, 1870.

37. Chambers, 1967, 362.

38. 'A life-screed at Random' in Smith, 1869, 37.

39. *Glasgow Courier*, 11 July 1793.

40. *The Northern Looking Glass*, vol. 1, no. 4. A similar view (Fig. 5), less elegant in style and content, from the mid-1820s is reproduced in Oakley, 1967, 104. C. H. Robertson's print of Edinburgh Grassmarket at Hallowfair (*c*1820), by contrast, is filled with livestock, with just one booth in the background. Views of smaller fairs have few entertainers: David Wilkie's famous, albeit highly stylised, painting of Pitlessie Fair (1804) has a solitary peep-show proprietor and a fiddler. Alexander Carse's watercolours of Oldhamstock's Fair have in one case no

showmen, and in a later 1805 version just a couple of acrobats. The earlier can be found in Errington (1987), and the later is in Scottish paintings, watercolours and drawings offered for sale, Bourne Fine Art, July and August 2004, see Fig. 6.

41. The ancient town of Falkirk and a sketch of the cattle tryst, *Falkirk Herald*, 15 October 1867, 2.

42. 'All Hallow Fair', *The Scotsman*, 17 November 1827.

43. *Falkirk Herald*, 14 September 1867, 2. The issue of 8 November 1849 gives a similarly ambivalent account. It is quoted in Fraser, 1990, 239, which gives the wider context of popular recreation.

44. Scott, 1926, 131.

45. Hutchison, 1865, 286.

46. Chambers, 1967, 362; Anderson, 1910, 12.

47. *Glasgow Herald*, 15 July 1878.

48. For the decline of rural trysts and fairs, see Haldane, 1973, ch. 8 'The Trysts', 133-49, and Appendix F which is another lengthy contemporary description of Falkirk Tryst in 1849, 240-1, and Cameron, 1979, ch. XI 'Fairs and Trysts', 94-101. McCraw, 1994, describes the decline in the agricultural element of these fairs over the nineteenth century.

49. Irving, 1885, 267.

50. 'The shows at Vinegar Hill (By an old Foggie)', *Glasgow Evening News and Star*, 14 July 1887. The *Glasgow Herald*'s detailed account of Glasgow Fair in 1864 starts 'Glasgow Fair is evidently in the last stages of decline. It is afflicted with old age and poverty ...', 16 July 1864, reproduced in Worsdall, 1981, 136-41.

51. Leatham, 1924, 9. Edinburgh information gathered in Workers Educational Association (WEA): Oral history project, *Leisure and Entertainment*, 10 May 1990, copy in School of Scottish Studies, Edinburgh University, SS: SA1990.053-60.

52. The marriage of John Cadonie, 25 January 1830, in North Leith to Elizabeth Hart appears in the Old Parish Records and the 1841 christening of a John and Betsy Codona's daughter Betsy in Manchester is noted in the International Genealogical Index. This could have been a first marriage and child for John (who is given in later records as married to Louisa Lightfoot).

53. *North Wales Chronicle*, 23 November 1847.
54. 'Amusements of the mob' – 2nd article. In *Chambers Journal of popular literature, science and arts*, vol. VI, no. 148, 1 November 1856, 281-86.
55. For this and all other biographical information on William and Adelaide Codona, see Appendix 1.
56. Great London Circus bill for the 1879 tenting season, item C-128 in the Circus Poster Collection, Manuscripts Division. Department of Rare Books and Special Collections, Princeton University Library.
57. Quoted in the *Cedar Falls Gazette*, 12 September 1879.
58. The *Daily alta California*, 17 March 1855, 'One week later from the East', notes the arrival of the steamer *John L. Stephens* (a steamship that operated between San Francisco and Panama from 1853-60 for the Pacific Mail), with passengers including Messr Codona as well as two Austins (members of which family appear on subsequent circus bills with Mr Codona).
59. *Mountain Democrat* [Placerville, California], 14 April 1855. Their departure from San Francisco on the bark *Yankee* is noted in the *New York Times*, 31 October 1855. Of their stay in Honolulu, the *Sandwich Islands' Monthly Magazine*, comments: 'Lee & Marshall's National Circus have been performing during the season, and left for San Francisco with the New Year. Joy go with them! for they contributed in no small degree to the pleasantness of the shipping season. They seemed "to the manor born", and did not appear to "work for bread"; an idea that so often clogs the enjoyment of many a respectable performance.' ('Monthly Chit Chat – Amusements', January, 1856, 29). My thanks to Joan Hori, Hawaiian Collection University of Hawaii at Manoa Library for this and the next reference.
60. 'Reminiscences of Theatricals in Honolulu', in *Hawaiian Almanac and Annual* for 1881, 37.
61. The Honolulu bills are listed as items 2125-28 in Forbes, 2003, 151-3.
62. *Historical and Statistical Review of Sacramento*. In Colville's *Sacramento Directory*, vol VI, for the year commencing 1856, San Francisco, 1856, XII-XIII. Lee and Marshall's is advertised

in *Sacramento's Democratic State Daily Journal*, 21 February 1856, on 11 August 1856, and finally on 8 November 1856. My thanks to librarians of Sacramento Public Library for these references.

63. The Sacramento County Recorders office records the marriage on 17 August 1856 of Henry Codona to Emma Maria Freeth (aged under 18). No other details are given. My thanks to Cheryl Nelson for checking this. Details of Miss Freeth are from Stuart Thayer, *American Circus Anthology*: <http://www.circushistory.org/Thayer/Thayer.htm> which describes her as 'possibly the daughter, perhaps the sister of a West Coast showman of the 1870s'.

64. *Daily alta California*, 22 October 1855. Other mentions of the Caronis' appearances with Risley's Vatican at the Union Theatre are in the issues of 27-30 November.

65. Bills for Risley's Vatican subsequently appearing in Sacramento in November 1855 survive in Yale University Library. A show on November 21 has Signor Caroni 'in a scene entitled the four tables' and 'the tight rope by the Caroni family'.

66. For Franconi's Cirque National de Paris, see *Glasgow Herald*, 27 May 1850, *The Scotsman*, 13 July 1850 and 16 October 1850, and *Caledonian Mercury*, 21 October 1850; and for Henri Franconi with Pablo Fanque, see *The Scotsman*, 25 December 1852 and 1 January 1853. A connection between the Codonas is further suggested by the appearance in Scotland of Monsieur and Madame Tournaire in Batty's Circus in 1848 (*The Scotsman*, 23 December 1848). The Tournaires and Franconis were closely linked – Jacques Tournaire had been a pupil of Antoine, the first of the Franconi circus dynasty in France – and Tournaires appeared in Franconi's Hippodrome in New York in 1853. (For Jacques Tournaire and Antoine Franconi, see Disher, 1937, 172-3.) What makes this especially relevant is the fact that the Tournaire and Brown families (Frank Codona's employers in the 1820s) were also linked. According to her obituary, equestrienne Louisa Brown was taught under the Tournaire family, 'famous European acrobats and riders', and married Francoise Tournaire. She subsequently remarried William C. Brown and her only

daughter Millie Brown 'acquired a reputation as a rider' ('Mme Louisa Brown Dead; "Mother of the circus profession" and Famous Rider, expires in Philadelphia', *The New York Times*, 17 April 1901). That 'Codova, The Wizard of the World' who appeared in 1859 in a 'Mammoth Musical Festival and Fete Champetre' in Jones' Wood New York was in fact a Codona, is strongly indicated both by appearance on the same bill of 'Tournaire's Mammoth Circus' and also of 'Antonelli's Neapolitan Punch and Judy' and 'Jeronelli's Italian Fantoccini or Marionettes'. Both of these puppet genres were Codona specialities and the names Antonelli and Jeronelli were probably made up to give the impression of a bigger cast of performers – a common type of puff. A week later they are simply described as 'Two Fantoccinis and Punch and Judy (*The New York Times*, 16 July 1859 and 22 July 1859. Other adverts for this show appear throughout that July).

67. 'Circuses. The Tenting Season of '71', *New York Clipper*, 8 April 1871, quoted at:
<http://www.circushistory.org/clipper/Clipper1870-71.htm>
Also in 'Sheldenburger's European Menagerie and Grecian Circus' were riders Little Mary Brown and Madame Brown. 'Millie Tournor' [*sic* – probably Louisa Brown's daughter, see above] appeared with Amelia and Henry Codona in Ames' New Orleans Circus when it appeared in Blairsville, Pennsylvania (*Blairesville Press*, 10 September 1869).

68. See Slout, 2005. This website also includes references for Harry Codona appearing with his wife Amelia in 1871 from the *New York Clipper*. (Their son Dave was listed in 1868 as a pony rider and contortionist.) He remarried equestrienne Lizzie Marcellus on 9 July 1873.

69. *Blairesville Press* [Pennsylvania], 3 June 1869. A week later this journal gives prominent billing to Amelia and Harry in a large pictorial advert for Ames Circus.

70. *The Daily Herald* [Dubuque, Iowa], 17 June 1873.

71. Dan Rice had adopted Lizzie from her parents as a child in the 1860s. He was in Canada when he heard of the proposed marriage and disapproved either because he thought she was too young (she was still a teenager) or for other reasons and

sent a telegram trying to stop the marriage to no avail. For
more details, see Carlyon, 2005, 24-5.

72. For the Kansas appearance, see King, 2001, 342-3.

73. 'Death of an Aberdonian in America', *The Aberdeen Weekly
Journal*, 16 May 1900. See Appendix 1 for fuller biographical
information on J. W. Cardownie.

74. *The New York Times*, 26 June 1900.

75. *The Washington Post*, 29 July 1908, *Sacramento Bee*, 15 April
1905, *Hamilton Spectator*, 25 January 1907, and *The New
York Times*, 8 September 1907.

76. See the Internet Broadway database <http://www.ibdb.com/>
for details. The 1930 New York census also lists a Louise
Cardownie, aged 39, born in Scotland, father born in Italy,
mother born in Scotland, who immigrated in 1905 and is given
as an actress in vaudeville.

77. Impressive funeral service of the late Louis P. Codona. In *Peace
River Block News*, 1 October 1937. My thanks to Neil Staple
of *Obituary Daily Times* for this. Distorted confirmation of
the link between Adelaide and Eduardo comes in two other
sources. A report of Alfredo's death conflates his mother
and grandmother (Eduardo's mother): 'His mother, Adelaide
Codona, a Mexican, was a famous somersault rider in the early
days with P. T. Barnum. She was also one of the first women
to work on the flying trapeze' ('Shots end circus romance',
Chicago Daily Tribune, 31 July 1937). Alfredo's mother
Hortense Buisley was from a family of aerialists and his grandmother Adelaide was the equestrienne. Also, a description of
Harriet Codona has her as niece of William and Adelaide
Codona (and so cousin of Eduardo) and aunt of Alfredo, which
fits if 'aunt' is taken in the looser sense of a female cousin of
his father, Perez Calvo, 2007, 115.

78. *La Tribuna* [Buenos Aires], 18 March 1873. They appeared in
the Teatro Colon, where they were touring with a Japanese
company. The advert is for their benefit night: 'Los Tres
Mejicanos … Magníficos juegos, equilibros asombrosos. Los
beneficiados ejecutarán la gran prueba del Puente del Niágra –
Los tres trapecios …'. (My thanks to César Ortega for this
reference.)

79. I am grateful to Johanan Codona for this information about his family. Several Codonas from different branches of the family mentioned a connection with Alfredo, but were unclear about the exact relationship. One family story claims that the Codonas were 'a mixture of Mexican and Italian. The first known person was Alfredo Cardrona, who came from Mexico, he was a trapeze artiste, and somehow when he was in Scotland, the name got changed to Codona on the billing boards. He decided to stick with this name, hence all the Codonas about now. There were two brothers ... one of them married an Italian. He was at least four generations before my father in law'. (Information from Mrs Jany Codona supplied by private correspondence.) The story may have become disordered in transmission, compressing the link with the Mexican Codonas with an older tradition concerning the origins of the family name, but it makes the connection, and moreover the use of the name 'Cardrona' once again raises the Cardona/i link – the original Frank was, in fact, five generations before the father-in-law. In his article based on an interview with John Codona in 1964, John Gibson, *op. cit.*, refers to 'others in the family' being 'hailed in America as the world's greatest trapeze artists', suggesting that John Codona may have remembered what the relationship was.

80. A full appreciation of the Mexican Codona family can be found in Cárdenas, 2004, 211-8.

81. William 'Codone' [1] is given as 'acter' in an 1825 entry for his baby daughter Johana (see Canongate Parish Burials, 1820-51 at:
<http://www.scotsfind.org/canongateburials_access/canongateburials.pdf>
and again as a strolling actor in the 1851 census. For the combination of acting and other skills deployed by popular Italian performers, see Richards and Richards, 1990, 15-31.

82. *The Era*, 9 December 1849, and for the rest of the month, *The Newcastle Courant*, 28 April 1854, and *The Era*, 7 September 1879. The parish register for St Martin in the Fields has Harriet Wilson Codona, minor (given as the daughter of John Codona, Artist), marrying Francisco Risarelli Lujan, Artist, on 27 June

1865 (see Appendix 1 for Harriet); and on 26 July 1868, *The Era* carried an advert for the Risarellis looking for artists to go to America, 'for particulars ... care of Madame Codona ...'. In 1870 Adelaide Codona shared a billing with Mdlle Rizarelli in Adams' Circus (*The Era*, 13 November 1870) and Mdlle Codona appeared with the Rizarelli family in Madrid in 1882 (*La Illustracion Espanola y Americana*, num. xxvi, 15 July 1883, 19).

83. *The Scotsman*, Wednesday 19 July 1843; 'Glasgow Fair' (from the *Glasgow Citizen* of Saturday).

84. McIsaac, 1910, no. 4.

85. For a full account of showmen and the marionette theatre, see McCormick, 2004.

86. *Glasgow Herald*, 13 July 1849. Already in 1845 the report of the fair observed that 'the great strength of the fair lies in the theatrical department, which has entirely superseded dear old Punch and Judy, the ground and lofty tumbling, and tight rope feats of other days' (18 July 1845). Similar sentiment is repeated in the report of 18 July 1851, which again mentions Codona as representative of the old guard and gives a lengthy description of a Penny theatre audience. For Penny theatres, see also King, 1987, 153-7 and Bell, 1998, 157-61.

87. 'Unlicenced Penny theatres', *Glasgow Herald*, 20 April 1846.

88. 'Police Court – Calvert's theatre', *Glasgow Herald*, 23 February 1849.

89. *The Professional Gazette and Advertiser*, 393, 1 January 1898.

90. Gilchrist, n.d., 17-8.

91. Carragher, 1906, 55.

92. Will Fyffe, in an interview with Wanda Dunbar, 'My memories of the geggies', *Glasgow Eastern Standard*, 4 March 1944.

93. J. Wilson McLaren, 'Show folks in the Capital', *Edinburgh Evening News*, 21 March 1936.

94. House, 1954.

95. 'Some Reminiscences of Springburn 40-50 Years Ago', typescript presented to the Mitchell Library by Charles Forsyth in September 1940, 18-19.

96. 'One-man Band's Farewell', *Edinburgh Evening News*, 30 October 1946.

97. Many thanks to Josephine Fox for information collected from her mother, Sarah Massar O'lone (*née* Johnston). Sarah's mother was Jessie Johnston (*née* Codona *c*1900-*c*1973), the daughter of William [4] and Catherine (Kate, *née* McBride). Among Sarah's other memories of William are that he referred to money as 'Denero' (a cant term) and the family belief that the Codonas came from Italy. Another story was that Buffalo Bill Cody came over and left a gift of two pearl-handled guns to William. Other family members included 'Tommy who boxed the pony' and 'the Inventor'. According to Josephine he was 'the grandfather of my related cousin who shares the same grandparents as we do. ... Our (cousin and I) grandparents were both sisters and brothers. Two Codona daughters married two Johnston sons and one Codona son married one Johnston daughter. All from the same two families. It is very confusing.' The Vinegar Hill site has gone, but descendants of this branch of the family still live in the east end of Glasgow.

98. Information supplied by Joy Codona. Her husband Alfred's family was based in East Lothian from the 1930s-50s and moved to Lanarkshire in the 1960s by which time they had left the shows. The memories of Kathleen Pinder, one of the 'Pinder Sisters', have been recorded for the National Sound Archive ('Oral History of the Circus', F10140-F10141), and are a valuable record of how the circus and fairground worlds continued to overlap until World War II.

99. 'One-Man Band's Farewell', *Edinburgh Evening News*, 30 October 1944. For the use of pan-pipes by Punch and Judy performers, see Speaight, 1990, 349, dating the arrival of the pan-pipes in England to 1803. Leach, 1985 has numerous illustrations of drum and pan-pipe-playing musicians accompanying shows.

100. Edinburgh, Museum of Childhood.

101. John Gibson, 'One man's music will be heard no more', *Edinburgh Evening News*, 16 January 1964; see also 'One man tradition fades out', *Daily Express*, 16 January 1964.

102. According to John Gibson (see above), John Codona's son Tom was carrying on the family tradition, but I have found no report of this after his father's death. The *Edinburgh Evening*

News, 26 March 1957, carries a reply to a query about John Codona, noting 'his son also plays the pipes and drum and makes the occasional appearance in the street'. A further report of John Codona's ill-health of 28 January 1959 states that 'his son has been seen doing the rounds occasionally'.

103. See Quennell, 1969, 445-534, for the world of the small-scale showmen, notably Punch, the Fantoccini Man, Acrobat or Street-posturer, and The Penny-gaff Clown.

104. Private e-mail.

105. My thanks to Mary Buisson for letting me quote from her unpublished memoir of life on Ann Street.

106. Edinburgh, Museum of Childhood.

107. 'The late Mr Frank Codona', *The World's Fair*, 6 August 1938.

108. Gordon Codona remembered the lines: 'Rumbo Jumbo I am my father's ghosto / Fall dideely hi doh fall dideely day' being recited in the show.

109. Anonymous and undated typescript in the family collection. Pepper's ghost refers to the originator of this polished-glass-based illusion, Professor John Henry Pepper. See 'Biddall's Ghost', ch. 5 in Brown, 2001, 52-67, for a detailed and well-illustrated account of 'Phantospectra Biddalls Ghosto-dramas' or Biddall's ghost show which travelled Scotland at the end of the nineteenth century. (Tommy Codona, as mentioned, worked for the Biddall family.) This book is a detailed history of the Freeman-Biddall family, who were active in Scotland, were connected by at least two marriages with Codonas, and whose history has many parallels with that of the Codonas.

110. J. Wilson McLaren, 'Show folks in the Capital', *Edinburgh Evening News*, 21 March 1936. The writer may only mean 'like the late Wilson Barret', but according to one of William Codona's great-grandsons, Jim McArdle, a group of his relatives met Barret's actor son after a performance and were told that his father knew William Codona well. Actor manager Wilson Barret (1846-1904) made a fortune with his play 'The Sign of the Cross', first produced in 1895, in which he played Marcus Superbus.

111. Scrivens and Smith, 1999, 77.

112. *The Era*, 7 August 1897.

113. *The Era*, 15 April 1899. For travelling bioscopes, see Scrivens and Smith, 1999. This has a snapshot of William Codona's Ghost Show and Cinematograph. See also Brown, 2001, ch. 7, 'There's no Fun like Work', 82-94, for the Biddall family involvement in cinema in Scotland; McBain, 1985, chs 1-3, 8-24, particularly for the Greens and Kemps, and McKillop and Hamilton, 2003.

114. 'Death of Mr William Codona at Tranent', *Edinburgh Evening News*, 11 August 1931, and *The World's Fair*, 15 August 1931.

115. 'Extraordinary Affair at Carstairs', *Hamilton Advertiser*, 2 September 1905. Accounts are also given in 'Extraordinary Affair at Carstairs', *Lanarkshire Examiner and Upper Ward Advertiser*, 2 September 1905, Lanark library scrapbook of cuttings, 1905, 44-5 (source unknown); 'Extraordinary affray at Carstairs', *The Scotsman*, 28 August 1905. My thanks to Iain D. MacIver of Lanark Library for these references.

116. 'The Carstairs shooting Affray – Trial at Lanark', *Hamilton Advertiser*, 21 October 1905. The trial is also reported in 'Exciting midnight shooting at Carstairs', *Lanarkshire Examiner and Upper Ward Advertiser*, 21 October 1905.

117. Another story concerning William Codona's Ghost Show in Northern Ireland was collected from his son Frank by J. Wilson McLaren: 'His father sent the show to the Chapel Fields, Belfast, where a bad riot occurred in 1898. The fairground was crowded at the time and the authorities had no control like those responsible in this country. Bricks and stones were thrown about, and Syd Braham, one of the showmen, threatened to let a lion out of a cage to disperse the hooligans as the police appeared to be helpless!' (J. Wilson McLaren, 'Show Folks in the Capital', *Edinburgh Evening News*, 21 March 1936). 'The Showman's World' column in *The Era* (16 April 1898) notes 'Cordona's ghost illusion with its new Klondyke front' in Belfast.

118. For a picture of Codona's Golden Dragons, see Thackray, 1993, 81.

119. See Baird, 2000, 248-9 for the Tower Amusements at 47 Tower Street and the Tower Hall at no. 62. The sites of both properties were owned by Harry Marvello, whose children's nanny

Cissie O'Donnell married William Codona's son Nathaniel. See Harry Marvello, 'My own show at Portobello', *The Dundee Evening Telegraph*, 25 February 1952.

120. Cathy was unsure about this; it could have been at Addiewell in West Lothian.

121. Baird, 2000, gives details of another venue, Cadona's Pictures and Varieties, a tent cinema on a fairground on Parliament Street, Leith, which was operating in 1912 and 1913 when the tent was replaced with a corrugated iron shed seating 200: 'He was stuck for a name for his new Picture House. This did not perturb Billy for long. He ran a competition ... the winner of which had the honour to pronounce the new name which was the Magnet. To celebrate the opening, Billy decorated the front of the "new house" with "Silver Magnets"' (202, 212-13).

122 Amongst the scant information on his marionette activity, *The Era* of 25 September 1897 has the following advert: 'Wanted, the address of Harry Ashington, Marionette proprietor, by W. Codona, Ghost Exhibition, Denny, Stirlingshire ...'. Perhaps, with the rest of his business growing, he was looking to sell his puppets.

123. See Baird, 2000, ch. 26, for the resort's places of entertainment. For its place in the history of tourism, see Durie, 1994, 206-16.

124. 'MC' in WEA: Oral history project, Leisure and Entertainment, 10 May 1990, School of Scottish Studies, Edinburgh University, ss: SA1990.053-60.

125. Telephone conversation with Jim McArdle (Snr), 4 July 2008.

126. My thanks to Archie Foley for collecting information from Melvyn Strand. Those living on the site included Melvyn's own family – father Robert Henry, wife and three sons, his uncle Billy Strand's family, Douglas Stewart's family and Stanley Sharp's family.

127. 'Fun City', Portobello, part of STV series 'Time out with Tennant' (1966, Scottish Screen Archive, T1131).

128. 'Fun City', Portobello, part of STV series 'Time out with Tennant' (1966, Scottish Screen Archive, T1131).

129. The kiln for Buchan's pottery can still be seen behind the Fun City.

130. For Albert Biddall (1874-1947), see Brown, 2001, *passim* and especially pages 90-1.

131. The Showmen's Guild regulated who had the rights to particular venues. See Toulmin, 2003, 2-4, for a brief introduction and further references.

132. William Codona's son Frank promoted a carnival at Meadowbank in the early 1930s (see below).

133. Maggie Swan, St James Fair, *The Scotsman*, 13 August 1894. This is already a considerable improvement from earlier in the century when, for example, arrivals at Paisley's St James Day Fair in 1828 are described as 'those nomadic hordes which itinerate with all their household attached to the flanks of some sorry jade' (*Paisley Advertiser*, 16 August 1828).

134. William Codona formed the firm of William Codona and Sons Ltd, which passed to his sons. When they split up, it came into the hands of his son Norman and then to Norman's children who still run fairgrounds, including those at Irvine Marymass festival and Galashiels Braw Lads' gathering.

135. For Ayr races, see White, 1990.

136. Carol McNeill, *Kirkcaldy Links Market* (Fife Council Community Services, 2004) is an excellent history with many Codona-related references and illustrations.

137. See Alfred Codona, Appendix 2, for Aberdeen and for the war years.

138. For Frank Codona and, in particular, his and his son Frank's business in and around Ayr, see White, 1990.

139. Typescript account, 'A Showman's contribution to the war effort', made by his son Jim (Jnr).

140. The continuing problems for travelling showpeople getting a school education are discussed in Jordan, 2000, 253-63. For some comparative research into the different modes of education and the values attached to them by both educationalists and showpeople in Australia, see Danaher, Moriarty and Danaher, 2002 and Danaher, Moriarty and Danaher, 2004, 47-66.

141. See Alfred Codona, Appendix 2.

142. See Marvello, 1952.

143. See Couper, 1996 for the fair established at Dunfermline by

John Codona's Pleasure Fairs [JCPF], and also for an account of the machines and transport used by the firm.

144. *The World's Fair* obituary tribute to John Codona describes him as follows: 'He was a showman proud of his calling, who always had the interests of the business close to his heart. Fully alive to the necessity of having up-to-date machines, he exploited each one he handled to the utmost. Never satisfied with even the best, as supplied by the makers, he always added that extra touch which gave it the John Codona hallmark. His acute sense of showmanship did not stop here, for he had a veritable "conjurer's bag of tricks" from which he could always produce something when working opposition, putting and keeping his machines one jump ahead all the time ...' (25 November 1948).

145. See Toulmin, 1999, 14-16, for the changing fashions in rides between the Wars. The Wall of Death arrived on fairgrounds in the late 1920s.

146. George Maxwell and Sons were based in Musselburgh.

147. Sid Farmer moved to George Maxwell's from the firm of Lakins. A fine example of his work on a 1950s Waltzer made by Maxwell's can be seen at: <http://www.fairart.co.uk/photogallery5.htm>

148. This refers to the first of a two-part feature by fairground historian Alan Ingram, describing the journey of John Codona's Pleasure Fairs to Woolwich Common for the coronation in 1952, with photographs of the Waltzer after alteration as well as much information on other Codona family history, rides and transport ('Coronation Scots: Outward bound', *The Fairground Mercury*, vol. 15, no. 4, March 1993 and 'Coronation Scots: The Return', *The Fairground Mercury*, vol. 16, no. 1, June 1993). Bob Couper, 1996 also describes Gordon's innovation.

149. See Alfred Codona's comments, Appendix 2.

150. This Frank Codona was the son of Gordon Codona's grandfather's brother Frank.

151. Gordon later told me that these were ex-army barrack huts, thousands of which were available just after the War. These were put onto four-foot high walls, raising them enough for maintenance work, including the building of bodies for the distinctive fleet of John Codona's Pleasure Fair lorries.

152. See Appendix 2.

153. Subi Brand.

154. See Alfred Codona, Appendix 2.

155. The *Edinburgh Evening News* carried the following front-page advertisement in the first week of 1931; 'Codona conquers Edinburgh with the largest and most spacious carnival ever staged in the capital at Edinburgh's new amusement park, Meadowbank, Abbeyhill. Continuing till 10th January. Admission Free. Opening 6.30. Figure 8 Railway, Noah's Ark, Wall of Death, Royal Grand Circus, Special performance New Year. Dare-Devil Peggy [in large capitals], Dragon's, Dodgem, Chairoplanes, &c. &c. &c. Visit the people's show. 19 of Britains largest roundabouts.'

156. See Toulmin, 1999, for the Stewart family and the world of fairground boxing.

157. Alfred Codona, interviewed in the *Aberdeen Evening Express*, 21 July 1977.

158. Alfred Codona, interviewed in the *Aberdeen Evening Express*, 21 July 1977.

159. The relevant minute approving this can be found in the Aberdeen Council Meeting records for 17 March 1969, 1109, no. 6.

160. For changing fashions in amusement machines, see Kurtz, 1991.

161. I am indebted to Mona Rhone for checking United States sources.

BIBLIOGRAPHY

Recorded Sources

Codona, Barry: interviewed 25 March 2004.
Codona, Gordon: interviewed 8 March 2002, 17 September 2003, 12 December 2003.
Codona, Justin: interviewed 20 March 2004.
Macintosh, Cathy: interviewed 18 August 2003, 13 October 2003.
Thomas, Catherine Codona: interviewed 25 February 2004.
'Fun City, Portobello', part of STV series 'Time out with Tennant' (1966), Scottish Screen Archive, T1131.
Workers Educational Association (WEA): Oral history project, Leisure and Entertainment, 10 May 1990, copy in School of Scottish Studies, Edinburgh University, SS: SA1990.053-60.

Select Newspaper Articles

Newspapers consulted at length include:

> *The Glasgow Constitutional*
> *The Glasgow Free Press*
> *Glasgow Herald*
> *The Glasgow Journal*
> *The Edinburgh Advertiser*
> *The Edinburgh Courant*
> *The Edinburgh Evening News*
> *The Era*
> *The Scotsman* (through its digital archive)
> *The World's Fair*

Several American newspapers were accessed through:

> <http://www. newspaperarchive.com>

Several other British newspapers were accessed through the British Library digital archive of nineteenth-century newspapers:

> <http://newspapers.bl.uk>

- 'All Hallow Fair', *The Scotsman*, 17 November 1827.
- 'Amusements of the mob' – 2nd article, *Chambers Journal of popular literature, science and arts*, vol. VI, no. 148, 1 November 1856, 281-6.
- 'Death of William Codona at Tranent', *Edinburgh Evening News*, 11 August 1931.
- 'Exciting midnight shooting at Carstairs', *Lanarkshire Examiner and Upper Ward Advertiser*, 21 October 1905.
- 'Extraordinary Affair at Carstairs', *Hamilton Advertiser*, 2 Sept. 1905.
- 'Extraordinary Affair at Carstairs', *Lanarkshire Examiner and Upper Ward Advertiser*, 2 September 1905.
- 'Fraud on the public', *Paisley Advertiser*, 13 September 1828.
- 'Most Beautiful girl with the circus', *The Fort Wayne Sentinel* [Indiana], 8 July 1910.
- '"Old Malabar." (By an old play-goer)', *North British Daily Mail*, c1871, an interview with showman and juggler Patrick Feeney pasted into a Mitchell Library Glasgow cuttings book, *The dark side of Glasgow*, 17-19.
- 'One-man band's Farewell', *Edin. Evening News*, 30 October 1946.
- 'The ancient town of Falkirk and a sketch of the cattle tryst', *Falkirk Herald*, 15 October 1867.
- 'The Biters Bit', *The Edinburgh Advertiser*, 23 September 1828.
- 'The Carstairs shooting Affray – Trial at Lanark', *Hamilton Advertiser*, 21 October 1905.
- 'The late Mr Frank Codona', *The World's Fair*, 6 August 1938.
- 'The old fairs at Pittenweem', *East of Fife Record*, 10 August 1908.
- 'The shows at Vinegar Hill (By an old Foggie)', *Glasgow Evening News and Star*, 14 July 1887.
- Will Fyffe interviewed by Wanda Dunbar: 'My memories of the geggies', *Glasgow Eastern Standard*, 4 March 1944.
- John Gibson: 'One man's music will be heard no more', *Edinburgh Evening News*, 16 January 1964.
- J. House: 'Codona; the royal family of the fairground', two-part feature in the *Evening News*, 1 December and 2 December 1954.
- J. W. McLaren: 'Show Folks in the Capital', *Edinburgh Evening News*, 21 March 1936.
- H. Marvello: 'My own show at Portobello', *The Dundee Evening Telegraph*, 25 February 1952.
- M. Swan: 'St James Fair', *The Scotsman*, 13 August 1894.

Books and Journals

The Life of Billy Purvis the extraordinary, witty and comical show-man, Newcastle, [facsimile of 1875 edition] 1981.

Scottish paintings, watercolours and drawings offered for sale, Bourne Fine Art, July and August 2004.

Anderson, R. *Aberdeen in Bygone Days*, Aberdeen, 1910.

Bell, B. The Twentieth Century. In Findlay, B. ed., *A History of the Scottish Theatre*, Edinburgh, 1998, 137-206.

Baird, G. *Edinburgh Theatres, Cinemas and Circuses, 1820-1963*, privately printed typescript first published in 1964 and re-set by George F. Baird in 2000.

Brown, F. *Fairground Strollers and Showfolk,* Taunton, 2001.

Bruce, F. 'You had to be game to stay in yon business': A working life in variety theatre, 1920-1950, *Oral History*, vol. 24, no. 2, Autumn 1996, 67-74.

Burnett, J. Glasgow Fair: the Hail Week, *Scottish Local History*, vol. 45, Spring 1999, 31-7.

Byrom, M. *Punch in the Italian puppet theatre,* Fontwell, 1999.

Chambers, R. *Traditions of Edinburgh*, Edinburgh and London, [1868] 1967.

Cameron, D. K. *The ballad and the plough; a portrait of the life of the old Scottish farmtouns,* London, 1979.

Cárdenas, J. R. *La Fabulosa historia del circo en Mexico*, Mexico, 2004.

Carlyon, D. Wisconsin circus woes and the great Dan Rice, *Wisconsin Magazine of History*, Summer 2005, 24-5.

Carragher, P. C. *'Red-light' recollections. Representing the … story of forty years of Fairport [i.e. Arbroath] from the footlights / told … by P. Charles Carragher [with plates, including a portrait]*, Arbroath, 1906.

Couper, R. Always the Best, *Fairground Mercury*, vol. 19, no. 2, September 1996.

Court, A. *Puck of the Droms; The lives and literature of the Irish tinkers*, Berkeley, 1985.

Danaher, G., Moriarty, B. and Danaher, P. A. Co-operative communities and problem-based lifelong learning: issues in educational delivery to Australian circus people, paper presented to the *International Lifelong Learning Conference*, Yeppoon, Central Queensland, Australia, 16-19 June 2002.

Danaher, P. A. Travellers under the Southern Cross: Australian show people, national identities and difference, *Queensland Review*, 8(1), 2001, 77-85.

Danaher, P. A., Moriarty, B. and Danaher, G. Three Pedagogies of Mobility for Australian Show People: Teaching about, through and towards the questioning of sedentarism, *Melbourne Studies in Education*, 45(2), 2004, 47-66.

Disher, M. W. *Greatest show on earth, as performed for over a century at Astley's – afterwards Sanger's – Royal Amphitheatre of Arts, Westminster Bridge Road, etc. [with plates, including portraits],* London, 1937.

Durie, A. J. The development of the Scottish coastal resorts in the central Lowlands, *c*1770-1880: from Gulf Stream to golf stream', *The Local Historian*, November 1994, 206-16.

Errington, L. *Alexander Carse, c1770-1843*, Edinburgh, 1987.

Forbes, D. W. *Hawaiian National Bibliography, 1780-1900*, Honolulu, 2003.

Forsyth, C. *Some Reminiscences of Springburn 40-50 Years Ago*, unpublished typescript presented to the Mitchell Library by Charles Forsyth in September 1940.

Fraser, W. H. Developments in leisure. In Fraser, W. H. and Morris, R. H. *People and society in Scotland*, vol. II, 1830-1914, Edinburgh, 1990, 236-64.

Giannone, P. *Histoire Civile du Royaume de Naples*, The Hague, [1723] 1742, vol. III.

Gilchrist, A. *Naethin' at a'; stories and reminiscences*, Glasgow, no date.

Haldane, A. R. B. *The Drove Roads of Scotland*, Newton Abbot, [1952] 1973.

Highfill, P. H., Burnin, K. A. and Langham, E. A. *A biographical dictionary of actors, actresses, musicians, dancers, managers and other stage personnel in London, 1660-1800* (Carbondale and Edwardsville), vol. 15, 1993.

Hutchison, W. *Tales, traditions and antiquities of Leith*, Revised Edition, Leith, 1865.

Ingram, A. Coronation Scots: Outward bound, *The Fairground Mercury*, vol. 15, no. 4, March, 1993a.

Ingram, A. Coronation Scots: The Return, *The Fairground Mercury*, vol. 16, no. 1, June, 1993b.

Irving, J. Dumfries Rood Fair. In *The West of Scotland in history:*

being brief notes concerning events, family traditions, topography, and institutions, Glasgow, 1885, 265-67.

Jordan, E. The exclusionary comprehensive school system: the experience of Showground families in Scotland, *International Journal of Educational Research 33*, 2000, 253-63.

King, E. Popular culture in Glasgow. In R. A. Cage, ed., *The working class in Glasgow 1750-1914*, London, 1987, 142-85.

King, O. C. *Only big show coming, Vol. 1; 1853-78*, Philadelphia, 2001.

Kurtz, B. *Slot machines and coin-op games; a collector's guide to one-armed bandits and amusement machines*, London, 1991.

Leach, R. *The Punch and Judy show; history, tradition, meaning*, London, 1985.

Leatham, J. *Shows and showfolk I have known north and south of the Tweed*, Turriff, 1924.

McArdle, J. (Jnr). *A Showman's contribution to the war effort*, (unpublished autobiography dictated by Jim McArdle [Snr]), no date.

McBain, J. *Pictures past; Recollections of Scottish cinemas and cinema-going*, Edinburgh, 1985.

McCormick, J. *The Victorian Marionette Theatre*, Iowa, 2004.

McCraw, I. *The fairs of Dundee*, Dundee, 1994.

MacGilp, M. Puppets and Glasgow Fair from the 1770's until the 1850's, *The Puppet Master*, Autumn 2008, 30-2.

McIsaac, G. H. M. *Chryston and its worthies*, Kirkintilloch, 1910.

McKillop, J. and Hamilton, J. *The Ritz Cinema Lesmahagow, Vol. 1: The Palmers, the pictures and the pies*, Wishaw, 2003.

McNeill, C. *Kirkcaldy Links Market*, Fife, 2004.

Miller, D. P. *The life of a showman: to which is added, managerial struggles*, London and Leeds, 1849.

Modignani, A. and Mantovani, S. *Il circo della memoria; storie, numeri e dinastie di 266 famiglie circensi Italiane*, Trento, 2002.

Morris, J. The Scottish Fair as seen in Eighteenth and Nineteenth Century Sources, *Scottish Studies*, vol. 33, 1999, 89-109.

Oakley, C. A. *The second city*, Glasgow, 1967.

Perez Calvo, L. R. *Norteamericanos en la Argentina*, Buenos Aires 2007.

Quennell, Peter, ed. *Mayhew's London; Being selections from 'London Labour and the London Poor' by Henry Mayhew*, London, [1851] 1969.

Richards, K. and L. Richards (1990): *The Commedia dell'arte; a documentary history* (Oxford).

Sanger, Lord George. *Seventy years a showman*, London, [1910] 1926.

Sayer, I. S. *Annie Oakley and Buffalo Bill's Wild West*, Mineola, 1981.

Scott, A. and Lindsay, M., eds. *The comic poems of William Tennant*, Edinburgh, 1989.

Scott, H. *Fasti Ecclesiae Scoticanae ... Volume VI, Synods of Aberdeen and of Moray*, New Edition, Edinburgh, 1926.

Scrivens, K. and Smith, S. *The travelling cinematograph show* Tweedale, 1999.

Shaw, J. Storytellers in Scotland: Content and Function. In *Scottish Life and Society, Oral Literature and Performance Culture*, Edinburgh, 2007, 28-48.

Smith, J. *Poems, Songs and Ballads*, 3rd Edition, Edinburgh and Glasgow, 1869.

Speaight, G. *The history of the English puppet theatre*, Carbondale and Edwardsville, 2nd Edition, 1990.

Speaight, G. The Origins of Punch and Judy: a new clue, *Theatre Research International*, vol. 20, no. 3, Autumn 1995, 200-6.

Sponza, L. *Italian Immigrants in Nineteenth Century Britain: Realities and Images,* Leicester, 1988.

Thackray, S. *British Fairgrounds; A photographic history,* Norwich, 1993.

Tobin, T. Popular entertainment in seventeenth century Scotland, *Theatre Notebook*, 23:1, Autumn 1968, 46-54.

Turner, J. *Victorian Arena; the performers – A dictionary of British circus biography, Volume One*, Formby, 1995.

Turner, J. *Victorian Arena; the performers – A dictionary of British circus biography, Volume Two*, Formby, 2000.

Toulmin, V. *A fair fight; an illustrated review of boxing on the fairground*, Oldham, 1999.

Toulmin, V. *Pleasurelands; All the fun of the fair,* Sheffield, 2003.

White, R. Days at the races, *The Fairground Mercury*, vol. 13, no. 2, September 1990.

Whiteley, H. A. A. *Memories of Circus Variety etc. as I knew it*, George Speaight, ed., London, 1981.

Worsdall, F. A. *Glasgow Keek Show; glimpses of city life,* Glasgow, 1981.

Zucchi, J. E. *The little slaves of the harp; Italian child street musicians in nineteenth-century Paris, London and New York*, Liverpool, 1999.

Internet

American digital Newspaper Archive:
   <http://www.newspaperarchive.com>

British Library archive of nineteenth-century British newspapers:
   <http://newspapers.bl.uk/blcs/>

Official government source of genealogical data for Scotland:
   <http://scotlandspeople.gov.uk>

Slout, W. L. (2005): *Olympians of the Sawdust Circle: A biographical dictionary of the nineteenth century American circus*, to be found at:

   <http://www.circushistory.org/Olympians/Olympians.htm>

[All websites in this book were accessed in March 2010]

GLOSSARY

This selective list contains terms found in the text that may require explanation:

Ben Hur: platform ride modified from Ark rides (below) that by the mid-1930s were ubiquitous; a dramatic scene of racing charioteers was reproduced on a large front piece; traditional Ark figures were replaced by horses alternating with chariots.

Cake-Walk: introduced *c*1909, named after a dance; customers walked along boards moved by cranks in contrary directions; speed could be altered according to the music.

Dodgems: electrically powered 'bumper' cars driven on flat platform, first introduced to Britain in 1928.

Figure 8: large railway-style ride on elaborate raised wooden trellis in the shape of the number 8.

flattie: showfolk term for those not in, or born into, the business.

geggie: minor theatre, either travelling, semi-permanent or permanent, popular until the early 1900s.

Jets: rotating ride with jets on the ends of arms that can be partly controlled by the rider.

Mad Mouse: type of roller-coaster with small cars, seating four or less; takes tight, flat turns at modest speeds, but with high sideways force.

Matador: distinctive flat-fronted artillery tractor built by the Associated Equipment Company during World War II and adopted as fairground transport.

Mont Blanc: introduced 1932; circular platform-based ride; riders in suspended 'cars' that swung outwards as the ride revolved; one of several thrill rides introduced in the 1930s.

Moon Rocket: introduced 1936; a huge circular machine with a circle of rocket-shaped cars driven around an inclined circular track.

Noah's Ark: introduced 1930; circular platform-based ride with animal-themed carriages; spectacular décor; one of the most popular roundabouts of the inter-war years.

Panotrope: loudspeaker system used for broadcasting music on fairgrounds.

Roundabout: catch-all term for rotating rides.

Skid/Swish: introduced late 1920s; also known as the Swirl; cars similar to Waltzer, but smaller and on flat surface; cars could pivot, but a brake pedal controlled degree of swing.

slanging: exhibiting at a fairground.

Speedway/Motorcycle Speedway: introduced 1937; version of the Ark with motorcycle mounts, exploiting popularity of motorcycle speedway racing.

spieling: patter associated with rides and side-shows.

Twist: produced from 1959; ride rotates in one direction, with car groups going in counter direction, creating wave effect.

Wall of Death: side-show featuring drum or barrel-shaped wooden cylinder in which stunt motorcyclists rode and did tricks; first known example in Britain appeared in 1929.

Waltzer: introduced in 1933; circular platform ride revolving around an undulating track; riders in tub-shaped cars that could spin on their axis.

INDEX